CSR, Sustainability, Ethics & Governance

Series editors

Samuel O. Idowu, London Metropolitan University, London, UK
René Schmidpeter, Cologne Business School, Cologne, Germany

More information about this series at http://www.springer.com/series/11565

Weikang Zou

Corporate Governance in the Banking Sector in China

 Springer

Weikang Zou
School of Public Administration
University of International Business
and Economics
Beijing, China

ISSN 2196-7075   ISSN 2196-7083 (electronic)
CSR, Sustainability, Ethics & Governance
ISBN 978-981-13-3509-9   ISBN 978-981-13-3510-5 (eBook)
https://doi.org/10.1007/978-981-13-3510-5

Library of Congress Control Number: 2018962780

© Springer Nature Singapore Pte Ltd. 2019
This work is subject to copyright. All rights are reserved by the Publisher, whether the whole or part of the material is concerned, specifically the rights of translation, reprinting, reuse of illustrations, recitation, broadcasting, reproduction on microfilms or in any other physical way, and transmission or information storage and retrieval, electronic adaptation, computer software, or by similar or dissimilar methodology now known or hereafter developed.
The use of general descriptive names, registered names, trademarks, service marks, etc. in this publication does not imply, even in the absence of a specific statement, that such names are exempt from the relevant protective laws and regulations and therefore free for general use.
The publisher, the authors and the editors are safe to assume that the advice and information in this book are believed to be true and accurate at the date of publication. Neither the publisher nor the authors or the editors give a warranty, express or implied, with respect to the material contained herein or for any errors or omissions that may have been made. The publisher remains neutral with regard to jurisdictional claims in published maps and institutional affiliations.

This Springer imprint is published by the registered company Springer Nature Singapore Pte Ltd.
The registered company address is: 152 Beach Road, #21-01/04 Gateway East, Singapore 189721, Singapore

Foreword

Doing well in business in the twenty-first century regardless of whether you are based in the east, west, north, or south of planet Earth requires business leaders to be proficient in a number of socially responsible leadership styles and issues. This was certainly not the culture in place some 50 or more years ago. This statement is of course not an attempt by us to make you our readers of this piece, and believe or assume that we were businessmen or in business or knew how businesses were run 50 years ago—far from it. Having said this, we are all too aware of a number of happenings, events, transformations, and re-orientations that have come to the fore in the business arena globally since Howard R. Bowen's landmark book in 1953 on the social responsibilities of business people—was added to the literature. Not only that, a number of corporate malfeasances around the globe—Enron, Walmart, Parmalat, even the global financial crisis of 2008 which brought our world to its very knees—have meant that the issue of corporate governance in all sectors is one that should be taken seriously and not toyed with.

Before Corporate Social Responsibility (CSR) came into prominence, corporate leaders' performance in running the business was judged simply on the single bottom line—economic responsibility. There was no notion of the triple bottom line or *stakeholders*—corporate strategies were formulated around the interests of the very few providers of capital—the shareholders, all other actors in business arena were irrelevant! But in the UK, for instance, the *Corporate Report* of the *Accounting Standard Steering Committee (ASSC)* (1975) changed that, and it gave recognition to the needs of all legitimate stakeholders of the business. Nearly a decade after that, Ed Freeman's world-class piece on stakeholder strategic management (1984) laid the foundation for the debate and serious research on the issue of stakeholders. These two events took place toward the end of the twentieth century. The two documents in our view gave credence to the global recognition of the term *stakeholder* in both the literature and the world at large. Understanding the needs of modern stakeholders and ensuring that corporate entities are run and directed effectively with no wrongdoings and reckless risk taking by those at the helm of governance meant that all will be well for the entity concerned.

This author's book on *Corporate Governance in Chinese Banking Sector* is a timely addition to the literature, and it fills in a big gap in both the markets on how Chinese banks are governed at the board level. The book highlights a number of issues which are of interest to scholars, practitioners, and anyone interested in Chinese corporate governance. Not only that, the book also makes contributions to the existing theories in the literature which future researchers in the area will find interesting.

The era we now live in is a very different era from what was in place fifty years ago. It is an era of responsibility, transparency, and accountability regardless of which sector of an economy you operate in on Zou's masterpiece on the issue of corporate governance with reference to the largest economy in the world has touched on a number of noteworthy issues that all practitioners and corporate governance scholars cannot but take cognizance of if the debate on the impacts of governance style in different sectors around the globe is to be raised to the next level.

We take this opportunity to congratulate Zou for this addition to the literature and having browsed through it carefully, and we are delighted to recommend it as a must-have companion to today's governance scholars, practitioners, and research students that reside in the length and breadth of our world, not just in China. We are delighted to recommend the book to you all unreservedly.

London, UK
Samuel O. Idowu
Guildhall School of Business and Law
Cologne, Germany
René Schmidpeter
October 2018
Cologne Business School

Contents

Part I Theoretical Framework in Corporate Governance of Banking Organizations

1 Introduction 3
    1.1   Background and Research Problems 3
    1.2   Theory and Concepts 4
           1.2.1   Extant Theories on Corporate Governance 4
           1.2.2   Discursive Institutional Approach 5
           1.2.3   New Understanding of Corporate Governance
                   with Discursive Institutional Approach 10
           1.2.4   Theories of Corporate Governance in Banking
                   Organization 12
           1.2.5   Theories of Corporate Governance in Banking
                   Organizations in China 14
    1.3   Overview of the Chapters 16
    1.4   Contribution 20
    References 21

2 A Discursive Institutional Approach to Corporate Governance ... 25
    2.1   Introduction 25
    2.2   Varieties of Capitalisms Analysis 26
    2.3   Theories of Institutionalism 30
           2.3.1   Defining Discursive Institutionalism 31
    2.4   Three Levels of Discursive Institutionalism and Application
           in Corporate Governance in VoC Context 33
           2.4.1   Legitimacy 33
           2.4.2   Paradigm 36

vii

viii   Contents

	2.4.3	Frame	38
	2.4.4	Dynamics Between Legitimacy, Paradigm, and Frame	39
2.5	Conclusion		40
References			41

Part II   Corporate Governance in Banking Organizations: Legitimacy

3   Legitimizing Corporate Governance in Banking Organizations ... 47

3.1	Introduction		47
3.2	The Anglo-Saxon Model		48
	3.2.1	Bank and Economy	48
	3.2.2	Financial Regulation	55
	3.2.3	Financial Re-regulation and De-re-regulation	60
	3.2.4	Legal Intervention	61
	3.2.5	Implication of Legitimacy on Paradigm and Frame in Corporate Governance in Banking Organizations	62
3.3	The Continental Model and State-Affected Model		64
	3.3.1	Continental Model	64
	3.3.2	State-Affected Model Countries	69
3.4	Conclusion		71
References			71

4   Legitimacy of Corporate Governance in Chinese Banking Organizations ... 75

4.1	Introduction		75
4.2	Bank and Economy		77
	4.2.1	Bank and Economic Development	77
	4.2.2	Bank and Industries	81
	4.2.3	Bank and Enterprises, SOEs Versus SMEs	83
4.3	Bank and Administrative Control, Governance and Financial Regulation		86
	4.3.1	Financial Control and Administrative Governance	86
	4.3.2	Deregulation	87
4.4	Bank and Legal Influences		90
	4.4.1	Judicial Passivism	90
	4.4.2	Judicial Activism	92
4.5	Bank and International Influence		93
4.6	Implication for Paradigm and Specific Governance Structure		96
4.7	Conclusion		98
References			98

Contents ix

Part III Corporate Governance in Banking Organizations: Paradigm

5 Paradigm Discourses on Corporate Governance in Banking Organizations 105
  5.1 Introduction 105
  5.2 General Models of Corporate Governance Around the World 106
    5.2.1 The Anglo-Saxon Model 106
    5.2.2 The Continental Model 107
    5.2.3 Other Models and Relevant Theories 108
  5.3 Paradigm Discourses in Corporate Governance in Banking Organizations 109
    5.3.1 The Anglo-Saxon Model: The Shareholder Primacy Theory Refined 109
    5.3.2 The Continental Model and the State-Affected Model 113
  5.4 Conclusion 117
  References 117

6 The Paradigmatic Analysis on Corporate Governance in Banking Organizations in China 121
  6.1 Introduction 121
  6.2 The Enhanced Shareholder Primacy Theory in China 121
    6.2.1 The Paradigm of the Enhanced Shareholder Primacy 121
    6.2.2 The Agency Problem 124
  6.3 The Diversified Stakeholder Theory 125
    6.3.1 General Theory on Stakeholders 125
    6.3.2 Stakeholders of Different Kinds 128
  6.4 Conclusion 138
  References 139

Part IV Corporate Governance in Banking Organizations: Frame

7 The Board of Directors in Bank Governance in China 143
  7.1 Introduction 143
  7.2 Study on Board of Directors in Generic Corporate Governance Arrangement 143
    7.2.1 The Organization and Behavior of Board of Directors 143

7.3	Understanding the Board of Directors in the Context of Bank Governance	146
	7.3.1 The Orientation of the Bank Board	147
	7.3.2 The Size of the Bank Board	149
	7.3.3 The Board Independence in Banking Organizations	151
7.4	The Board of Directors in Corporate Governance of Chinese Banking Organizations	153
	7.4.1 Organization of the Board of Directors	153
	7.4.2 The Board Independence	157
	7.4.3 The Arrangement of the Supervisory Board	160
7.5	Conclusion	161
References		161

8 Financial Regulation on Executive Pay in Chinese Banks 165

8.1	Introduction	165
8.2	Regulation of Executive Pay	165
	8.2.1 The Composition of Executive Pay	167
	8.2.2 Regulation on Executive Pay	169
8.3	Regulation on Executive Compensation	172
	8.3.1 Composition of the Compensation	172
	8.3.2 Regulation on Executive Pay	176
8.4	Conclusion	180
References		181

9 Risk Management System in Corporate Governance in Banking Organizations in China 183

9.1	Introduction	183
9.2	Risk Management in General Banking Organizations	183
	9.2.1 General Risk Management Structure	185
	9.2.2 Variance in Risk Management in Different Model Countries	188
9.3	Risk Management in Chinese Banking Organizations	195
	9.3.1 Overall Risk Management Framework	195
	9.3.2 Risk Appetite and Specific Risk Management Mechanism	197
9.4	Conclusion	200
References		200

10 Legal Duties in Chinese Bank Governance 203

10.1	Introduction	203
10.2	Legal Duties in Generic Corporate Governance	203
10.3	Legal Duties in Corporate Governance in Banking Organizations	207
10.4	Legal Duties in Corporate Governance of Chinese Banks	210

	10.4.1	Legal Compliance Practices	210
	10.4.2	Fiduciary Duties in Corporate Governance in Banking Organizations in China	213
10.5	Conclusion		221
References			221

11 Book Conclusion 223
    11.1 Key Findings 223
    11.2 Policy Recommendation 226
    11.3 Limitations of the Book and Further Research 228

Abbreviations

BIS	Bank for International Settlements
CBA	China Banking Association
CBRC	China Banking Regulatory Commission
CCP	Chinese Communist Party
CFWC	Communist Party Central Financial Work Commission
CIRC	China Insurance Regulatory Commission
CSRC	China Securities Regulatory Commission
IMF	International Monetary Fund
LTI	Long-term incentive
MoF	Ministry of Finance
NPLs	Nonperforming loans
PBC	People's Bank of China
RMB	Renminbi, Chinese currency
SAFE	State Administration of Foreign Exchange
SASAC	State-owned Assets Supervision and Administration Commission
SHSE	Shanghai Stock Exchange
SMEs	Small- and micro-sized enterprises
SOEs	State-owned enterprises
SZSE	Shenzhen Stock Exchange

List of Figures

Fig. 1.1	VoC and discursive institutional approach	6
Fig. 1.2	Dynamics of three levels of ideas	10
Fig. 1.3	Three layers of discourses and interactions	11
Fig. 2.1	Dynamics of three-level ideas	39
Fig. 3.1	Capital and banking markets around the world (2010). *Source* Mc Kinsey & Company, McKinsey Global Institute (2011)	51
Fig. 3.2	Traditional model of banking process. *Source* Bair (2007)	52
Fig. 3.3	Securitization process of banking in US. *Source* Bair (2007)	53
Fig. 3.4	2000–2012 difference between total bank deposits and loans in US banks (unit: billion US dollars). *Source* Tyler (2012)	54
Fig. 3.5	Contribution of financial sector to GDP across countries—1998, 2008. *Source* OECD, ONS, and bank calculation (2011)	56
Fig. 3.6	UK banking sector assets as % of GDP from 1880 to 2006. *Note* The definition of UK banking sector assets used in the series is broader after 1966, but using a narrower definition throughout gives the same growth profile. *Source* Haldane (2009)	57
Fig. 3.7	US bank's legal costs 2012. *Source* The Economist, Oct 13, 2012	63
Fig. 3.8	Changes of bank loans by German banks from 2007 to 2012. *Source* The Economist, November 10, 2012	66
Fig. 4.1	2003–2012 total assets and total liabilities of Chinese banking industry unit: trillion RMB. *Source* CBRC (2013)	81
Fig. 8.1	CEO remuneration packages in companies with revenue (including banks) between 1 and 3 billion US dollars (including banking organizations), 2009. *Source* Watson Wyatt (2009)	168

List of Tables

Table 3.1	Discourse of corporate governance in banking organizations in three models	49
Table 3.2	Capital market-based model and bank-based model of financial capitalisms	50
Table 3.3	Amounts announced or pledged for financial sector support by country (in percent of 2009 GDP unless otherwise noted)	58
Table 3.4	Donations to the conservative party from 2005 to 2010 UK	59
Table 3.5	Summary of charges by SEC against the financial industry and the collection of fines and compensation	62
Table 4.1	Discursive analysis of corporate governance in banking organizations in China	77
Table 4.2	Statistics on bank loans by Chinese banking industry and financial institutions in facilitating the Chinese National '40 Trillion Stimulus Package' in 2009 unit: billion RMB	79
Table 4.3	2011 international business expansion by the sampled bank (including Hong Kong, Macau, and Taiwan), unit: billion USD	95
Table 6.1	Investment in large-sized sampled banking organizations by CHI on behalf of the state in 2012, unit: billion	123
Table 6.2	2011 Bank B CSR report on protection for different stakeholders	126
Table 6.3	2011 Bank B CSR exchange programs with stakeholders	127
Table 6.4	2009–2010 training sessions for employees in Chinese Banks	130
Table 6.5	Statistics for energy-saving and environmental protection programs by financial institutions in Chinese banking industry 2007–2010	134
Table 6.6	Statistics on loans to green economic areas by Bank B (2011), Unit RMB 100 million	134

Table 7.1	Boards of directors of selected banks from FTSE Top 200 and top 5 largest national banks (total assets).	150
Table 7.2	2003–2008 yearly summary statistics (mean) on board characteristics in US—board size	151
Table 7.3	2003–2008 yearly summary statistics (mean) on board characteristics in US—board independence	152
Table 7.4	2011 statistics on board of directors of sampled banks in China in 2011	155
Table 7.5	Supervisory board of sampled banks 2011	160
Table 8.1	Disclosure requirements for companies with revenue between 1 and 3 billion US dollars across different model countries, 2009	171
Table 8.2	2011 Bank B compensation for senior management. Unit 10 thousand RMB	173
Table 8.3	The overall compensation (before tax) for the chairman of the board of directors and CEO in sampled banks in 2014–2015. Unit 10 thousand RMB.	177
Table 9.1	Selected key guideline, principles, and rules for risk management in banking organizations by BIS under Pillar I, II, and III.	190
Table 10.1	2011 Bank B statistics on attendance by board directors at board meetings and meetings by board special committees	215

Abstract

In contrast to conventional economic, political, and institutional studies of corporate governance, this book brings together varieties of capitalism (VoC) and discursive institutional approaches in order to analyze how corporate governance is constituted in Chinese banking organizations. The discursive institutions which produce and reproduce national arrangements of corporate governance in banking are analyzed as operating across three related levels, namely legitimacy, paradigm, and frame. By comparison with the existing national models of corporate governance in banking, the book holds that the corporate governance of Chinese banks has a hybrid form that combines elements of the Continental stakeholder model, the Anglo-Saxon shareholder model, and the State-affected model. The book finds that the Chinese discursive institutional configuration largely shapes bank governance and is thus crucial to establishing a governance structure that is clearly distinguishable from other models.

Specifically, the book demonstrates that the embedded discursive institutions that legitimate relations between banking and the national economy, forms of financial regulation, and legal provisions in the Chinese context also legitimate a particular form of corporate governance in Chinese banking organizations. In terms of paradigm, the book shows how the legitimacy discourse is manifested in the competing paradigmatic shareholder and stakeholder models which are combined and integrated into the Chinese context. At the frame level, the present study elaborates on the key practical discourses in bank corporate governance in China—the board of directors, regulation of executive pay, risk management, and legal obligations—and finds that they are broadly consistent with the distinctive national discourses of the legitimacy and paradigm. For instance, implicated by the enhanced shareholder model and the stakeholder model, the bank board is oriented toward sustainable profitability to the shareholders, active support for economic development, and balance of interests of various stakeholders. The composition of the bank executive pay and specific regulatory measures, on the other hand, reveals the influence of close financial regulation and the state as the controlling shareholder in Chinese context. In risk management, echoing the paradigm of the stakeholder theory, Chinese banks have moderate risk appetites and concentrate on long-term profitability, real economic investment, and sustainable development, which also represents the concerns for the financial stability by the regulators and their close supervision of the banks. For legal duties, which include the compliance duty and the fiduciary duty, the manifestation of a strong financial regulation is present, typically exemplified in shaping various standards and qualifications of legal duties.

Part I
Theoretical Framework in Corporate Governance of Banking Organizations

Chapter 1
Introduction

I started from my sleep with horror; a cold dew covered my forehead, my teeth chattered, and every limb became convulsed: when by the dim and yellow light of the moon, as it forced its way through the window shutters, I beheld the wretch - the miserable monster whom I had created.

—Mary Shelly, Frankenstein

1.1 Background and Research Problems

As the post-2007 global financial crisis has unfolded, renewed attention is being paid to defects and deficiencies in corporate governance of banking organizations. Such attention is, to Mary Shelley's phase, part of a wider questioning of how these man-made financial giants have turned into the monster of *Bankenstein*. Scholars, regulators, and the public alike start to review and reconsider key issues in banking, such as the role of the bank in modern society, the function of the bank's boards of directors, the regulation on bank executives' pay, risk management and legal obligations, along with the arrangement of macroprudential financial regulation. And various changes and reforms are actively proposed and promoted worldwide to re-enhance corporate governance in banking organizations (UK Walker Review 2009; US Blueprint, Department of Treasury (2008); US, Dodd-Frank Act 2010).

However, before all these proactive measures can be effectively implemented, a more fundamental understanding of corporate governance in banking organization is needed. And it is in this context that the book offers an institutional analysis of corporate governance issues in banks. Specifically, it aims to analyze the changing face of corporate governance in banking organizations in China. To this end, the key questions to be addressed range from the general and broad to the particular and specific. How is corporate governance in Chinese banking organizations initiated and developed? In what ways does corporate governance in Chinese banking

© Springer Nature Singapore Pte Ltd. 2019
W. Zou, *Corporate Governance in the Banking Sector in China*, CSR, Sustainability, Ethics & Governance, https://doi.org/10.1007/978-981-13-3510-5_1

organizations conform to the principal models that circulate in academic analysis? What are the key factors contributing to Chinese distinctiveness, and how might we distinguish it from other model countries? But before answering these questions in the specific Chinese national configuration, a few fundamental questions need our attention. For instance, how is corporate governance in banking organizations conceptualized? How is corporate governance in banking organizations constituted and changed? What are the main models of corporate governance in banks? And how do variances in bank governance develop in different national institutional settings?

1.2 Theory and Concepts

1.2.1 Extant Theories on Corporate Governance

In the extant literature, a great variety of theories are elaborated by scholars on the study of corporate governance. Typically, an economic theory is employed, which focuses upon the ownership structure, maximization of shareholder interests, and elimination of agency problems (Jensen and Meckling 1976; Shleifer and Vishny 1997; Barca and Becht 2002). Based upon the famous separation of ownership and management (Berle and Means 1932), the well-known shareholder primacy model is developed and actively promoted, arguing for maximizing the shareholders' rights and interests while subordinating interests and claims of other stakeholders. Its major concern is how to eliminate agency problems and achieve best returns to the investors (Shleifer and Vishny 1997). In contrast, the stakeholder model, which is said to typically prevail in Continental European countries, argues for sufficient protection for the stakeholders' interests in addition to maximizing the shareholders' returns (Cochran and Wartick 1988). And instead of being troubled with the principal–agent problem, more attention is given to the principal–principal conflict, where the majority shareholders may exploit the minority ones due to their overwhelming power in the ownership structure (Shleifer and Vishny 1997).

Within the economic analysis of corporate governance, La Porta et al. (1998, 1999, 2000) further develop a financial–legal theory, which focuses upon the legal protection for investors, especially the minority shareholders. According to their survey across a wide range of countries, they find that common-law countries have the strongest protections for investors while French-civil-law provides weakest legal protection, leaving Scandinavian-civil-law countries located in the middle (La Porta et al. 1998). In this context, they argue that 'the legal approach is a more fruitful way to understand corporate governance and its reform than the conventional distinction between bank-centered and market-centered financial systems' (La Portaet al. 2000, p. 3).

In contrast with economic and financial–legal theories, Roe (2003) applies political analysis to corporate governance issues. He argues a concentrated ownership structure may result from major political determinants which prefer stakeholder interests rather than pure maximization of shareholders' values. In contrast, weak political forces always favor a dispersed ownership structure rather than concerns for the stakeholders' interests. Countries that 'fit' the Anglo-Saxon model, especially USA, fear the existence of influential economic powers—the concentrated shareholders—and respond with bans on the formation of such ownership structures through various legal mechanisms, even if this adversely affects the rights of shareholders (e.g., restrictions on solicitation of votes by shareholders, or burdensome procedures required on shareholders in derivative suits). Such worries are rare in the Continental model countries. However, although political forces may contribute to the existence of different models, there are problems with simply regarding political forces as a singular causal variable. For instance, it is quite possible for a dispersed ownership structure to co-exist with a political orientation and policies which favor the general welfare of stakeholders (Brian 2001). Other scholars employ an institutional approach, explicitly or implicitly, in addressing institutional settings for the status quo of corporate governance, its continuity, and changes (Jackson 2003; Lane 2003, 2005; Bebchuk and Roe 1999). For instance, by applying the concept of 'path dependence,' a core notion in historical institutionalism, Bebchuk and Roe (1999) stress upon the significance of the initial ownership structure in corporate governance and its subsequent impacts on the present one (the structure driven path).

Such theories seem inadequate, however, when explaining the diverse arrangement of corporate governance in banking organizations. Their focuses on particular aspects of corporate governance—economic, legal, or political—seem to both separate out and overlook other factors which also play significant roles in the development of corporate governance. Meanwhile, these theories understate the way in which the governance arrangement in a certain institutional setting is a consequence of joint forces by many factors, though with different weights. Moreover, with excessive concentration on shareholder issues and performance of the firm, the theories tend to neglect what happened to the stakeholders of various kinds in the recent financial crisis. Furthermore, the lack of detailed analysis on how institutions and orientations affect and are represented in the business practices and activities in the framework of corporate governance may limit the empirical significance of these theories.

1.2.2 Discursive Institutional Approach

Seeking for a wider and in-depth understanding of corporate governance in banking organizations, the book brings together the institutionalization of the variety of capitalisms (VoC) approach with a discursive institutional approach. This combination advances knowledge of why corporate governance is divergent in different national configurations, and how such distinctions are formed, oriented, and applied in various institutional settings. Figure 1.1 provides a summary of the theoretical approach taken by this book.

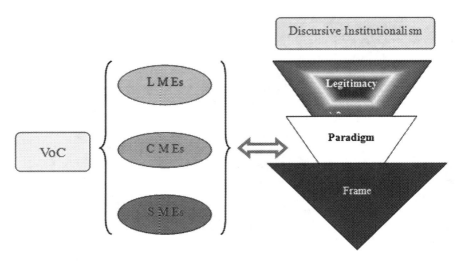

Fig. 1.1 VoC and discursive institutional approach

As a way to understand the institutional diversity of different national capitalisms, VoC is developed in explaining key issues in comparative political economy, such as financial markets and corporate governance (Hall and Soskice 2001a, b; Streeck and Yamamura 2001; Yamamura and Streeck 2003; Schmidt 2003; Amable 2003; Morgan 2005). The recognized strength of VoC lies in categorizing and explaining how different institutional formations produce variances in economic, financial, and political activities. And it is in this context that VoC will be employed in this book for explaining the existing variances of corporate governance of banking organizations in different national institutional settings.

According to a threefold typology, VoC are mainly categorized into liberal market economy (LME), coordinated market economy (CME), and state-affected market economy (SME). Theoretically, LME is said to be characterized with the prevailing ownership of private property, pro-competitive disengagement attitude by the government, and highly developed legal protections for various property and contractual rights (Hall and Soskice 2001a). In contrast, CME relies on non-market relationships, coordination and collaboration, credible commitments, and deliberative calculation on the part of firms. Specifically, there is a close coordination between the government and the industries, and the government is more actively involved in industrial adjustment process by coordinating the policies across the industrial sectors. Private ownership is less prevalent and often has a strong social nature, and the legal protection, to some extent, is comparatively weaker (Hall and Soskice 2001b). SME, exemplified by France, prioritizes upon the state's capacity to devise, orchestrate, and implement economic policies aimed at modernizing industries and achieving macropolicy objectives (Scmidt 2002, 2003; Coates 2000; Boyer 1997; Weiss 1999). Such self-legitimized state intervention in industries and economic process may well enfeeble the private ownership while over-prevailing the 'public ownership' by the

1.2 Theory and Concepts

sovereign. Moreover, even the legal protection may have a strong flavor of public interests, though there are hidden 'rent-seeking' schemes by dominant interest group who maximize their own interests in the disguise of 'public good' (Hall and Soskice 2001a).

Though VoC is advantageous in explaining how corporate governance may be differentiated due to varied national institutions, it is less powerful in illustrating how the specific orientation or governance arrangements are constituted in corporate governance across different categories of capitalisms. And it is in response to this deficiency that this book draws upon discursive institutionalism. Traditionally, institutionalism is widely used in political science and social science as an analytical approach, and institutional explanations remain popular in policy and governance studies as well as individual-level behavior analysis. Institutionalism, theoretically, is divided into the old institutionalism school (Broderick 1970; Wilson 1898; Bates et al. 1998) and the new institutionalism school (Peters et al. 2005; March and Olson 1989; Steinmo et al. 1992). And within the latter, more precise categorizations are made distinguishing between historical institutionalism, rational choice institutionalism, sociological institutionalism, and discursive institutionalism (Schmidt 2010).

As the newest of the 'new institutionalisms,' discursive institutionalism focuses on the substantive content of ideas and the interactive processes of generating and communicating them to the public (Schmidt 2000). Closely connected to sociological institutionalism (Campbell 1995) and the historical institutionalism (Pierson and Skocpol 2002; Pierson 2000), discursive institutionalism pays more attention to discourses which illustrate the ways in which actors engage in the process of generating, deliberating, and/or legitimizing ideas about social activities.

As the core of discursive institutionalism, ideas/discourses are regarded as foundations for the formation and change in institutional arrangements. Defined as causal beliefs which are products of cognition and connected to the material world via interpretation of the surrounding environments, ideas are said to provide guides for actions and specific ways to address problems and challenges (Jolly et al. 2005). Not infrequently, ideas can take many forms, such as high-profile public frames, discourses and ideologies at the foreground of the cognition (Schon and Rein 1994; Campbell 2004), or a lower-profile assumptions and paradigms that remain at the backgrounds of the arena (Hall 1993). Similarly, this book seeks to categorize ideas as operating at three levels that can be analytically distinguished. I will call these three levels or layers of ideas legitimacy, paradigm, and frame.

First, as the broad foundations of institutions, ideas take the form of legitimacy which comprises public sentiments and assumptions, and this takes into account various social entities, actors, factors and extends to the political, economic, legal institutions. Typically, legitimacy may embrace the relationship between citizens and the state, the rights and obligations in political, social, and economic institutions, and public sentiments based upon the common language, culture, and historical identity (Hay 2001). However, there is an intricate relationship between the legitimacy and the actor. On one side, the actor is bound by legitimacy if he or she intends his/her activities to be regarded as institutionally acceptable and publicly desirable. On the flip side, due to broadness and lack of clarity, legitimacy in general cannot provide a specific option or solution to a problem. Meanwhile, it may be played on or even maneuvered by powerful actors, like political leaders, influential businessmen or public figures, (Hay 2008).

In the context of corporate governance, legitimacy varies in different national institutional settings. In the Anglo-Saxon countries, which largely fall under the LME variety of capitalism, the legitimacy of corporate governance lies in the prevailing ownership of private property, a pro-competitive hands-off posture by regulators, and strong legal protections for property and contractual rights. In contrast, in the Continental European countries which approximate to the CME variety of capitalism, legitimacy is characterized by the coordination between the government and the industries, banks and enterprises, active involvement by the regulator in industrial adjustment process, and comparatively limited judiciary protection for private property rights. In the State-affected countries, which are largely consistent with SME variety of capitalism, legitimacy is characterized by the state's controlling ownership and active intervention in industries and economic process, the regulator's strong orientation for promoting national economic development, and comparatively weak legal protection for private investment.

Secondly, ideas take the forms of paradigms. In social activities, paradigms produce opportunities for actors in the process of forming their own ideas, and in pursuing the solution to problems. These may be a totally unconscious process, as paradigms are generally rooted in actors' cognitive backgrounds and underlying theoretical and ontological assumptions about how the world runs. For instance, they may be formed through textbooks and case studies in schools and universities, seminars and influential publications by master scholars in the fields, or one's experience from his family, working place, and increasingly powerful social media (Campbell 1998).

In the context of corporate governance, different paradigms are distinguished by varied models and theories in various national institutional settings, based upon the legitimacies as discussed above. In the Anglo-Saxon countries, paradigmatic ideas in corporate governance are categorized as the Anglo-Saxon model and said to be dominated by the shareholder primacy theory, which is characterized by maximizing the interests of the investors, mitigating agency costs, and enhancing the performance of the corporation. Such paradigm well echoes the legitimacy of prevailing of private ownership, disengagement by the government for competition, and strong legal protection of private interests. In the Continental countries, however, the paradigm in corporate governance is labeled as the Continental model and characterized with the stakeholder theory, which contends for equally protecting the interests of the corporate stakeholders, such as the employees, creditors, suppliers, while limiting the maximization of economic interests for the shareholders. This largely resonates with the legitimacy of coordination of interests of different players by the state, limitation on the priority of private ownership, and weak legal protection in CME. And for the State-affected countries, which is classified as the State-affected model and said to be the hybrid of the shareholder primacy theory and stakeholder theory, the paradigm lays specific emphasis upon national economic development and endeavors to harmonize the interests by the shareholders, the stakeholders, and the national

1.2 Theory and Concepts

economic growth. This is consistent with its legitimacy of preference for the state intervention and active involvement in corporate operation and governance structure, with the pursuit of national economic objectives.

Thirdly, ideas operate at the level of frames, which include norms, codes, and rules of thumb in routine practices, and are designed to diagnose specific problems encountered in social life, sort out most efficient solutions, and achieve certain objectives. Not infrequently, a frame is expected to be clear, concise, and behave as an efficient 'short-cut' among a great variety of options and ideas (Campbell 1998). In corporate governance context, frames mainly constitute the key practices on the specific governance arrangement, such as the ownership structure, the organization and behavior of the board of directors, code of corporate governance, and legal duties of relevant parties. Effectively, frames resonate strongly and are nested within the aforementioned levels of legitimacy and paradigm and are analytically significant as they often illustrate the impacts of 'taken for granted' ideas.

For instance, despite its general function as 'the brain and heart' of the corporation, the board of directors varies in different models regarding its organization, practice, and duties. In the Anglo-Saxon model, the board of directors is oriented toward the best performance of the corporation, effective monitoring over the management, and higher standards of the fiduciary duties. These frames are broadly representative of the paradigm of corporate governance in the Anglo-Saxon model, especially as it emphasizes upon the shareholder primacy and the legitimacy discourse of the prevailing private ownership. In contrast, the board of directors in the Continental model stresses on it's relational role with the shareholders, strong connections with the stakeholders such as mandatory labor participation, and less burden of legal obligations. These well reflect its paradigm of protecting the stakeholders' interests and the legitimacy of coordinating interests among various parties in the framework of corporate governance. The board of directors in the State-affected, though similar to that in the Continental model, is distinguished by the state's influence on the board of directors, its strong political connections, and orientations for promoting the national economic development. These are consistent with the paradigm in the State-affected model (the hybrid of shareholder primacy theory and stakeholder theory) and legitimacy of strong state intervention and concerns for national economic growth. Similar dynamics can be observed in other frames of corporate governance, such as the ownership structure, code of corporate governance, and legal duties.

As in Fig. 1.2, a general path, spiraling from legitimacy, paradigm and then down to frame, is illustrated for better understanding of different levels of ideas in the cognitive background and foreground. Meanwhile, dynamics between and among these different levels of ideas abound and are more complicated than they first appear. **On one side, there is a logical order of ideas, funnelling down from legitimacy, to paradigm and then to frame, from the cognitive background to the cognitive foreground.** For instance, the paradigm is mainly built upon what is legitimate in the sense of being widely accepted by the public as socially desirable. And the frame, oriented by the paradigm, may directly integrate the paradigm in the form of norms like specifically designed documents, guidance, or codes.

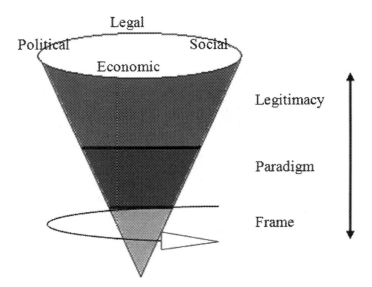

Fig. 1.2 Dynamics of three levels of ideas

On the flip side, however, such logic may deviate or even be reversed, as illustrated in Fig. 1.3. A paradigm may divert from what is widely seen as legitimate due to the aggressive promotion by policy makers, think tanks, and academia. Frames can deviate from the paradigm and legitimacy to a larger scale. First, there is some cognitive 'distance' between the frame and the paradigm and even farther the legitimacy, which enables the frame to be fairly independent and stretch away from the bounds of the paradigm and legitimacy. This typically happens when the frame is maneuvered by certain interest groups for the sake of their own benefits. Secondly, it may happen when the frame is more about specific practices and technical issues, like developments of mathematic models, patterns, or equations targeted at certain business. In a more drastic form, there will be a 'rebel' of the frame when, under the powerful influences by certain interest groups. Nevertheless, when this happens, there may already have been some changes going on in paradigm and legitimacy which are consistent with the changing frame.

1.2.3 New Understanding of Corporate Governance with Discursive Institutional Approach

With the VoC and discursive institutional approach as the analytical tools, the present book, distinguished from the extant literature, summarizes corporate gov-

1.2 Theory and Concepts

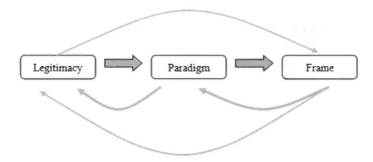

Fig. 1.3 Three layers of discourses and interactions

ernance into the following three views, the micro/microscopic, meso/telescopic, and macro/kaleidoscopic (Preda 2009), which resonate with the three levels of discursive institutionalism, the frame, the paradigm, and legitimacy. The microscope view of corporate governance, the discourse of frame, observes mainly the endogenous and micro-aspects of the corporation while intentionally isolating other entities, actors or elements, such as the protection of returns of the financial investment by the investors/shareholders (Shleifer and Vishny 1997), mitigation of the agency problem (Jensen and Meckling 1976; Fama and Jensen 1983), and various specific governance issues like the ownership structure, the board of directors, the legal duties. The kaleidoscopic view of corporate governance, or the discourse of legitimacy, observes the corporation in its relationship to broader economic, social, and political institutions (Dignam and Galanis 2008). And, this view often highlights the divergence of corporate governance in different countries which have their own specific political, economic, legal, social, and cultural arrangements (Hermes et al. 2007; Okike 2007; Aguilera and Cuervo 2009). A meso- or telescope view of corporate governance, categorized as paradigm in the present discursive institutional analysis, observes the relationship between corporation and other entities and actors like the creditors, regulators, and employees. It defines corporate governance as a set of rules or a mechanism regarding the relationship among the shareholders, management, stakeholders, and the society. And a good governance structure should provide an efficient framework to achieve the corporate objectives, monitor the corporate performance (Williamson 1984), and consider the overall interests of different stakeholders apart from the shareholders (Freeman 1984; Donaldson and Preston 1995).

The present book, instead of favoring any of the aforesaid conceptions of corporate governance, argues that corporate governance is a composite of the 'three scopes' views. First, from the micro-perspective, corporate governance is a well-designed structure 'through which the objectives of the company are set, and the means of attaining those objectives and monitoring performance are determined' and it is expected to 'provide proper incentives for the board and management to pursue objectives that are in the interests of the company and its shareholders, and should facilitate effective monitoring' (OECD 2004, p. 11). Secondly, illustrating the meso-view, corporate governance involves a set of complicated relationship 'between a company's management, its board, its shareholders and other stakeholders' (OECD 2004, p. 11) and is greatly influenced by the dynamics between these diversified participants. Thirdly, corporate governance is also shaped by the macro factors, such as the economic, legal, and regulatory environments, which can be further categorized into macro economic policies (OECD 2004).

1.2.4 Theories of Corporate Governance in Banking Organization

Corporate governance in banking organizations is not, however, merely constituted through the same discursive institutions of legitimacy, paradigm, and frames that operate in corporate governance more broadly. It is certainly the case that distinctive country-level governance arrangements legitimize both financial and non-financial sectors, especially considering increased competitions and higher threats from the market for corporate control in the financial industry. And these force banks to take more effective governance structures for the sake of maximizing shareholders' interests and improving banks' performance, and push the bank's governance structure to evolve toward the general governance system used by generic unregulated firms (Belkhir 2008). Yet, although 'Sectoral orientation will generally reflect national orientation,' it may also present some distinctive features and 'reflect the bias of the dominant agency or agencies in the sector and this may reflect the agencies' particular history, mission, or jurisdictional responsibilities' (Vogel 1996, p. 22). Hence, while the governance arrangements in banking organizations are largely consistent with those of generic firms at the country level, specialties abound in the banking sector due to its specific characteristics and business activities. These specifics may be more significant in the constitution of certain governance mechanisms in banking organizations (Adams and Mehran 2003, 2008). The specific discourses on banks may cover issues such as the bank's role as a unique financial intermediary providing liquidity services, its highly leveraged capital structure, more opaqueness and lack of transparency compared with the generic corporations, vulnerability to bank runs and hence causing possible systematic financial risk, and being heavily regulated.

Referring to the specialty of the banking industry and the three-level perspectives of generic corporate governance, the book summarizes corporate governance of banking organization as a composite of micro-, meso-, and macroviews. At the micro-level, corporate governance of the bank 'involves the manner in which the business and affairs of banks are governed by their boards of directors and senior management, which affects how they set corporate objectives; operate the bank's business on a day-to-day basis; meet the obligation of accountability to their shareholders' (Basel 2010, p. 7, 2015). In the terms we set out in discussion in discursive institutionalism, this is what we have called the specific 'frame' of the governance structure of the bank. Meanwhile, corporate governance in banking organizations

1.2 Theory and Concepts

demarcates an emphasis on the arrangement of various stakeholders' interests, such as the protection of the interests of the depositors, creditors, and the state. This boundary of corporate governance goes beyond the profitability of the bank and the maximized return to its shareholders, and takes into account of the bank's influences upon its constituencies. In our terms, the meso-view leads to the construction of 'paradigms,' which focus on how the bank's governance structure should be oriented toward the protection of its various stakeholders, typically the depositors, creditors, and the economy BIS (2010, 2015). The macroview, moreover, emphasizes that corporate governance in banking organizations should 'align corporate activities and behavior with the expectation that banks will operate in a safe and sound manner and in compliance with applicable laws and regulations' (Basel 2010, p. 7, 2015). And, in doing so, it concentrates more on the functions of the banking sector for the sake of economic growth and stability, and addresses the macroeconomic implications of the bank's governance structure, such as contagion risks, impacts on payment systems, liquidity problems, and bank runs. For us, this macroview is a question of producing the 'legitimacy' of corporate governance arrangements at work in banking organizations.

Integrating the micro-, meso-, and macroperspectives in conceptualizing corporate governance in banking organizations, the discursive institutional approach, along with the implicit VoC analysis, develops a dynamic three-tier canvass of governance structure in banks, proceeding from legitimacy, paradigm, to frame. At the legitimacy level, the VoC analysis is specifically used to approach different institutional settings. It pertains to how corporate governance in the bank is legitimized by the discourse on the relationship between the bank and the economy, especially as this is manifested in financial regulation and the role of legal interventions. For instance, the government plays a significant role in 'creating and shaping' the banks' behavior and activities, and, apart from its prevalent regulatory and supervisory function, the government actually 'creates and constitutes what banks are and what banks do' (Rethel and Sinclair 2012). In relation to the other levels of our analysis, the different paradigms and models of corporate governance in banking organizations, summarized as the shareholder primacy model, the stakeholder theory model, and the state-affected model, can thus be seen to appear as socially and economically appropriate. Moreover, the discursive institutions of legitimacy also contribute to the shaping of the specific governance frames in the bank, such as differences in the organizational structure of the board of directors, the extent of regulation on executive pay, risk management arrangements employed, and legal obligations.

At the paradigm level, and referring to different models in generic corporate governance, the book explores different models in the context of the banking industry. The shareholder primacy model takes on some industrial specialties for banking organizations, such as the acuteness of agency problems and intensive conflict of interests between residual claimants and fixed claimants. For the stakeholder model, an umbrella of the social responsibility for the bank comes into the analytical picture, especially as that covers the interests of various stakeholders. And, for the state-affected model, as a hybrid of the shareholder primacy model and stakeholder model, the paradigm for corporate governance in banking is marked by the state's positioning of the bank as playing an active role in support of national economic development.

At the level of frames, manifesting the varied legitimacies and paradigms, specific corporate governance structures in banks are developed in different national institutional settings and models. Though there are a great variety of frames to be studied for bank governance, four pivotal issues are selected in the present research. These embrace the organization and behavior of the board of directors, regulation on executive pay, risk management, and legal duties. The discussion of the board of the bank illustrates how different paradigms and legitimacy discourses are manifested in framing the orientation of the board of directors, the size of the board, and the board's independence. The regulation on executive pay, on the other hand, presents the implication of varied paradigm and legitimacy on the composition of the executive remuneration and differentiated regulative measures. The analysis of risk management, as the pivotal issue in the banking industry, manifests how the converged international influence and divergent national legitimacy and paradigm discourses co-function to constitute the conceptions of different risks, the overall risk management framework, and the specific risk management arrangement. The legal duties of the bank, mainly the compliance duty and fiduciary duty, represent the influence of different paradigm and legitimacy in shaping the boundary of the bank's responsibilities and the potential liabilities by the bank board directors and managers.

1.2.5 Theories of Corporate Governance in Banking Organizations in China

Applying the discursive institutional approach to corporate governance in Chinese banking organizations, along with comparing and contrasting with different models, the book explores specifically how corporate governance is constituted in banks in Chinese national configuration. This is achieved from the three-tier discourse analysis of legitimacy, paradigm, and frame. At the level of legitimacy, corporate governance in Chinese banks will be shown to be a hybrid of the Continental model, the State-affected model, and the Anglo-Saxon model, which is apparent in the discourse on the Chinese banks' integration into the national economy, their close relationships with industries, and intertwining with enterprises. Regarding discourses of financial regulation, running in parallel is continued close control and administration by the government and an increasing orientation for opt for deregulation. In terms of legal intervention, meanwhile, the courts in China are legitimated as playing a paradoxical role of passivism and activism and frequently influenced by political discourses. Meanwhile, the discourse of international influence is increasingly significant in legitimating particular corporate governance arrangements in China, especially as it refers to China's active presence in international economic organi-

1.2 Theory and Concepts

zations, competitions from foreign banks, and increasing overseas expansions by Chinese banks.

Understanding the specific form taken by this hybridization of legitimacy in corporate governance in banking organizations in China requires, however, that we pay attention to the ways in which the broader discourses and institutions that legitimate banking practices in Chinese context are manifested in many deviations from the aforesaid paradigms. As such, an enhanced shareholder primacy model will be shown to develop through the specific concerns of the Chinese state as a majority shareholder of the banks, and this leads to attempts to balance the maximization of the shareholders' investment returns with the protection of the stakeholders' interests, and to a specific agency problem. The diversified stakeholder model, on the other hand, highlights banks' serious concerns for the interests of a great variety of stakeholders, from general economy to individual employees, from the regulators to the clients, and from the environmental protection to the social welfare at large.

Echoing the legitimacy and paradigm as so discussed, a specific set of corporate governance frames will be shown to have developed in Chinese banks, especially pertaining to frames for the organization and behavior of the bank board, regulation on executive pay, risk management, and legal duties. The organization and behavior of the bank board embraces the orientation of the board directors, its composition, the board size, and its independence. Manifesting the hybrid of the paradigm discourses of the enhanced shareholder primacy and the diversified stakeholder model and relevant legitimacy discourses, for instance, the board of directors in Chinese banks is oriented toward sustainable profitability to the shareholders, active support for economic development, and balance of interests of various stakeholders. Similar hybrid manifestations can be observed in the board composition, the board independence and impediments, and arrangement of supervisory board of directors. The exploration on regulation on executive pay in Chinese banks embodies the composition of the compensation, and the specific regulatory measures and mechanisms. It reflects the embeddedness of the legitimacy discourses of close financial regulation, exemplified by mandatory requirements on the composition, proportion, and terms of the executive remuneration. Meanwhile, it illustrates the implication of the paradigm discourse of the stakeholder model by the high proportion of performance-related bonus, adequate fixed salary, and generous welfare package for the sake of the long-termism by the bank management. Also, it presents concerns for the stakeholder interests by setting the social indicator as a compulsory standard for assessing the executives' performance.

As a key issue of corporate governance in Chinese banks, risk management focuses on the analysis of the discourses from international influence and regulators in shaping the general framework of risk control, risk appetite, and specifically developed risk management mechanisms. Reflecting the paradigm discourse of the stakeholder model, the dominant role of the state as the controlling shareholder, and the legitimacy discourse of strict financial regulation, for instance, Chinese banks set moderate appetites for their risks. Meanwhile, due to the legitimacy of Chinese bank's intimate relationship with economic development, industries and enterprises, credit risk management takes a specific place in Chinese banks and is targeted in particular at issues like lending to financing platforms by local governments, industries like real estate and environmental protection, and the small and micro-enterprises (SMEs). Last but not the least, legal duties in Chinese bank governance embrace the compliance duty and fiduciary duty expected of the board directors and management. The compliance duty of the bank is more a public law obligation and closely connected with risk management and internal control. The fiduciary duty of the bank, frequently rooted in private law terrain, pertains to the board directors, senior management, and shareholders, and embraces the duty of care, duty of loyalty, and duty of disclosure. Due to limited roles of the judiciary in China, many of the standards and requirements come from various regulations and rules by financial regulators. The legal obligation in Chinese banking organizations reveals strong regulatory discourses while limited role of the court.

The book reviews and explores the general practice of the overall corporate governance in Chinese banking industry. However, for the sake of China's specific institutional embedment and the general framework of the financial market, the present research selects and prioritizes corporate governance arrangement, in particular, of certain sampled Chinese banks, mainly the large-sized commercial banking organizations which are typical and representative of the present Chinese banking industry, considering their large proportion in the total assets of the banking sector, great influence industrial wide as well as to national economy, and modeling effects for other banks.

1.3 Overview of the Chapters

In general, the present book is divided into four parts. Part I, including the present chapter and Chap. 2, aims to introduce the book and set up the theoretical approach to be taken for analyzing corporate governance in banking organizations. As the prelude of the whole book, this chapter introduces specifically the purpose, theoretical framework, and general content of the book, and specifies the unique conceptual analytical toolkit of financial institutionalism related to corporate governance in banks across the world and China, such as the legitimized institutional settings, the dominant paradigmatic model, and the varied frames in practice. Moreover, the chapter will present the outline of the book and its arrangement. Chapter 2 unveils the unique theoretical framework in investigating corporate governance in banking organizations, which, ranging from macro, meso to micro, takes into account the financial institutional settings of bank governance, the dominant paradigms, and the specific arrangement and structure. The chapter mainly reinvigorates the implicit institutionalism of the VoC literature by drawing on the recent development of discursive institutional theory and analyzes corporate governance by differentiating and exploring three levels of discourses: legitimacy, paradigm, and frame. Legitimacy in corporate governance is shown to involve the public sentiments and popular cognitions present in diverse forms of capitalisms, which constitute the legitimate roles that corporations are expected to perform across varieties of capitalisms. The paradigm

1.3 Overview of the Chapters   17

is, as sedimented institutional arrangements, typically referred to as different models of corporate governance. Such models are specifically useful in explaining the constitutive and competing conceptions of how corporate governance can and should be organized, including the so-called shareholder model, stakeholder model, and state-affected model. The frame, embedded in routine and mundane practices, includes specific governance arrangements like the ownership structure, the organization and activities of the board of directors, the code of corporate governance, and legal duties.

Part II, comprising Chaps. 3 and 4, proceeds to discuss the details of corporate governance in banking organizations through the institutional lenses provided by the discursive institutionalism toolkit. Chapter 3 explores corporate governance in banking organizations at the level of legitimacy across countries and understands how the specific financial institutions will work on the production of the paradigmatic models and practices on bank governance. 'Playing with the financial institutions,' the chapter analyzes the specific legitimate grounds for governance in banks in different financial models by looking into the relationship between the bank and the economy, the financial regulation, deregulation, and re-regulation, the role of legal interventions by the court and the authorities, as well as the role of financial globalization. The chapter also reflects on the impacts of such legitimacy upon the constitution of the paradigm and frame in bank governance. On this basis, Chap. 4 goes further and focuses upon the legitimacy of corporate governance in Chinese banks. With a comparative view, the chapter explores the institutional legitimacy represented by Chinese banks' close ties with the macroeconomy and national economic development, their intimate intertwining with industries and enterprises of different kinds, strong policy orientation in the context of administrative control and governance by the regulator, gradual and careful financial deregulation, increasing though limited legal intervention, and strong international impacts. Such legitimacy also provides a deep discursive ground for Chinese banks' operating paradigms and specific governance arrangement.

Part III, composed of Chaps. 5 and 6, focuses on the next level of the discursive analysis, the prevalent paradigm of bank governance which is largely shaped by the varying institutional embedment. Chapter 5 illustrates the paradigms and philosophical thinking about the models of corporate governance in banking institutions. Reviewing the generic models of corporate governance, the chapter explores the changes and transformation in the prevalent models against the backdrop of the banking industry and the specialty of the bank governance, summarizes henceforth the acute shareholder primacy model, the enhanced stakeholder model, and the state-affected model. The paradigm discourse, as constitutive ideas, provides great significance in shaping the specific arrangement and practice in bank governance. In turn, Chap. 6 explores the specific model of corporate governance in banking organizations in China and finds there develops a hybrid and national-specific paradigm of bank governance. The chapter demonstrates that influenced by the prevalent models of corporate governance, though to different degrees, the paradigm of bank governance presents a hybrid feature in China. Nevertheless, considering the institutional specialty and national configuration, transformations and new features abound which constitute a 'Chinese model' of bank governance, typified by the enhanced shareholder model, the more diversified stakeholder model, and intertwined state-affected model. Moreover, this Chinese specific paradigm of corporate governance in banking organization, not frequently, serves as a working orientation for varied practice in corporate governance arrangement of Chinese banks.

Part IV, from the 'frame' perspective, provides in-depth canvass of corporate governance in banking organizations and includes Chaps. 7, 8, 9, and 10. First and foremost, Chap. 7 looks into various organizational and behavioral issues of board of directors in banking organizations. Comparing and contrasting with the board of directors in generic firms, the chapter figures out some specific features of the bank board due to the industrial specialties. And in analyzing the arrangement of board of directors in banks in different financial models, the chapter focuses on the comparative analysis of some key issues like the orientation the board of directors, its composition, the board size, and its independence, which is found to be closely connected with responding institutional settings and paradigms. Based on such cross-examination, this chapter goes on to analyze the key settings and activities of the bank board in Chinese configurations, and the underlying operating paradigms and financial institutions with Chinese specialty. Chapter 8 studies another critical issue in bank governance during and *ex post* the global financial crisis, the financial regulation on executive's pay. The chapter reviews and compares the regulatory measures on executive pay in banking institutions in varied financial models, especially in the aftermath of 2007–2009 financial crises. Starting from the comparative study of the pay composition, the chapter explores different sets of regulations on banker's pay across varied model countries, which include the cap on the bonus and overall compensation package, the restriction on the vesting of stock options and shares, 'Say on Pay' by shareholders, the disclosure mechanisms, and the use of the compensation committee. Taking into account of the ruling orientation and the institutional embedment in China, especially the overwhelming role of the regulatory agencies, this chapter presents further analysis of the specific regulatory framework on the executive pay in Chinese banks. Chapter 9 reads and discusses about the risk management settings in banking institutions in varied financial models, covering several subjects specially emphasized *ex post* the global financial crisis. And based on such comparing framework, this chapter looks into the overall risk management system in Chinese commercial banks and focuses specifically on the key issues such as production of the bank's risk appetite/tolerance, the development of the mixed risk method, the renewal and update of the special risk management mechanisms, and the related measures and governance arrangement. Specifically, the chapter reflects upon the influences of Chinese financial institutions and the role of the changing paradigm in shaping the bank's risk management structure. Last but not the least, Chap. 10 concentrates upon and analyzes the legal obligations and liabilities in banking institutions in different model countries, which includes the increasingly important compliance duty with public features and the fiduciary duties falling into the private sector. While the former reproduces how the bank should comply with a great variety of new norms after 2007–2009 financial crisis regarding its legitimate business operations, anti-money laundering campaigns, and anti-corruption efforts, the latter reshapes the fiduciary duties against the backdrop of the banking industry, which covers the duty of care, duty of loyalty, and duty of disclosure. The chapter, based on such comparative theoretical framework, explores further the specialties of the legal duties in Chinese banking institutions and the responding institutions and ruling paradigms.

Chapter 11 concludes and generalizes the theoretical and pragmatic implications of the book's exploration on corporate governance in banking institutions based on the multi-level analysis and provides a new and alternative understanding on the production and reproduction of bank governance in varied financial institutional settings.

Part I Theoretical Framework in Corporate Governance of Banking Organizations

Chapter 1   Introduction
Chapter 2   A Discursive Institutional Approach to Corporate Governance

Part II Corporate Governance in Banking Organizations: Legitimacy

Chapter 3   Legitimizing Corporate Governance in Banking Organizations
Chapter 4   Legitimacy of Corporate Governance in Chinese Banking Organizations

Part III Corporate Governance in Banking Organizations: Paradigm

Chapter 5   Paradigm Discourses on Corporate Governance in Banking Organizations
Chapter 6   The Paradigmatic Analysis on Corporate Governance in Banking Organizations in China

Part IV Corporate Governance in Banking Organizations: Frame

Chapter 7   The Board of Directors in Bank Governance in China
Chapter 8   Financial Regulation on Executive Pay in Chinese Banks
Chapter 9   Risk Management System in Corporate Governance in Banking Organizations in China
Chapter 10 Legal Duties in Chinese Bank Governance
Chapter 11 Conclusion

1.4 Contribution

In contrast with the more popular study on corporate governance of generic firms in China, the book focuses on the less explored specific governance structure in Chinese banking organizations, which are in many aspects unique due to the industrial specialty and the bank's tremendous influence on the economy and society at large, best represented in the 2007–2009 financial crises. Distinguished from the peer research on corporate governance in Chinese banks, which largely concentrates on certain aspects of the governance structure, the book contributes by presenting a rich, in-depth, and dynamic study on the key mechanisms in corporate governance in Chinese banking organizations, including the organization and behavior of the board of directors, regulation on executive pay, risk management and the legal duties, all of which are in hot debate by scholars from fields of corporate governance, finance, and banking ever since the passing financial crisis. A unique contribution by the present book lays in the innovative analysis of corporate governance in Chinese banks from more paramount institutional angles, which explore the specific Chinese institutional national settings, dominant orientations in Chinese banks, and their manifestation in the key practices of corporate governance arrangement.

Theoretically, the present book contributes to the study on corporate governance in banking organizations by applying the discursive institutional approach, which is distinguished from the conventional economic, political, or institutional approach. By bringing together the VoC analysis with the discursive institutional analytical framework, the present research presents an in-depth, dynamic and reinvigorating view on how corporate governance in banking organizations is constituted from three levels of discourses. At the level of legitimacy, the present research intends to innovate an exploration on how corporate governance in banking organizations is legitimized and accepted at large in Chinese national institutional settings, involving the interrelationship between the bank and the economy, the financial regulation, and the legal obligation. Such legitimacy, as the discourse at the background of cognition, provides a profound implication for the discourses at the level of paradigm and frame as the foreground of ideas. At the next level of ideas, the book demonstrates how corporate governance in banks is conceptualized and constituted through the paradigm, which resonates with the legitimacy while providing further implications for the formation of specific governance in Chinese banks. With extensive elaboration on the discourse of frame, the book highlights on how the solutions are sorted out for specific corporate governance mechanisms in banking organizations in the context of different legitimacy and paradigm. Meanwhile, the book also reflects on the dynamics between these three levels of discourses.

References

Adams, R., & Mehran, H. (2003). Is corporate governance different for bank holding companies? *Economic Policy Review, 9*, 123–142.

Adams, R., & Mehran, H. (2008). Corporate performance, board structure, and their determinants in the banking industry, Staff Report no. 330, Federal Reserve Bank of New York, June 2008.

Aguilera, R. V., & Cuervo-Cazurra, A. (2009). Codes of good governance. *Corporate Governance: An International Review, 17*(3), 376–387.

Amable, B. (2003). *The diversity of modern capitalism*, Oxford: Oxford University Press.

Bates, Robert, H., Rui, J. P., De Figueiredo, Jr., and Barry, R. Weingast (1998). The politics of interpretation: rationality, culture and transition, Politics and Society, *26*(4), 603–642.

Barca, F., & Becht, M. (2002). *The control of corporate Europe*. Oxford University Press.

Bebchuk, L. A., & Roe, M. J. (1999). A theory of path dependence in corporate ownership and governance. *Stanford Law Review, 52*(1), 127–170.

Berle, A. A., & Means, G. C. (1932). *The modern corporation and private property*. New Brunswick, N.J.: Transaction Publishers.

BIS, Basel Committee on Banking Supervision Switzerland (2010). *Principles for enhancing corporate governance*. Switzerland: Basel Committee on Banking Supervision.

BIS, Basel Committee on Banking Supervision Switzerland (2015). *Corporate governance principles for banks*. Switzerland: Basel Committee on Banking Supervision.

Boyer, R. (1997). French statism at the crossroads. In C. Crouch & W. Streeck (Eds.), *Political economy of modern capitalism: Mapping convergence and diversity*. London: Sage.

Brian, R. C. (2001). History and the global corporate governance revolutions: The UK perspective. *Business History, 43*, 87–118.

Broderick, A. (1970). The French Institutionalists: Maurice Hauriou, Georges Renard, Joseph T. Delos.

Campbell, J. L. (1995). Review of forging industrial policy. *Contemporary Sociology, 23*, 822–823.

Campbell, J. L. (1998). Institutional analysis and the roles of ideas in political economy. *Theory and Society, 27*(3), 377–409.

Campbell, J. L. (2004). *Institutional change and globalization*. Princeton: Princeton University Press.

Coates, D. (2000). *Models of capitalism: Growth and stagnation in the modern era*. Cambridge: Polity Press.

Cochran, P. L., & Wartick S. L. (1998). Corporate governance: A review of the literature, Financial Executives Research Foundation.

Dignam, A. J., & Michael, G. (2008). Corporate governance and the importance of macroeconomic context. *Oxford Journal of Legal Studies, 28*(201), 213–214.

Donaldson, T., & Preston, L. E. (1995). The stakeholder theory of the corporation: concepts, evidence, and implications. *Academy of Management Review, 20*, 65–91.

Fama E. F., & Jensen M. C. (1983). Separation of ownership and control, *The Journal of law and Economics, 26*(2): 301–325.

Freeman, R. E. (1984). *Strategic management: A stakeholder approach*. Boston: Pitman.

Hall, P. A. (1993). Policy paradigms, social learning and the state. *Comparative Politics, 23*, 275–296.

Hall, P. A., & Soskice, D. (2001a). *'Introduction' in varieties of capitalism*. New York: Oxford University Press.

Hall, P. A., & Soskice, D. (Eds.). (2001b). *Varieties of capitalism-the institutional foundations of comparative advantage*. Oxford: Oxford University Press.

Hay, C. (2001). The "crisis" of Keynesianism and the rise of neoliberalism in Britain. In J. L. Campbell & O. K. Pedersen (Eds.), *The rise of neoliberalism and institutional analysis*. Princeton, NJ: Princeton University Press.

Hay, C. (2008). Constructivist institutionalism. In Raw Rhodes, S. Binder & B. Rockman (Eds.), *Oxford Handbook of Political Institutions*. Oxford: Oxford University Press.

Hermes, N., Postma, T. J., & Zivkov, O. (2007). Corporate governance codes and their contents: An analysis of Eastern European codes, *Journal for East European Management Studies*, *12*, 53–74.

Jackson, G. (2003). Corporate governance in Germany and Japan: Liberalization pressures and responses during the 1990s. In K. Yamamura & W. Streeck (Eds.), *The end of diversity? Prospects for German and Japanese capitalism?* New York: Cornell University Press.

Jensen, & Meckling, W. H. (1976). Theory of firm—managerial behavior, agency costs and ownership structure. *Journal of Financial Economics*, *3*(4), 305–360.

Jolly, R., Emmerij, L. J., & Weiss, T. G. (2005). *The power of UN ideas: Lessons from the first 60 years*. New York: United Nations Intellectual History Project.

Lane, C. (2003). Changes in corporate governance of German corporations: Convergence to the Anglo-American model? *Competition & Change*, *7*(2–3), 79–100.

Lane, C. (2005). Institutional transformation and system change: Changes in the corporate convergence of German corporations. In G. Morgan, R. Whitely, & E. Moen (Eds.), *Changing capitalisms: Internationalism, institutional change, and systems of economic performance?* New York: Oxford University Press.

La Porta, R., Lopez-de-Silanes F., Shleifer, A., & Vishny, R. W. (1998). Law and finance, *Journal of Political Economy*, *106*, 1113–1155.

La Porta, R., Lopez-de-Silanes F., Shleifer, A., & Vishny, R. W. (2000). Investor protection and corporate governance, *Journal of Financial Economics*, *58*, 3–27.

La Porta, R., Lopez-de-Silanes, F., & Shleifer, A. (1999). Corporate ownership around the world. *Journal of Finance*, *54,* 471–517.

Mohamed, B. (2008). Board of directors' size and performance in the banking industry. *International Journal of Managerial Finance*, *5*(2), 201–221.

Morgan, G. (2005). Institutional complementarities, path dependency, and the dynamics of Firms. In G. Morgan, R. Whitely, & E. Moen (Eds.), *Changing capitalisms: Internationalism, institutional change, and systems of economic performance*. New York: Oxford University Press.

OECD, Organization for Economic Co-operation and Development. (2004). *Principles of corporate governance*. Paris: Organization for Economic Co-operation and Development.

Okike, E. N. M. (2007). Corporate governance in Nigeria: The status quo. *Corporate Governance: An International Review, 15,* 173–193.

Peters, B. Guy, Pierre, Jon & King, Desmond S. (2005). The politics of path dependency: Political conflict in historical institutionalism, *Journal of Politics*, *67*(4), 1275–1300.

Pierson, P. (2000). The limits of design: Explaining institutional origins and change. *Governance*, *13,* 475–499.

Pierson, P., & Theda, S. (2002). Historical institutionalism in contemporary political science, In Milner Henry and Katznelson, Ira 2002, Political Science- The State of the Discipline, eds. New York and Washington, DC: Norton and the American Political Science Association.

Preda, A. (2009). *Framing finance-the boundaries of markets and modern capitalism*. Chicago: The Chicago University Press.

Rethel, L., & Sinclair Timothy, J. (2012). *The problem with banks*. London: Zed Books.

Roe, M. J. (2003). *Political determinants of corporate governance—political context, corporate impact*. London: Oxford University Press.

Schmidt, V. A. (2000) Values and discourse in the politics adjustment. In F. W. Scharp & V. A. Schmidt (Eds.), *Welfare and work in the open economy volume I: From vulnerability to competitiveness*. Oxford: Oxford University Press.

Schmidt, V. A. (2002). *The futures of European capitalism*. New York: Oxford University Press.

Schmidt, V. A. (2003). French capitalism transformed yet still a third variety of capitalism. *Economy and Society, 32,* 526–554.

Schmidt, V. A. (2010). Taking ideas and discourse seriously: Explaining change through discursive institutionalism as the fourth 'new institutionalism'. *European Political Science Review, 2*(1), 1–25.

Schon, D. A., & Rein, M. (1994). *Frame reflection: Toward the resolution of intractable policy controversies*. New York: Basic Books.

References

Shleifer, A., & Vishny, R. W. (1997). A survey of corporate governance. *Journal of Finance, 52*(2), 737–783.

Steinmo, S., Thelen, K., & Longstreth, F. (1992). *Structuring politic—historical institutionalism in comparative analysis.* Cambridge: Cambridge University Press.

Streeck, W., & Yamamura, K. (2001). *The origins of nonliberal capitalism—Germany and Japan in comparison.* Ithaca: Cornell University Press.

UK. (2009). *Walker review.*

US. Department of Treasury (2008). A blueprint for a modernized financial regulation structure, Washington D.C.: Department of Treasury. Available at: http://www.treas.gov/press/releases/reports/Blueprint.pdf. Accessed 18 November 2009.

US. (2010). *Wall street reform and consumer protection act of 2010 (Dodd Frank Act).*

Vogel, S. K. (1996). *Free markets, more rules, regulatory reform in advanced industrial countries.* Ithaca and London: Cornell University Press.

Weiss, L. (1999). State power and the Asian crisis. *New Political Economy, 4,* 317–342.

Williamson, O. (1984). Corporate governance. *Yale Law Journal, 93,* 1197–1230.

Wilson W. (1898). *The State.* Heath.

Yamamura, K., & Streeck, W. (Eds.). (2003). *The end of diversity? Prospects for German and Japanese capitalism.* New York: Cornell University Press.

Chapter 2
A Discursive Institutional Approach to Corporate Governance

2.1 Introduction

In contrast with the extant literature on corporate governance, this chapter sets out an alternative approach which reinvigorates the implicit institutionalism of the variety of capitalisms (VoC) literature by drawing, in particular, on the recent development of discursive institutional theory. It is an approach that is taken in order to further interrogate the processes through which nationally diverse corporate governance arrangements are actually constituted over time and across space. This is quite different from the extant literature which posits and explores changes within different 'models' of corporate governance, but tells us very little about how these models are produced and reproduced in practices. Specifically, the chapter develops the implicit institutionalism of the VoC literatures by differentiating and elaborating on three levels of discourses: legitimacy, paradigm, and frame. Implicit or explicit within the VoC literature, legitimacy in corporate governance is shown to involve the public sentiments and popular cognitions present in diverse forms of capitalisms, from the 'free market capitalism' to the 'coordinated capitalism'. Such sentiments and cognitions constitute the legitimate roles that corporations are expected to perform across varieties of capitalism. Paradigm for corporate governance, on the other hand, pertains mainly to more abstract orientations and ideas which are best represented in forms of models and patterns on varied corporate governance structures. Such models are not simply passive descriptions of diverse and path-dependent institutional realities, but are constitutive and competing conceptions of how corporate governance can and should be organized, including the shareholder model, the stakeholder model, and the state-affected model. But, corporate governance arrangements are also constituted through the norms, ideas, codes, standards or 'frames' embedded in routine and mundane practices that include the ownership structure, the organization and activities of the corporate board of directors, code of corporate governance, and legal duties.

© Springer Nature Singapore Pte Ltd. 2019

W. Zou, *Corporate Governance in the Banking Sector in China*, CSR, Sustainability, Ethics & Governance, https://doi.org/10.1007/978-981-13-3510-5_2

2.2 Varieties of Capitalisms Analysis

As 'a new framework for understanding the institutional similarities and differences among the developed economies' (Hall and Soskice 2001b, p. 2), their continuity and changes, VoC is developed in explaining economic activities in comparative institutions (Hall and Soskice 2001a, b; Streeck and Yamamura 2001; Yamamura and Streeck 2003; Schmidt 2003; Amable and Gatti 2004; Morgan 2005). With its emphasis on 'system coordination' and the idea of 'institutional complementarities,' VoC argues that 'correctly calibrated' sub-systems, such as financial system, labor market, interfirm relations, can reinforce the 'comparative institutional advantage' of the firm (Hall and Soskice 2001a; Kang 2006). And, it is in this context that VoC is employed in the present book for studying the variances of corporate governance of banking organizations in diverse national configurations.

Several models of capitalisms are developed by VoC, mainly categorized as the liberal market economy (or LME), the coordinated market economy (or CME), the state-affected market economy (SME). LME, typically represented by US and UK, is said to be founded upon the institutional settings of the prevailing ownership of the private property, pro-competitive disengagement by the government, and highly developed legal protections for various property and contractual rights (Hall and Soskice 2001a). In LME, 'firms coordinate their activities primarily via hierarchies and competitive market arrangements' and 'market relationships are characterized by the arm's length exchange of goods or services in a context of competition and formal contracting' (Hall and Sockie 2001b, p. 9). In this context, market institutions frequently play dominant roles in coordinating activities by the economic actors. And, the government is expected to confine its role in setting the rules, providing regulatory and legal infrastructures for efficient functions of the capital market and supplying a basic safety net for the unemployed and the old as well as settling the conflicts (Hall and Soskice 2001a). These are typically observed in UK, for instance, when the **Thatcher's governments** adopted a fairly hands-off relationship with both business and labor (King and Wood 1999; Wood 2001; Schmidt 2002), and promoted 'liberation of the financial markets with the "big bang" in 1986, privatized business with the massive sell-off of monopolistic public enterprise as well as state-owned firms in the competitive sector, deregulated business by replacing voluntary self-governing arrangements and formal government–industry relationships with independent regulatory agencies and radically decentralized the labor markets through deregulatory labor policies that reduced unions' organizing and strike powers while increasing employers' ability to hire and fire at will. And, as a result, the "liberal" British state became even more liberal, and acted primarily as an agent of market preservation by providing framework legislation to locate decision-making power in companies, and limit the power of organized labor' (Schmidt 2003, p. 532).

Meanwhile, as a key player in LME, the court exerts unusual influences on business activities and is purported to provide strong legal protection which 'supports formal contracting and encourages relatively complete contracts' (Hall and Sockie 2001b, p. 10). Characterized with the legal system of judge-made-law, the court in LME

2.2 Varieties of Capitalisms Analysis

takes a prominent place. Frequently, the rules and principles established by the court, in forms of precedents which are legally binding, are carefully considered by the corporation and integrated into its article of incorporation or practices to avoid further legal suits under the similar cause of action. Meanwhile, the regulators are active in launching legal actions against malpractices and legal violations by the corporations, though these cases largely end in settlements and their merits are questioned (Bauma et al. 2007).

The CME variety of capitalism, on the other hand, relies more on the non-market relationships, coordination and collaboration, and credible commitments among various market participants, and is well exemplified by Germany and Japan. In contrast with the overwhelming market institutions in LME, in CME, 'firms depend more heavily on non-market relationships to coordinate their endeavors with other actors and to construct their core competencies,' which pertain to 'more extensive relational or incomplete contracting, network monitoring based on the exchange of private information inside networks, and more reliance on collaborative instead of the competitive relationships to build the competencies of the firm' (Hall and Sockie 2001b, p. 9). As the firms in this model mainly achieve their goals through strategic interactions, specific institutions apart from the market competition are needed which are expected to 'reduce the uncertainty actors have about the behavior of others and allow them to make credible commitments to each other' (Hall and Sockie 2001b, p. 10), such as better exchange of information, efficient monitoring of behavior, and penalty for defection from cooperative endeavor (Ostrom 1990; Hall and Sockie 2001b). And, in practice, these institutions embrace 'powerful business or employer associations, strong trade unions, extensive networks of cross-shareholding, and legal or regulatory systems designed to facilitate information-sharing and collaboration' (Hall and Sockie 2001b, p. 11).

In CME, the state is legitimized in taking its position as 'enabling' to enhance economic competitiveness, while without 'jeopardizing the non-market coordinating institutions, — in which regulatory authority was vested in private bodies, including employers' associations and unions' (Schmidt 2003, p. 533). The state prefers to help coordinate the relationships between various participants in economic activities and foster coherence between the business and labor. In this context, the rules are jointly decided by the key participants, conflicts are harmonized between the management and labor, and the collaboration is achieved through a combination of external institutions with abundance of low-cost capitals and labors (Hall and Soskice 2001b). And, even in the instance of economic reforms, the government may take a slow step and coordinate with various economic actors such as business, labor, and local communities governments. Meanwhile, the legal system in CME model, which is frequently labeled as the Continental legal system, is said to provide weak protection for property rights and the court is less active in intervening in the economic activities (Shleifer and Vishny 1997). Nevertheless, the court in this model takes on some specialty due to the dominant coordinative institutions. In Germany, for instance, 'the character of legal regulation is said to facilitate many kinds of non-market coordination' and the court is expected to 'effectively employ regulatory contract law doctrines based on social market economy norms that are routinely dismissed by US legal experts as untenable' (Hall and Soskice 2001b, pp. 388–389). This attributes to the strategic capacity of German firms to create interfirm relations and non-market forms of coordination, which 'consist of sophisticated but standardized contractual structures that facilitate the construction of new forms of industrial organization within the economy. And, once firms collectively develop these frameworks, courts in Germany use them to impose strong legal regulation' (Hall and Soskice 2001b, p. 390). Meanwhile, applying the regulatory approach, German courts 'have much higher information requirements' and 'must take into account broader societal norms regarding fair contracting when adjudicating disputes and, moreover, assess information pertaining to the relationship as a whole' (Hall and Soskice 2001b, p. 392).

The state-affected capitalism (SME), or the state-led/state-enhanced capitalism, are epitomized by France, Italy, and Korea (sometimes Japan is included considering its close business–government relationship), which are based on the continuing influential role of the state, though drastic changes are taking place (Schmidt 2002, 2003; Coates 2000; Boyer 1997; Weiss 1999). Although this third model of capitalism is argued to be either 'on the road' to LME (Morin 2000) or CME (Hancké 2001; Rhodes and Van Apeldoorn 1997) due to financial globalization and deregulation, there is 'continuing importance of the state or state-related institutions in the economic management systems of countries', in which the state, having played a highly directive role in the past, continues to exercise significant albeit less direct influences on economic development (Schmidt 2003, p. 527).

In contrast with the overwhelming market institutions in LME, or influential non-market coordination in CME, economic activities in SME are frequently state oriented. The state directs the economic process and business activities according to its own needs and wishes, acts either in place of, or takes the place of, the market, and guides the economy by various means, like nationalizing industries, planning and promulgating industrial policies (Schmidt 2002). For instance, in France in 1990s, 'the state mediated inter-firm relations, set medium-term corporate strategies through planning and industrial policy and underwrote the investment of traditionally undercapitalized business, sometimes demanding no financial return at all if the state's medium-term goals were being fulfilled, such as maintaining employment or increasing production in strategic areas' (Schmidt 2003, pp. 529–530). Even in the process of drastic economic reforms when the state retreats from the leadership of business, such as financial market liberalization, business deregulation, privatization and labor market decentralization, the government may continue to play a dominant role due to its 'capacity to impose reforms without crippling protests, — and a discourse that spoke to the necessity of reform in the face of economic crisis and its appropriateness in terms of national sacrifice' (Schmidt 2003, p. 533). Though the reforms in SME have actually transformed the state from 'a leadership role to an "enhancing" role,' the state continues to 'intervene strategically to protect business and/or labor from the worst effects of the markets' even if the market institutions are becoming increasingly significant (Schmidt 2003, p. 533). Meanwhile, the state may intervene in hard times to protect its large enterprises from bankruptcy by means of bailout and obstruct foreign takeovers by outlawing takeover measures (Schmidt 2002). These strong government postures and powerful political influences, not infrequently, may

2.2 Varieties of Capitalisms Analysis

lead to a weaker role of judiciaries in business activities in SME in contrast with the LME or CME model. And sometimes, the court may even subdue to the political interests and lose its independence in significant economic cases (The World Bank, Doing Business Report 2004).

Though VoC is well developed in analyzing the comparative institutional advantages, significant limitations are said to be present (Peck and Theodore's 2007; Kang 2006; Jackson and Deeg 2006). Like its advantages in explaining the varieties of capitalisms, the VoC analysis is equally defective in lack of varieties of capitalisms. For instance, major differences can be observed in key institutional aspects among countries roughly categorized as the same capitalism. Though Japan is categorized with Germany in the same CME capitalism, its government plays a more intervening role in economic activities, which makes it more fitful to be categorized as the SME capitalism like France. Meanwhile, there are problems in applying VoC analysis to the transitional economies, which cannot fit neatly into the pigeonholes designed by the VoC scholars as they present some hybrid or derivative features of the existing capitalisms (Howell 2003).

Meanwhile, VoC is also less competent in accommodating the changes in institutions. Largely built upon comparatively static institutions, VoC classifies and describes various capitalisms based on the presumed institutional stability (Howell 2003; Allen 2004), and implicitly excludes the influences of the changes in the institutional settings to retain its theoretical intactness. For instance, it cannot adequately handle the changes in the existing categories of capitalisms. Since 1990s, some capitalisms (like France) underwent massive institutional changes and did not properly fit into the original category. Instead, they are 'stuck' in a transitional gap between different capitalisms, a state of the different subgroup. In more drastic cases, they may 'jump' to totally different categories of capitalisms. VoC often cannot provide a sound explanation for such institutional changes and update its categorization on capitalisms (Jackson and Deeg 2006).

Moreover, VoC lays special emphasis on the analysis of formal institutions like the capital market and labor relationships, while gives limited consideration to informal institutions like norms, usages, and practices by the firms. This may cause problems as sometimes the informal institutions play a far more important role in shaping the activities of the firm. For instance, though there is apparent formal institutional stability in a certain national configuration, the firms may, based on their own discourses and preferences, pursue a specific strategy which is in substance inconsistent with the existing formal institutions. In this context, the formal institutions may be used differently by the firms and give away to those informal institutions (Morgan 2005; Hall and Thelen 2005).

To overcome the limits of the VoC analysis, this book brings in as well the discursive institutionalism as the analytical framework. In contrast with the VoC analysis, the discursive institutional approach is more efficient in explaining institutional changes by analyzing the role of ideas in shaping and changing the activities of the actors. With extensive elaboration on legitimacies, paradigms, and frames, the discursive approach provides a much wider exploration on institutions, from micro to macro and from static to dynamic. Specifically, focusing on the role of ideas, this institutional approach takes into account both formal and informal institutions. Meanwhile, acknowledging the diversities in institutional settings, the discursive institutional approach uses a more flexible categorization method and addresses effectively the dynamics and changes between different model countries.

2.3 Theories of Institutionalism

Traditionally, institutionalism is widely used in political and social science as an analytical approach, and institutional explanations have become popular in policy and governance studies. Applied in this book, it presents a useful analytical framework for better understanding of how the institutional settings constitute and change the corporate governance system. Specifically, it illustrates how different corporate governance arrangements are legitimized in diverse national institutional settings by considering the variety of capitalisms, how such legitimacy influences the key orientation in the form of paradigm, and how these legitimacy and paradigm affect the various norms and practices, or frame in general, in the operations of business organizations.

Theoretically, institutional approach can be divided into the old institutionalism school and the new institutionalism school. The former focuses on formal institutions like law and statutes, and their roles in governing. It argues for the dominance of structure and its bounds upon individuals and stresses upon the historical foundations for institutional analysis (Bates et al. 1998). The latter, on the other hand, develops a further understanding and argues that the institution is a structural feature of the society or polity, which can be formal as in the form of legislature or informal like norms, values, or usages. As a 'stable existence,' the institution can be used to predict behaviors apart from its binding effects upon the individuals. Also, the institution can lead to some senses of shared values and meanings of members within its range (Peters et al. 2005; March and Olson 1998; Steinmo et al. 1992).

Within the new institutional tradition, moreover, there are further and more precise categorizations which typically distinguish between the historical institutionalism, rational choice institutionalism, sociological institutionalism, and discursive institutionalism. While broadly united by their emphasis on institutions of all kinds, these different institutionalisms vary greatly in terms of key analytical questions. For instance, historical, sociological, and rational choice institutionalisms are somewhat static and typically emphasize continuity over change. In contrast, discursive institutionalism is more dynamic and capable of analyzing changes (Schmidt 2010).

The historical institutionalism argues that the initial institution will have a continuing and lasting determinative influence over institutions far into the future (Pierson and Skocpol 2002; Thelen 1999) and is mainly characterized with its argument for path dependence and the asymmetrical allocation of powers by different interest groups (Krasner 1984; Dryzek 1994; Pierson 2000). The rational choice institutionalism, in contrast, argues that utility maximization is always the primary motivation of individuals and their goals can be achieved most effectively through institutional

2.3 Theories of Institutionalism   31

action (Peters et al. 2005). This embraces both internal and external elements, such as
the actor's fixed set of preferences, strategic extensive calculations (Kenneth 1989),
and the specific set of structures, procedures, or mechanisms provided by the external
institutions. The sociological institutionalism is said to be the widest institutionalism
in explaining the origin and function of the institutions, which defines that institutions
embrace not only the usual formal rules, procedures, or norms, but symbol systems,
cognitive scripts, and moral templates. Besides, culture here is also regarded as
an institution instead of external factor to traditional 'institutions' (Campbell 1995).
Hence, the relationship between institutions and actors is approached with a 'cultural
approach,' which develops a highly interactive and mutually constitutive relationship
between the institutions and actors. In this context, the actors, consciously and sub-
consciously, engage themselves in socially meaningful activities as social players
and in turn reinforce the institutional norms they stick to. They work and rework
with available institutional templates to devise a course of action.

2.3.1 Defining Discursive Institutionalism

The discursive institutionalism, in contrast with other three new institutionalism, is
'an umbrella concept for the vast range of works' which takes account of 'the substantive content of ideas and the interactive processes by which ideas are conveyed
and exchanged through discourse' (Schmidt 2010, p. 3). At the substantive level, the
discourse pertains to ideas 'about "what is and what ought to be" at different levels
of generality' (Schmidt 2010), which extends from the specific and implementable
policy ideas (Hall 1989), to paradigms (Hall 1993; Berman 1998) and to deeper
philosophic ideas or public sentiments (Campbell 2004). Moreover, the discourse
can also be categorized into cognitive ideas (Hall 1993; Schmidt 2002) and norma-
tive ideas (Schmidt 2000), with the former focusing on interests and necessity and
the latter centered on values and appropriateness (Schmidt 2010). At the interactive
dimension, the discourse is distinguished between a coordinative process and communicative process, where ideas are constructed and communicated differently. In
coordinative discourse, the ideas are jointly constructed by various participants. In
contrast, the communicative discourse involves a wide range of actors who 'bring
ideas developed in the context of the coordinative discourse to the public deliberation and legitimization' (Schmidt 2010, p. 3). Distinguished from other institutionalisms focusing on ideas like ideational institutionalism (Hay 2001), constructivist
institutionalism (Hay 2008), or strategic constructivism (Jabko 2006), the discursive
institutionalism stresses that 'discourse is not just ideas or "text" (what is said) but
also context (where, when, how, and why it was said). The term refers not only to
structure (what is said, or where and how) but also to agency (who said what to
whom).' (Schmidt 2008, p. 305).

Based on the multi-facet analysis of the institutions by connecting the 'macro with
the micro,' the discursive institutionalism lays special emphasis upon the role of the
ideas and discourses on the social activities. And, it is powerful in generating, delib-

erating, and/or legitimizing ideas about social activities in the institutional context and provides effective explanations for the dynamics of institutional changes, which illustrates when and how ideas in discursive interactions may efficiently enable actors to overcome constraints that are regarded as institutional impediments (Krook 2007). Meanwhile, an intricate relationship can be observed between the discourse and the institutions. On one side, the discourse is carefully distinguished from the institutions, as the latter is said to play a decisive role in shaping the discourse (Schmidt 2002; Fischer 2003). On the flip side, however, discourses and institutions are frequently intertwined and may 'unfold as ideas are articulated and, over time, are turned into rules-based systems of concepts and conceptions' 'Institutions, in turn, are authorized and sanctioned discourse. The set of rules governing a discourse are referred to as institutions when these rules, through processes of institutionalization, have attained some degree of authority and been linked to sanctions' (Lynggaard 2007, p. 294). Typically, the power of the discourse may go beyond explaining the reality as it may be the major force in constituting most part of the reality (Fischer 2003).

As a 'young' institutionalism, however, the discursive institutionalism has its limitations. For instance, from the epistemological perspective, the discourse is comparatively abstract and hard to be tracked down. And it is sometimes not easy to find solid evidence of its causal impacts on social activities and outcomes. This becomes more difficult when there are a great variety of ideas drifting around in a specific social context or when ideas are only a part of a broad social ideology or public philosophy. Meanwhile, ideas may have different levels of abstractions, and there may be certain unconscious ideas at work in people's mind (Parson 2003). Thirdly, there may be some confusion about ideas as either *explanans* (the explanation) or *explanandum* (what needs to be explained). On one side, ideas may become major causal factors in explaining the social activities on their own. On the other side, however, powerful institutional factors may constrain the production and dissemination of ideas (Schmidt 2002; Walsh 2000).

The discursive institutionalism has a complicated relationship with other new institutionalisms. For instance, conflicts are unavoidable in considering the interrelationship between the discursive institutionalism and rational choice institutionalism, especially when ideas, the core of the former, are being forayed into the latter and act as 'switches' which funnel interests down specific directions (Bates et al. 1998) or even substitute the interests in explaining the constructions of institutions as 'shared mental modes' (North 1990). On the other hand, complementary relation can be observed between the historical institutionalism and discursive institutionalism, especially considering the strength of ideas in explaining changes and as a heritage down the history (Blyth 2003). This is further evidenced by acceptance of ideas by historical institutionalism scholars who gradually combine ideas into their historical institutional analysis (Peters 2009). The discursive institutionalism has an intimate relationship with the sociological institutionalism, constructivist institutionalism (Hay 2008), and economic constructivism (Abdelal et al. 2007) due to its focus on ideational analysis. On one side, there is a strong 'family resemblance' in these institutionalisms as ideas, acting as the basis of the institutionalism, are argued to constitute the norms, paradigms, and frames which help construct the actor's under-

2.3 Theories of Institutionalism 33

standings of interests and redirect their actions within the institutions. On the flip side, however, the discursive institutionalism is distinguished by its further emphasis on the interactive process of generating and communicating ideas to the public and the dynamics between the discourse and the institution.

2.4 Three Levels of Discursive Institutionalism and Application in Corporate Governance in VoC Context

As the core of the discursive institutionalism, ideas are regarded as foundations for the formation and changes of the institutional arrangements. Defined as causal beliefs which are products of cognition and connected to this material world via interpretation of the surrounding environments, ideas are said to provide guides for actions and specific ways to address problems and challenges (Jolly et al. 2005). Not infrequently, ideas can take many forms, such as high-profile public frames, discourses, and ideologies at the foreground of the cognition (Schon and Rein 1994; Campbell 2004) or a lower-profile assumptions and paradigms that remain at the backgrounds of the arena (Hall 1993). Generally, ideas in the discursive institutionalism 'tend to occur at three main levels of generality,' i.e., policy solutions, general programs underpinning the policy ideas, and public sentiments which 'undergird the policies and programs with organizing ideas, values, and principles of knowledge and society' (Schmidt 2008, p. 306). In this framework, the discourses are categorized logically into three levels, namely legitimacy, paradigm, and frame, which can be innovatively used in analyzing the generic corporate governance system in varied models by combining the VoC theories.

2.4.1 Legitimacy

First, as the foundation of the institution, ideas take the form of legitimacy comprising public sentiments and public philosophy (Campbell 1998, 2004). Like observation through the kaleidoscope, the legitimacy is rich in 'colors and shapes' by taking into account various social entities, actors, factors and extends to the political, economic, legal institutions. In its dazzling display, key features of the legitimacy for a period of time in a certain place may be sorted out due to the dominance of certain elements, which are then distilled by the actors and become taken-for-granted public assumptions. For instance, legitimacy may take into account the relationship between citizens and the state, the rights and obligations in political, social and economic institutions, and public sentiments based on the common language, culture and historical identity (Hay 2001).

However, there is always an intricate relationship between the legitimacy and the actor. On one side, the actor is bound by legitimacy if he intends his activities are institutional acceptable and public desirable. This restricts his choices and options *ex ante* as he has to take same or similar attitudes and stands with the public. In times of uncertainty or instability, specifically, the legitimacy can become overwhelming and even dictate the activities of the actor (Campbell 1998). On the flip side, however, due to the broadness and lack of clarity, legitimacy in general cannot provide a specific option or solution but supplement to the decision making of the actor. Meanwhile, it may be played or even maneuvered by the powerful actor, like the political leader, influential businessman, or public figure, to turn his own ideas into legitimacy and promote to the public. For instance, neoliberal ideas create neoliberal policies and in turn become legitimate for the public in US and UK. The globalization may become something of a self-filling prophecy and behaving as if it was a reality. Actually, it is the policy makers across countries that makes the globalization happen (Hay 2008).

When applied to analyzing the corporate governance structure in business organizations, legitimacy is found to vary in different national institutional settings. In the Anglo-Saxon countries, which largely fall under the LME as represented by US and UK, the legitimacy is well manifested in strong orientation toward the prevailing private ownership and higher economic efficiency, maximization of the private wealth under equal situations, pro-competitive deregulation stance by the government, and strong legal protections by independent court systems. And, the institutional settings are largely characterized by an arm's length relationship between different entities, like regulators, corporations, and banks (Hall and Sockie 2001b). For corporate finance, the capital markets take a most prestigious place and funnel major financing to corporations of various kinds. Although bank relations are also significant, especially in hard times, the bank–firm relationship follows an arm's length pattern and the bank is less powerful in monitoring and controlling the invested corporations. The shares of the corporation are highly dispersed, either held by individual investors or institutional investors, and are actively traded in the capital market (Vogel 1996; Allen and Gale 2002). To mitigate the effects of information asymmetry in such decentralized market, a high level of transparency is demanded. For instance, financial reporting is required to be prepared by the auditors and periodically reviewed by the investors and analysts. Fight for corporate control, always in the form of antagonistic merger and acquisition, is fairly active and mainly exercised through the takeover markets. The state, as a 'passive participant,' frequently recesses to the corner in the process of economic and business activities and pledges a pro-competitive disengagement attitude, though in times of economic crisis it prefers to be more active and engaging and take up the Keynesianism (Hall and Sockie 2001b; Allen and Gale 2002). And, the court is highly valued by the private parties in settling economic disputes and expected to render sufficient legal protections for property and contractual rights.

2.4 Three Levels of Discursive Institutionalism and Application …   35

In contrast, in the Continental countries which approximate to the CME, legitimacy is characterized by the coordination and close relationship between the government, banks, corporations, and labor, as typically represented in Germany and Japan (Hall and Sockie 2001a). Private ownership is more or less tinged with certain social nature, and legal protection for private rights is, to some extent, hindered and comparatively less developed. Though the government, apparently, takes a liberal posture and promotes self-regulation by the corporation, it is more actively involved in, as a 'coordinator,' industrial adjustment process by coordinating the policies across the industrial sectors, smoothening relationship between the banks and the enterprises, and facilitating business activities and overall economic development. Capital markets are comparatively less developed and restricted in size, and the corporations are mainly financed by the retained earnings and bank loans. The former may result from institutional and legal incentives, which encourage the corporations to accumulate their own reserves, such as high corporate taxation and allowance for accelerated depreciation. The latter originates from the bank's active lending activities to the generic firms and its unique status in corporate governance of the enterprises (Allen and Gale 2002). In this context, concentrated ownership, typically in forms of block holding and cross-holding, is quite popular in the Continental countries and the bank-industrial cross-holding relationship is much stronger. These result from a closer collaborative system where the government bureaucrats, corporate managers, bankers, and political parties have some shared aims for the sake of economic development. Targeted at long-term interests and sustainable development, the corporate management is encouraged to hold the investors 'patient' and focus on returns of capital gains and collateral business in the long run, rather than paying immediate high dividends to the investors (Vogel 1996; Allen and Gale 2002). Due to the existence of active and controlling shareholders, there is less need for transparency, and information disclosure is only drawn up to meet tax and reporting obligations rather than informing the public shareholders. Meanwhile, the corporate control market is inactive and takeovers are fairly rare. Even in events of merger and acquisition, the transactions are mainly based on inside information and friendly negotiation instead of the hostile takeover which marks the Anglo-Saxon model (Hall and Sockie 2001a; Allen and Gale 2002).

In the State-affected countries, which are largely consistent with the SME legitimacy is characterized by the state's controlling ownership, active intervention in industries and economic process and promotion of the national economic development. Such intervention is intentionally biased against the private ownership while prioritizing the 'public ownership' by the sovereign for the sake of national economy. The institutional settings are mainly characterized by the dominant role of the government in controlling corporations by means of state ownership, direct appointment of quasi-official directors in banks and public corporations, and strict regulations (Goyer 2001). The funding of the corporation is mainly provided by the bank, while the development of the capital market is comparatively limited. In particular, it is always the state that controls the key commercial banks, and a state-controlled pattern is set in place in allocating credit resources to the corporations and determines the price of such credit. Other funding channels, like policy loans, government subsidy, and tax preference treatment, are also provided to encourage the development of specific sectors, industries, or corporations, which are considered as strategically important for national economy (Chang 1996; Deyo 1989; Woo and Woo-Cumings 1991). Meanwhile, senior managers in the corporation are frequently assigned by the government and initiated by bureaucratic promotion. And, instead of pursuing short-term profit maximization, the corporate managers hold themselves as long-term committed, seek the long-termism of the corporation development, and are accountable for the national economic development (Kang 2006). In addition, close inter-connectivity through informal state networks, based on state-related education and experience, helps form better inter-corporation coordination, information sharing, and cooperation on corporate strategies (Schmidt 2002). The market for corporate control is significantly affected by the government, and in the instances of takeover battles, financial regulators frequently play a determining role in the outcome (Hall and Sockie 2001b). The legal system also has a strong flavor of public interests and may sometimes give away to regulatory influences.

2.4.2 Paradigm

At the next level of the discursive institutionalism, ideas take the form of paradigms, exemplified as the 'underlying assumptions or organizing principles orienting policy' (Schmidt 2008, p. 306). Different paradigms and their relationship can be compared to observing the planets and stars through the telescope, separate but connected. Implicated by different legitimacy discourses, paradigms appear to be isolated from each other and maintain their independence and boundary as separate entities. Nevertheless, due to invisible interactions, especially the similar goal to be achieved, the varied paradigms are somehow closely connected and may affect each other from time to time, resembling interactions between the planets because of gravity despite the fact that they revolve 'lonely' in their own orbits.

In social activities, paradigms frequently produce opportunities for actors in the process of forming their own ideas and in pursuing the solutions to problems. These may be a totally unconscious process, as paradigms are generally rooted in actors' cognitive backgrounds and underlying theoretical and ontological assumptions about how the world runs. For instance, they may be formed through textbooks and case studies in schools and universities, seminars, and influential publications by master scholars in the field, which shape the 'discursive path and terrain' of the actor. Or they are shaped by one's experience from his family and working place. Meanwhile, the increasingly powerful social media, especially the Internet social networks like blogs, twitters may greatly influence the actor's mindset by its frequent, overwhelming and persuasive existence (Campbell 1998).

For paradigms, there are dominant and subordinate, which may coexist but with different weights and influences. However, the dominance of the paradigm in policy, academic popularity, and public acceptance may not be decided by its proximity to truth, but frequently how efficiently it is promoted and sold. This is well evidenced

2.4 Three Levels of Discursive Institutionalism and Application ... 37

by the history of science, from Bruno to Galileo, where the acceptance of the law of nature lagged far behind its discovery as the actively promoted or arbitrary paradigm of the pseudolaw never easily gave away its throne. In social science, the game is even fanatically played when the 'truth' is 'relative' while the orientations and interests of the players, academia, policy makers, and practitioners alike are 'absolute.' Frequently, the popularity and dominance of certain paradigms are closely connected to the continuous endeavors by the scholars, think tanks, and policy makers. Like salesman, they design, package, and market the distilled, simplified, and easy-to-read set of ideas in their aggressive approaches, in forms of commercial ads, brief policy position papers, popular books, journal articles, radio and television appearances, and newspapers, which create an air of 'salesmanship' instead of 'scholarship.' Sometimes, instead of generating new ideas, they just cram the government and the public with their favored academic conceptions and theories (Campbell 1998).

In the context of corporate governance study, paradigms are distinguished by varied models and theories in various national institutional settings, resonating with the legitimacy discourses discussed as above. In the Anglo-Saxon or LME countries, the paradigm in corporate governance is categorized as the Anglo-Saxon model and is said to be dominated by the shareholder primacy theory. The ideas of maximizing the interests of the investors, mitigating agency costs, and enhancing the performance of the corporation are actively 'advertised' to the public by academia, policy makers, and practitioners. It well echoes the legitimacy of the prevailing private ownership, disengagement by the government for competition, and strong legal protection of private interests. The sub-current theories, like the stakeholder theory which argues for the protection of stakeholders and corporate social responsibilities, are less accepted and believed in despite their merits. Even if they are recognized to a certain degree, they are largely theories on the paper and implemented poorly.

In the Continental countries, the paradigm in corporate governance is labeled as the Continental model and characterized with the stakeholder theory. In contrast with the shareholder primacy theory in the Anglo-Saxon model, it contends for equally protecting the interests of the stakeholders of the corporation, such as the employees, creditors, suppliers, while limiting the maximization of the interests of shareholders. This largely resonates with the legitimacy of coordinating the interests of different players by the state, limitation on the priority of private ownership, and weak legal protection. Although there are scholars arguing for the convergence toward the Anglo-Saxon model and stressing on the maximized investment returns to the shareholders and best performance of the corporation, such subordinate paradigm exerts limited influences upon the existing policy or legislation.

For other types of countries, relevant paradigms are developed, either as a hybrid or derivative of the afore-discussed models. For instance, the paradigm for the State-affected countries is classified as the State-affected model, which is said to be the hybrid of the shareholder primacy model and stakeholder model. On one side, it is oriented toward the enhancement of the shareholders' interests, as in the Anglo-Saxon model. On the flip side, it is also targeted to the protection of the interests of various stakeholders similar to the Continental model. However, such paradigm discourse lays specific emphasis upon the national economic development. Always, with the state being the controlling shareholder, the paradigm aims to harmonize the interests by the shareholders, the stakeholders, and national economic growth. This is consistent with its legitimacy of preference for the state intervention and active involvement in corporate operations and governance structure, with the pursuit of national economic objectives.

2.4.3 Frame

At the empirical level of the discursive institutionalism, ideas take the form of the frame, which embodies a great variety of norms, codes, and usages in routine practices. As the manifestation of the legitimacy and paradigm discourses, the frame may 'involve specific policies, measures, guidance developed to tackle the practical problems' encountered in social life, which is purported to sort out most efficient solutions and achieve designated objectives (Schmidt 2010, p. 5). Not infrequently, the frame is expected to be clear, concise, and behave as an efficient 'short-cut' among a great variety of options and ideas (Campbell 1998).

When applied to corporate governance analysis, the frame mainly focuses upon certain key practices of the governance arrangement in generic corporations, such as the ownership structure, the organization and behavior of the board of directors, code of corporate governance, and legal duties. Other issues may be of greater significance in the context of corporate governance in banking organizations, such as the regulation on executive pay and risk management arrangement. Effectively, the frame resonates with the afore-discussed legitimacy and paradigm discourses in corporate governance system and illustrates the impacts of these 'taken-for-granted' and abstract ideas. For instance, implicated by divergent legitimacy and paradigmatic discourses, the board of directors varies in different models regarding its organization, practice, and duties despite its general function as 'the brain and heart' of the corporation. In the Anglo-Saxon model, the board of directors is organized in one-tier structure for higher efficiency. It is strongly oriented toward best performance of the corporation, effective monitoring upon the management, and higher standards of fiduciary duties. These well represent the paradigm in the Anglo-Saxon model of the shareholder primacy and legitimacy of prevailing private ownership. In contrast, the board of directors in the Continental model is characterized with the two-tier board structure, which stresses upon the relational role with the shareholders, strong connections with the stakeholders, and less burden of legal obligations. These well reflect the paradigm of protecting the stakeholders' interests in the Continental model and legitimacy of coordinating interests among various parties in the framework of corporate governance. The board of directors in the State-affected, similar to that in the Continental model, is distinguished by the state's influence in the boardroom its strong political connections, and orientations for promoting national economic development. These are consistent with the paradigm of the State-affected model (the hybrid of shareholder primacy theory and stakeholder theory) and legitimacy of strong state intervention and concerns for national economic growth. Similar dynamics can be observed in other practices of corporate governance, such as the ownership structure, code of corporate governance, and legal duties.

2.4.4 Dynamics Between Legitimacy, Paradigm, and Frame

In Fig. 2.1, a general path, spiraling from the legitimacy, paradigm and then down to frame, is illustrated for better understanding of different levels of ideas in the cognitive background and foreground. However, interactions and dynamics between and among different level of ideas are more complicated than it appears. On one side, there is a logical order of ideas funnelling down from the legitimacy, to paradigm and then to frame, from the cognitive background to the cognitive foreground. For instance, the paradigm is mainly built upon the legitimacy widely accepted by the public as socially desirable. The frame, oriented by the paradigm, may directly integrate the paradigm in the form of norms like specific designed documents, guidance, or code and gains its justification by relating to the legitimacy. On the flip side, however, such logic may deviate or even be reversed. For instance, the paradigm may diverge from the legitimacy due to the aggressive promotion of by the policy makers, the think tanks, and the academia, especially when ideas in legitimacy are less clear and broader. Frame can go further and vary from the paradigm and legitimacy to

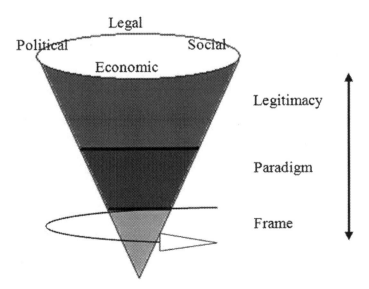

Fig. 2.1 Dynamics of three-level ideas

a larger scale. First, there is some cognitive 'distance' between the frame and the paradigm and even farther for the legitimacy, which enables the frame to be fairly independent and stretch far away from the bounds of the paradigm and legitimacy. This typically happens when the frame is maneuvered by a certain interest group for the sake of its own benefits. Secondly, it may happen when the frame is more about specific practices and technical issues, like developments of mathematic modules, patterns, or equations targeted at certain business. In a more drastic form, there will be a 'rebel' of the frame when, under the powerful influences of a certain interest group, it can defy against the present paradigm and legitimacy and even reshape them. Nevertheless, when this happens, there may already have been some changes going on in the paradigm and legitimacy which are consistent with the changing frame.

2.5 Conclusion

Contrasting with the traditional theoretical framework of corporate governance across different countries, the present chapter innovatively develops the discursive institutionalism as an analytical tool for better understanding of the corporate governance system. By bringing in the VoC analysis for diversified institutional settings, the chapter prepares the models for institutional analysis on the production and reproduction of corporate governance in varied institutional embedment. This is reinforced by the development of the discursive institutionalism, which explores the functions of institutions from macro- to micro-level and the significant role of ideas in shaping and changing corporate governance. Divided into three levels, ideas may take the form of legitimacy, paradigm, and frame. The legitimacy lays a 'take-for-granted' and socially desirable ground for the institutional settings of corporate governance. The paradigms, originating and distilled from the legitimacy, provide a clear orientation and certain preferences in corporate governance. And the frame, targeted at solving specific problems, pertains to the guide, norms, and practice in the corporate governance structure. Represented in different forms, ideas may play a dominant role in the development and changes of corporate governance in different institutional settings. And, the discursive institutionalism developed in this chapter will be used as a powerful toolkit and applied to corporate governance in banking organizations around the world and then China in the following chapters.

References

Abdelal, R., Blyth, M., & Parsons, C. (2007). *Constructivist political economy*, manuscript. Available at http://ducis.jhfc.duke.edu. Accessed May 08, 2010.

Allen, F., & Gale, D. (2002). *Comparing financial systems*. Beijing: Ren Min University Press.

Allen, M. (2004). The varieties of capitalism paradigm: Not enough variety? *Socio-Economic Review, 2,* 87–108.

Amable, B., & Gatti, D. (2004). Product market competition, job security, and aggregate employment. *Oxford Economic Papers, 56*(4), 667–686.

Bates, R. H., De Figueiredo Jr, R. J. P., & Weingast, B. R. (1998). The politics of interpretation: Rationality, culture and transition. *Politics and Society, 26*(4), 603–642.

Bauma, D. J., Palmiter, R. A., & Partnoy, F. (2007). *Corporations law and policy* (6th ed.). NY: West Publisher.

Berman, S. (1998). *The social democratic develoment*. Cambridge: Harvard University Press.

Blyth, M. (2003). Structures do not come with an instruction sheet: Interests, ideas, and progress in science. *Perspectives on Politics, 1*(4), 695–706.

Boyer, R. (1997). French statism at the crossroads. In C. Crouch & W. Streeck (Eds.), *Political economy of modern capitalism: Mapping convergence and diversity*. London: Sage.

Campbell, J. L. (1995). Review of forging industrial policy. *Contemporary Sociology, 23,* 822–823.

Campbell, J. L. (1998). Institutional analysis and the roles of ideas in political economy. *Theory and Society, 27*(3), 377–409.

Campbell, J. L. (2004). *Institutional change and globalization*. Princeton: Princeton University Press.

Chang, S. J. (1996). An evolutionary perspective on diversification and corporate restructuring: Entry, exit, and economic performance during 1981–89. *Strategic Management Journal, 17*(8), 587–611.

Coates, D. (2000). *Models of capitalism: Growth and stagnation in the modern era*. Cambridge: Polity Press.

Deyo, F. C. (1989). *Beneath the miracle: Labor subordination in the new Asian industrialism*. University of California Press.

Dryzek, J. S. (1994). *Discursive democracy: Politics, policy, and political science*. Cambridge University Press.

Fischer, F. (2003). *Reforming public politics*. Oxford: Oxford University Press.

Goyer, M. (2001). Corporate governance and the innovation system in France: 1985-2000. *Industry and Innovation, 8*(2), 135–158.

Hall, P. A. (1989). *The political power of economic ideas: Keynesianism across nations*. Princeton NJ: Princeton University Press.

Hall, P. A. (1993). Policy paradigms, social learning and the state. *Comparative Politics, 23,* 275–296.

Hall, P. A., & Soskice, D. (2001a). *'Introduction' in varieties of capitalism*. New York: Oxford University Press.

Hall, P. A., & Soskice, D. (Eds.). (2001b). *Varieties of capitalism-the institutional foundations of comparative advantage*. Oxford: Oxford University Press.

Hall, P. A., & Thelen, K. (2005). The politics of change in varieties of capitalism. In: Conference Paper in American Political Science Association Annual Meeting, September 1–4, 2005. New York: Washington, D.C.

Hancké, B. (2001). Revisiting the French model: Coordination and restructuring in French industry. In P. A. Hall & D. Soskice (Eds.), *Varieties of capitalism: The institutional foundations of comparative advantage*. Oxford: Oxford University Press.

Hay, C. (2001). The "crisis" of Keynesianism and the rise of neoliberalism in Britain. In J. L. Campbell & O. K. Pedersen (Eds.), *The rise of neoliberalism and institutional analysis*. Princeton, NJ: Princeton University Press.

42 2 A Discursive Institutional Approach to Corporate Governance

Hay, C. (2008). Constructivist institutionalism. In R. Rhodes, S. Binder & B. Rockman (Eds.), *Oxford handbook of political institutions*. Oxford: Oxford University Press.

Howell, C. (2003). Varieties of capitalism: And then there was one? *Comparative Politics, 36*(1), 103–124.

Jabko, N. (2006). *Playing the market—a political strategy for uniting Europe 1985–2005*. NY: Cornell University Press.

Jackson, G., & Deeg, R. (2006). How many varieties of capitalism? Comparing the comparative institutional analyses of capitalist diversity, MPIFG Discussion Paper 06/2, April 2006.

Jolly, R., Emmerij, L. J., & Weiss, T. G. (2005). The power of UN ideas: Lessons from the first 60 years. New York: United Nations Intellectual History Project.

Kang, N. (2006). A critique of the "Varieties of Capitalism" approach. Research paper series, Nottingham University. http://www.nottingham.ac.uk/business/ICCSR. Accessed 26 June 2011.

Kenneth, A. S. (1989). Studying institutions: Some lessons from the rational choice approach. *Journal of Theoretical Politics, 1*(2), 131–147.

King, D., & Wood, S. (1999). The political economy of neoliberalism—Britain and the United States in the 1980s. In K. Herbert, L. Peter, M. Gay, & S. John (Eds.), *Continuity and change in contemporary capitalism*. New York: Cambridge University Press.

Krasner, S. D. (1984). Approaches to the state: Alternative conceptions and historical dynamics.

Krook, M. L. (2007). Candidate gender quotas: A framework for analysis. *European Journal of Political Research, 46*(3), 367–394.

Lynggaard, K. (2007). The institutional construction of a policy field: A discursive institutional perspective on change within the common agricultural policy. *Journal of European Public Policy, 14*(2), 293–312.

March, J. G., & Olsen, J. P. (1998). The institutional dynamics of international political orders. *International Organization, 52*(4), 943–969.

Morgan, G. (2005). Institutional complementarities, path dependency, and the dynamics of firms. In G. Morgan, R. Whitely, & E. Moen (Eds.), *Changing capitalisms: Internationalism, institutional change, and systems of economic performance*. New York: Oxford University Press.

Morin, F. (2000). A transformation in the French model of shareholding and management. *Economy and Society, 29*(1), 36–53.

North, D. C. (1990). A transaction cost theory of politics. *Journal of Theoretical Politics, 2*(4), 355–367.

Ostrom, E. (1990). *Governing the common—the evolution institutions for collective action*. New York: Cambridge University Press.

Parsons, C. (2003). *A certain ideas of Europe*. Connell University: Connell University Press.

Peck, J., & Theodore, N. (2007). Variegated capitalism. *Progress in Human Geography, 36*(6), 731–772.

Peters, B. G., Pierre, J., & King, D. S. (2005). The politics of path dependency: Political conflict in historical institutionalism. *Journal of Politics, 67*(4), 1275–1300.

Peters, B. G. (2009). *Institutionalism*, reprinted. London: Sage Publications Ltd.

Pierson, P. (2000). The limits of design: Explaining institutional origins and change. *Governance, 13*, 475–499.

Pierson, P., & Theda, S. (2002). Historical institutionalism in contemporary political science. In M. Henry I. & Katznelson (Eds.), *Political science—the state of the discipline*. New York and Washington, DC: Norton and the American Political Science Association.

Rhodes, M., & Van Apeldoorn, B. (1997) Capitalism versus capitalism in Western Europe. In M. Rhodes, H. Paul, & W. Vincent (Eds.), *Developments in West European politics*. London: St. Martin's Press.

Schmidt, V. A. (2000). Values and discourse in the politics adjustment. In F. W. Scharp & V. A. Schmidt (Eds.), *Welfare and work in the open economy volume I: From vulnerability to competitiveness*. Oxford: Oxford University Press.

Schmidt, V. A. (2002). *The futures of European capitalism*. New York: Oxford University Press.

References

Schmidt, V. A. (2003). French capitalism transformed, yet still a third variety of capitalism. *Economy and Society, 32,* 526–554.

Schmidt, V. A. (2008). Discursive institutionalism: The explanatory power of ideas and discourse. *Annual Review of Political Science, 11,* 303–326.

Schmidt, V. A. (2010). Taking ideas and discourse seriously: Explaining change through discursive institutionalism as the fourth 'new institutionalism'. *European Political Science Review, 2*(1), 1–25.

Schon, D. A., & Rein, M. (1994). *Frame reflection: Toward the resolution of intractable policy controversies.* New York: Basic Books.

Shleifer, A., & Vishny, R. W. (1997). A survey of corporate governance. *Journal of Finance, 52*(2), 737–783.

Steinmo, S., Thelen, K., & Longstreth, F. (1992). *Structuring politic—historical institutionalism in comparative analysis.* Cambridge: Cambridge University Press.

Streeck, W., & Yamamura, K. (2001). *The origins of nonliberal capitalism—Germany and Japan in comparison.* Ithaca: Cornell University Press.

Thelen, K. (1999). Historical institutionalism in comparative politics. *The Annual Review of Political Science, 2,* 396–404.

Vogel, S. K. (1996). *Free markets, more rules, regulatory reform in advanced industrial countries.* Ithaca and London: Cornell University Press.

Walsh, J. I. (2000). When do ideas matter? Explaining the successes and failures of Thatcherite ideas. *Comparative Political Studies, 33*(4), 483–516.

Weiss, L. (1999). State power and the Asian crisis. *New Political Economy, 4,* 317–342.

Woo, J. E., & Woo-Cumings, M. (1991). *Race to the swift: State and finance in Korean industrialization.* Columbia University Press.

Wood, S. (2001). Business, government, and patterns of labor market policy in Britain and the Federal Republic of Germany. In P. A. Hall & D. Soskice (Eds.), *Varieties of capitalism-the institutional foundations of comparative advantage.* Oxford: Oxford University Press.

The World Bank. (2004). Doing business—smarter regulations for small and medium-size enterprises 2004. Washington. DC. http://www.worldbank.org. Accessed on 18 July 2012.

Yamamura, K., & Streeck, W. (Eds.). (2003). *The end of diversity? Prospects for German and Japanese capitalism.* New York: Cornell University Press.

Part II
Corporate Governance in Banking Organizations: Legitimacy

Chapter 3
Legitimizing Corporate Governance in Banking Organizations

3.1 Introduction

Innovatively combining the institutionalism theoretical framework and the category of the VoC analysis, as prepared and developed in last chapter, this chapter explores the institutional embedment for corporate governance in banking organizations in varied financial/governance models, i.e., the Anglo-Saxon model, the Continental model, and the State-affected model. Justified as the legitimacy background, institutional settings frequently play a fundamental role in producing and reproducing corporate governance in banking institutions in different financial models which, not infrequently, embrace the complicated relationship between the bank and the real economy, the approaches of the financial regulation and posture of the regulators, the role of the court, and the international influences. The interaction between the banking organization and a country's economy elaborates the function of the bank in national economic development, its contribution to GDP growth and progress in general economic welfare, and its connections with the enterprises of different sizes. The positioning of the financial regulators, varied as it is across different financial models, compares the diversified regulation and supervision orientations and practices over banking institutions, and the dynamics and interaction between financial authorities and the governed banks. The role of the court, from a unique perspective, demonstrates the legal constraints and motivations for the banking organizations to design and develop their own specific business activities and governance arrangement in certain scenarios. Meanwhile, considering the trend of convergence in corporate governance across countries, though debated, the chapter also looks into the international influences on the reproduction of the domestic corporate governance system in banks in certain countries.

© Springer Nature Singapore Pte Ltd. 2019
W. Zou, *Corporate Governance in the Banking Sector in China*, CSR, Sustainability, Ethics & Governance, https://doi.org/10.1007/978-981-13-3510-5_3

3.2 The Anglo-Saxon Model

From a kaleidoscope view, institutional settings play a 'legitimizing' role in shaping corporate governance of banking organizations. These mainly pertain to the relationship between the bank and the economy, the influence of the financial regulation, and the legal intervention, as listed in Table 3.1. In what is labeled as the Anglo-Saxon model countries or LME capitalisms, typically represented by USA and UK, legitimacy of corporate governance in banking organizations is characterized with the bank's loose ties with industry, separation from the real economy, a precompetition deregulative posture by the state (though accompanied with cyclical re-regulation movements), and active legal interventions by the court, regulators, and lawyers.

3.2.1 Bank and Economy

Historically, banks in the Anglo-Saxon model used to perform important functions for the state and were closely integrated into the economy in the early development of the capitalism. Typical examples can be observed in the expansion of the British Empire in colonial periods, its industrial revolution when banks contributed numerous funds for commerce, foreign trade, and the war (Vogel 1996; Allen and Gale 2002). Similarly, in the modernization progress of USA in the nineteenth century, banks played a pivotal role in providing funds to help build railway, dock, and tunnels which could not be accomplished by the capital held by the private households or even the government, especially in the absence of the modern capital market (Bauma et al. 2007). Even today, many banks in USA or UK, apparently, hold the belief that the banking organizations are helping the enterprises development by adequately raising and allocating capital. For instance, Goldman Sachs, acting as a typical investment bank, boasts that the bank is doing the 'God's work' by helping companies grow by means of providing needed funding, thus creating more job opportunities and contributing to the overall national economic growth and social progress (however, this is simply a modern myth coined by the giant banks and is challenged with hesitation) (Kay 2015, pp. 19–20).

However, banks gradually loosened their ties with the industry, became isolated from the general economy, and drifted to another trajectory. This attributes to several reasons. First and foremost is the booming of the modern capital market where the industry can obtain a large, better, and substitutive source of funding in forms of shares instead of debts and henceforth become less tied to banks, except in times of near insolvency or economic crisis. Such direct, less restrictive and fast financing from the capital market out-competes the traditional intermediate and demanding banking loans and turns the Anglo-Saxon model into the 'capital market-based model/system' of financial capitalism, as in Table 3.2 (Hellwig 1991; Rajan 1992; Zysman 1983; Allen and Gale 2002; Ergungor 2004, 2008; Levine 2002). In the context of such capital market-based model, there is observed a high percentage of

Table 3.1 Discourse of corporate governance in banking organizations in three models

Models of corporate governance in banking organizations	Typology of ideas as discursive institutionalism		
	Legitimacy	Paradigms	Frames
The Anglo-Saxon model	Loosened ties with industry, separation from the real economy, and aggressive financial disintermediation Pro-competitive deregulation by the government, self-regulations, and strong powers from banking industry Active legal interventions by various parties	Strongly oriented toward profit maximization and best performance Shareholder primacy theory Acute agency problems due to high-leverage capital structure Aggravated conflict of interests between the shareholders and fixed claimants Ineffective monitoring from significant stakeholders	High board independence, strong orientation for maximized profitability, and efficient board size Higher ratio of shareholding in the executive's pay, and preference for more market-oriented regulatory measures like shareholder's say on pay, higher disclosure requirement, and reinforced compensation committee High-risk preference, and specific risk management in credit risk, compliance risk More specified and detailed legal duties, typically the fiduciary duty of the board directors and management
The Continental model	Integration into the real economy and close ties with industries Coordinated financial regulation and moderate powers from banking industry Less legal interventions	Stakeholder theory Long-term interests oriented instead of short-term profits maximization or best performance Wider-ranged scope of stakeholders	Limited board independence, strong orientation for long-term profitability, and big board size Limited ratio of shareholding in the executive's pay, increased proportion of base salary and performance-related bonuses, and preference for stricter regulatory measures like cap on bonuses Moderate-risk preference, though sometimes amplified in worsening real economy and specific risk management in credit risk, compliance risk Less specified and detailed legal duties, typically the fiduciary duty of the board of directors and the management
The state-affected model	Close integrated or even affiliated relationship to industries and real economy Most restrictive and manipulative control by regulators, even in cases of financial reform, and limited powers from the banking industry Few legal interventions and subject to political influence	Hybrid of a modified shareholder supremacy theory and stakeholder theory Focusing upon policy objectives and pubic interests Long-term performance belief shared by both shareholders, management, and stakeholders	Moderate board independence, strong orientation for sustainable development, and support for real economy, and moderate big board size Increasing high ratio of shareholding in the executive's pay, equally higher base salary, and preference for stricter regulatory measures like cap on bonuses Moderate-risk preference, more frequently amplified in worsening real economy, and specific risk management in real economy Limited legal duties, typically the fiduciary duty of the board of directors and the management

50   3 Legitimizing Corporate Governance in Banking Organizations

Table 3.2 Capital market-based model and bank-based model of financial capitalisms

	Capital market-based model	Bank-based model
Capital markets	High percentage of financial sector assets More issuers and participants and high trading volume	Relatively small percentage of financial sector assets Relatively few issuers participants and lower trading volume
Non-financial firm financing	Mainly equity and bond issues	Mainly long-term bank loans
Household role	Household finances enterprise	Household finance bank, which finances enterprise
Concentration of financial sector	Relatively low	Relatively high
Qualitative nature of financial and non-financial firm interaction	Arm's length interaction	Relational exchange
Information	Higher transparency, and markets gather information	Protects opacity, and information is concentrated
Liquidity	Able to satisfy large financing needs and offers liquidity through robust capital markets	Relative illiquidity
Focus of risk	Enterprise insolvency	Bank insolvency

Source Hardie and Maxfield (2010)

financial sector assets, and low concentration of financial sectors, as illustrated in Fig. 3.1. In USA for instance, the stock market capitalization takes 26% in the whole financial system, while the bank loans (the non-securitized) only take 10%. And, the general capital market takes 73%, while the bank loans, including those securitized through the capital market, take only 27%.

Meanwhile, a great variety of issuers and participants are involved in the capital market, the trading volume is high, and the trading activities are fairly active (Antzoulatos et al. 2008). Against this backdrop, the non-financial enterprises can henceforth raise their funding more easily and directly from such robust capital market through direct financing by means of issuing equity and bonds. The household holds a high proportion of investment in the capital market while limited holding of the bank deposit. Moreover, this model of financial capitalism is characterized with the arm's length relationship between the banks and non-financial enterprises, where the enterprises are, except in cases of financial crisis and economic recessions, less dependent on banks. This brings in a stricter requirement on transparency and information disclosure, in which the market mechanisms function more efficiently. Such capital market-based model is said to be in a better position to satisfy large financing needs and offers liquidity through the assumed efficient capital market, except in times of financial crisis. And the key risk is supposed to arise out of the enterprise insolvency (Allen and Gale 2002).

3.2 The Anglo-Saxon Model 51

Exhibit 13

The structure of capital and banking markets varies widely between countries

Financial depth, year end 2010[1]
Percent; % of regional GDP

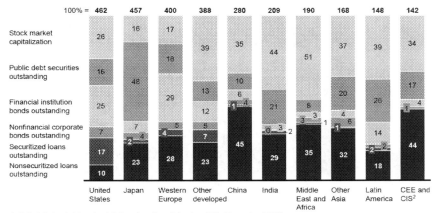

1 Calculated as total regional debt and equity outstanding divided by regional GDP.
2 Central and Eastern Europe and Commonwealth of Independent States.
SOURCE: Bank for International Settlements; Dealogic; SIFMA; Standard & Poor's; McKinsey Global Banking Pools; McKinsey Global Institute analysis

Fig. 3.1 Capital and banking markets around the world (2010). *Source* Mc Kinsey & Company, McKinsey Global Institute (2011)

In addition, the increasingly limited financing role by the banking organizations in the Anglo-Saxon world also results from the great changes in the commercial world in our modern times. On one side, this attributes to the shrinkage and deterioration of the industrial sectors in developed economies like USA or UK, where many manufactures and factories are closed down or relocated to other emerging economies and henceforth do not need or pursue earnestly the funding from the financial institutions typified by banks. On the other side, in the new era of economic development, many modern companies do not need to borrow voluminous money from the banks to invest in or purchase expensive real estates, for instance, as their base of business operation. Instead, they frequently rent buildings like offices, shops, or warehouses as their main business premises. Moreover, with the burgeoning of new high-tech firms or service-oriented enterprises, best exemplified as Apple, Google, or Facebook, intangible assets, instead of the traditional tangible ones, matter more to the ongoing of the modern business which again greatly reduce their financial dependence on bank financing. And, contrasting with the traditional companies like car manufactures or brewers which may frequently need financial lending from the banks for new projects or business expansion like building new plants, these new high-tech companies may even become good cash generators, especially by means of IPO in the capital market. Moreover, some big companies, especially those with good profits, can successfully raise funds internally for their growth rather than external bank borrowings. For instance, Exxon Mobile, one of the most profitable companies in USA, invested massively on exploration and infrastructure development, which amounted to 20 billion US dollars, and such investments are mainly financed internally by Exxon Mobile itself (Kay 2015, pp. 19–20). These changes, especially the loosened ties between the industry and the bank, force the bank to renovate its business model to efficiently use its assets and hence develop innovative financial products which are steps away from the real economy (Allen and Gale 2002).

Secondly, the government in this model becomes less competent, or unwillingly, in coordinating industrial policies and loses its control in guiding the efficient allocation of credit to the industry. This expedites the separation of the bank from the industry as its financial interests are less likely to coincide with the industrial ones in such 'standby' political climate. For instance, in the postwar era, UK government started an industrial policy for the financial sector, but without any financial policy for the industrial sector, which implied the government's strong support for London's role as an financial center while not intending to use the financial system as a tool of industrial policy (though the government might occasionally intervene in industrial finance or help the industries in cases of economic hard times or crisis) (Reid 1988). The latest example is the inability of UK government to effectively orient bank loans for funding to the business and industries after the 2007–2009 financial crises (The Guardian, March 5, 2013). Similar government positioning can be observed in USA, though with national and contextual variances.

Thirdly, the increasing financial disintermediation leads to further spin-off of the bank from the real economy. Deviating from the traditional capital-raising and risk-bearing intermediation roles, the bank in the Anglo-Saxon model is increasingly

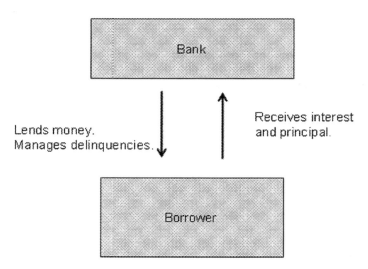

Fig. 3.2 Traditional model of banking process. *Source* Bair (2007)

3.2 The Anglo-Saxon Model

engaged in 'managing risks' and initiates the business pattern of 'originate to distribute,' best exemplified by transferring loan-related risks to third parties through the capital market and fanatic trading in a great variety of financial derivatives, typified as the credit default swap (CDS). A good example is the continuous and voluminous securitization process of the bank's loan before the global financial crisis. In traditional banking business as illustrated in Fig. 3.2, the bank issues loans to the borrower, monitors the credit situations of the borrower, and manages relevant delinquencies. The borrower repays the bank the principals and the interests agreed upon. In contrast, in the securitization process in Fig. 3.3, the traditional role of the bank as the lender is broken into several different independent components and the bank mainly 'underwrites and funds loans that are eventually sold to the SPE for inclusion in the securitization' and gets 'compensated by cash for the purchase of the loan and by fees' (Bair 2007). Instead of holding the loans on its balance sheet, the bank sells the loans to the issuer, the special purpose entity (SPE), which is formed to facilitate the securitization of the loan and in turn issues such securitized loans as securities to the investors.

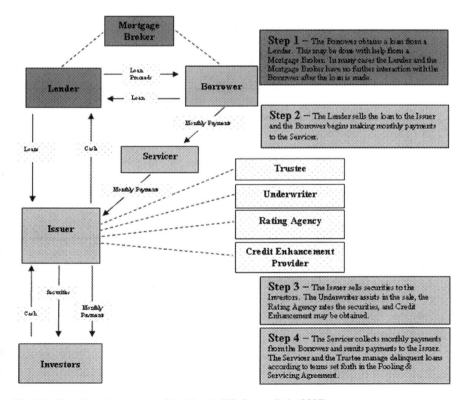

Fig. 3.3 Securitization process of banking in US. *Source* Bair (2007)

In the context, the bank will not bear any responsibilities for monitoring the economic situations of the borrower and managing the delinquency in case of default (Bair 2007). These result in the banks' retreat from the real economy. For instance, there has been less or even non-availability of finance provided to smaller businesses by UK banks (UK, Macmillan Report 1931) and the financial support for major infrastructure projects by banks is fairly limited (The Guardian, August 13, 2012). In some instances, the banks' role in the economy is criticized as 'socially useless' and or even 'economically damaging and socially destructive' (Mathiason, Newman and McClenaghan, July 9, 2012). Another prominent evidence of the bank's 'indifference' to the real economy in the Anglo-Saxon model can be observed in its reluctance to issue loans in times of economic difficulty after the 2007–2009 financial crisis. Though the government injects mountainous funds into the banking industry in times of financial crisis, the invested banks are holding the money back from the real economy and reduce their financing for industries, business, and infrastructure projects (Tyler 2012).

As illustrated in Fig. 3.4, from around the end of 2008 to November 2012, though the bank deposit in USA kept increasing to over 9.2 trillion, the bank loan issued in the same period declined from $7.27 to $7.15 trillion, a zero or negative loan issuance. Around 2 trillion have been held back by the banks which should have been issued to individuals, households, and small, medium, and large businesses to fund expansion and growth. Although the reluctance in financing the enterprises (specifically the SMEs) can be justified on cautious control of risks and the more

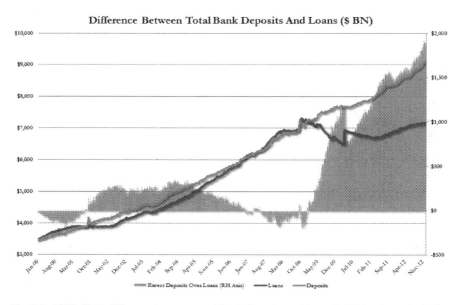

Fig. 3.4 2000–2012 difference between total bank deposits and loans in US banks (unit: billion US dollars). *Source* Tyler (2012)

conservative gesture in the austere economic environment during and after the global financial crisis, it nevertheless presents the long-held indifference by Anglo-Saxon banks in supporting the real economy. In a worse case, the banks may use the 'deposit to loan gap' to take on excessive risky activities, as best exemplified by the *London Whale Transaction* where JPMC bet on more fictitious financial derivatives and incurred over $60 billion losses (Tyler 2012).

3.2.2 Financial Regulation

Regarding the financial regulation in the Anglo-Saxon model, a deregulative environment is gradually developed and reinforced in the background of strong orientations for self-regulation and pro-competition, belief in the market as the efficient mechanism, and resistance to political intervention by the banking industry. First, there has been a traditional discourse, favored by either the regulators or the bank practitioners, for self-regulation which is said to be brewed in the context of 'long-term cultural homogeneity of the practitioners, geographical proximity of their offices and frequent informal meetings and contacts between bank industry and financial regulators' (Vogel 1996, p. 135). On one side, the regulators are proud and confident in this market-oriented regulatory approach as they can know the banks better and have an insider knowledge of the markets. On the other side, the bank practitioners prefer this market-oriented approach, which can effectively exclude the political intrusion into the financial industry (Vogel 1996).

Secondly, the constant financial innovations well challenge the regulator's competence to regulate. In USA, for instance, the financial institutions have been innovating fairly sophisticated financial products to take advantages of or circumvent the regulatory barriers, exemplified by the complicated securitization of loan obligations of various sorts and the dazzling financial derivatives, which frequently hinder the regulator to adequately and efficiently regulate due to their complexity, mix of a great variety of different risks, the volatility of the credit quality, and the involvement of too many participants. Meanwhile, as these financial products are traded through the capital markets, the banks and other intermediaries could transfer a core function of traditional intermediation from an industry subject to close, prudential supervision to one largely beyond regulatory oversight (Vogel 1996). In this context, the government is often incompetent to consolidate various issues into one single coherent debate and initiate an efficient financial regulation (Litt et al. 1990). The latest example is represented in the difficulty of implementing the Dodd-Frank Act in USA, where the presence of a great variety of complicated financial derivatives and new financial innovations perplexes the regulators in issuing a clear and finalized interpretation and implementation (USA, Dodd-Frank Act 2010).

Thirdly, there is an over-stress on the significance of the banking industry in national economy by the regulators in the Anglo-Saxon model, such as its contribution to the economy, and the proportion of its assets in GDP. As illustrated in Fig. 3.5, on measuring finance's contribution to GDP, financial services in the Anglo-Saxon

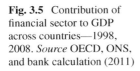

Fig. 3.5 Contribution of financial sector to GDP across countries—1998, 2008. *Source* OECD, ONS, and bank calculation (2011)

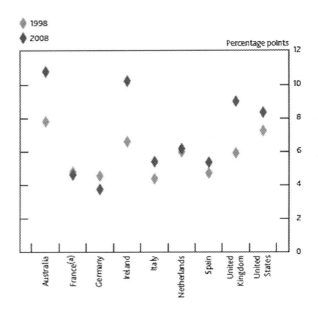

model seem to play a more important role to GDP than in its counterpart in either the Continental model or the State-affected model, with 9.5% in UK, 8.2% in USA, a little above 4% in Germany and France. Meanwhile, the total assets of the banks in the national GDP have been increasing drastically in the Anglo-Saxon model. In UK, for instance, the banks' assets as a percentage of GDP remained steady around 50% from the 1880s to 1970s, as in Fig. 3.6. However, from then on, it started to rise in size and rocketed over 500% of GDP by 2006. And it reached around 556% of GDP in 2012, much higher than that in German of 160% of GDP and France of 336% (Economist, November 10, 2012).

In this context, banks in the Anglo-Saxon model can get more government financial assistance in times of financial crisis than their counterparts in the Continental model or State-affected model, as listed in Table 3.3. For instance, in 2009, UK and USA pledged much higher support to the financial industries than the Continental model or State-affected model countries as a percentage of the national GDP, with UK pledging around 101%, USA 42%, Germany 27%, Japan around 21%, France 21%, and Italy 8%. All these lead to the abnormal and unique status of the banking organizations in the Anglo-Saxon model as 'Too big to fail' (Bernanke 2010), 'Too many to fail' (Acharya and Yorulmazer 2007; Mitchell 2001), and 'Too big to jail' (Mother Jones, January 2010), which are hardly possible in any other sectors. And, against this backdrop, the regulator in the Anglo-Saxon model is fairly resistant to employing strict financial regulation and fears such restrictions may force the banks to move to other countries, which will damage the country's comparative financial advantages and harm the economy as a whole (and, even if there are apparently harsh and stringent regulatory measures, their final implementation is always far

3.2 The Anglo-Saxon Model

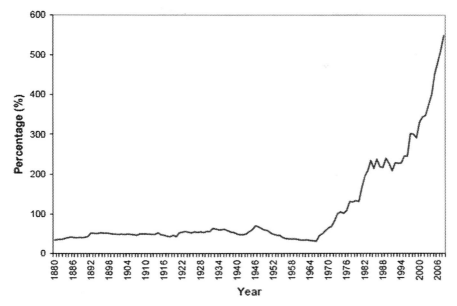

Fig. 3.6 UK banking sector assets as % of GDP from 1880 to 2006. *Note* The definition of UK banking sector assets used in the series is broader after 1966, but using a narrower definition throughout gives the same growth profile. *Source* Haldane (2009)

from satisfactory and less effective). For instance, UK financial regulators have been resisting restrictive financial reforms in EU, such as the financial transaction tax (The Tobin/Robinhood Tax) and the cap on the banker's bonus, and contended such reforms may damage its banking industry, henceforth its national economic interests. For USA, the regulators simply ignore such moves (The Guardian, February 27, 2013).

Fourthly, the regulator and government may frequently yield to the powerful banking industry by its aggressive lobbying and political influence. Banks in this model have gained massive powers from the cities they are located in, London in UK and New York in USA, both of which hold a very distinguished place in the national economy, politics, and especially the financial industry. This is typically observed in the case of the City of London, which is a metropolitan corporation of itself and has long steered the UK banking industry, and its own orientation is pivotal to UK financial industries as a whole and influential upon UK government regarding financial policies and regulations. Frequently, the city can persuade the government to provide a more *lassie faire* regulative environment to attract large foreign financial institutions (Vogel 1996).

Meanwhile, aggressive lobbying by banks in the Anglo-Saxon model may effectively impact on the financial legislation and policy making and exert great influences on politicians, regulators, and the government. For instance, UK financial service industry spent more than 92 million pounds in 2011 for lobbying politicians and reg-

Table 3.3 Amounts announced or pledged for financial sector support by country (in percent of 2009 GDP unless otherwise noted)

Model	Country	Capital injection	Purchase of assets and lending by treasury	Direct support	Guarantees	Asset swap and purchase of financial assets, including treasuries, by central bank	Upfront government financing	Total
		(A)	(B)	(A+B)	(C)	(D)	(E)	
Anglo-Saxon model	UK	8.2	3.7	11.9	40	28.2	8.7	100.7
	USA	5.1	2.3	7.4	7.5	12.1	7.4	41.8
Continental model	Germany	3.4	0	3.4	17.2	0	3.4	27.4
	Japan	2.5	4.1	6.6	7.2	0	0.4	20.8
State-affected model	France	1.3	0.2	1.5	16.9	0	1.1	21
	Italy	1.3	0	1.3	0	2.7	2.7	8

Note Columns A, B, C, D, and E indicate announced or pledged amounts and not actual uptake

Source IMF (2010)

3.2 The Anglo-Saxon Model

Table 3.4 Donations to the conservative party from 2005 to 2010 UK

Year	Total financial services industry cash contributions to CPCO	Yearly total cash donations to CPCO (all donors)	Financial service industry contribution as a % of total cash donations (%)
2005	£2,748,527	£11,142,090	24.67
2006	£6,196,999	£16,395,889	37.8
2007	£6,175,695	£1,6,728,005	36.91
2008	£5,364,319	£1,3,691,446	39.17
2009	£10,849,884	£20,813,184	52.12
2010	£11,420,974	£22,482,411	50.79
Total	£42,756,398	£101,253,025	

Source Mathiason and Bessaoud (2011)

ulators in 'an economic war of attrition' which achieved 'a string of policy victories,' such as slashing of corporation tax upon the bank's overseas branches, suffocating the government's plan for new corporate super-watchdog to further discipline the quoted corporation (Mathiason, Newman and McClenaghan, July 9, 2012). Further political impact by the banking organizations can be observed in the continuous and increasing political donation. In UK, for instance, the political donation doubled in 2010 in contrast with 2005, which took over 50% of all the cash donations, as listed in Table 3.4.

These lead to a series of deregulation movements and result in a more 'spoiling' regulatory environment for banks, which reached the peaks in the late 1980s and 1990s last century, when 'Big Bang' took place in UK in 1986 and Gramm–Leach–Bliley Act was passed in 1999 in USA. The financial deregulations are characterized with bold financial liberalizations, decentralizations of authority, and excessive self-constraints by the regulators, demolishing 'the wall' between the banking and brokerage business and affording the banking industry more freedom in their business. Evidence also abounds in the period preceding the 2007–2009 financial crises. Even if there were good signs of malpractices or excessive risky activities by the banks, such as the London Inter-Bank Offered Rate (LIBOR) manipulation, the highly risky sub-mortgage securitization, and mis-selling of various financial products like payment protection insurance (PPI), financial regulators in USA and UK took a fairly lax and standby stance (USA Today, July 18, 2012; The Guardian, June 29, 2012). Such deregulative posture even continues in the aftermath of the global financial crisis when the financial regulators are levying, apparently, much stricter and burdensome laws, rules, and policies on the governance structure, financial practice, and business activities of the banks, which leads to the development of a conflicting but cyclical de-re-regulation pattern, as to be discussed in the following.

3.2.3 Financial Re-regulation and De-re-regulation

However, accompanying the deregulative movements in the Anglo-Saxon model are the financial re-regulation campaigns, which are featured typically with imposing more regulatory constraints and restrictions, creating more new legal acts and laws, and setting up new regulatory bodies to accommodate the changes brought about by the financial liberalization. For instance, after the 1930s US financial crisis, 1933 Glass–Steagall Act was passed which separated the banking business from the investment business. In UK, the 'Big Bang' came hand in hand with a series of new re-regulations such as passing of the FSA, creation of new self-regulatory organizations and dozens of compliance departments, which aimed to establish a new and more extensive industrial system of financial regulations (Vogel 1996). Such financial re-regulation frequently takes place pro-cyclically with the financial crisis. And after the 2007–2009 financial crises, a new round of wide-ranged and prevalent re-regulations has been adopted by financial regulators in USA and UK. These are well evidenced by fanatic and overwhelming financial reforms and new legislations targeted at stricter regulation on the banking industry and protection of the customers, as typified by the Dodd-Frank Act in USA, UK's 'electrifying ring fence' of the banks, and a great variety of legal actions and penalty against the banks (UK Banking Reform 2013; US Dodd-Frank Act 2010). Secondly, new regulatory agencies are established, such as the Consumer Financial Protection Bureau (CFPB), the Financial Stability Oversight Council (FSOC) by US financial regulators (US Dodd-Frank Act 2010). Thirdly, there are more direct regulatory interventions in the bank's business activities, exemplified by prohibitions on the proprietary trading, the separation of the retail banking from investment banking, and the mandatory requirement of 'living will' for future solvency (US Dodd-Frank Act 2010). However, if perceived otherwise, the aforesaid re-regulatory moves in Anglo-Saxon model can be understood as the government's efforts in assuring a proper and smooth operation of the financial deregulation, a periodical self-rectification in the existing regulatory framework, and a baseline for the new round of deregulation.

However, though initiated for closer control and more stringent regulation over the banking industry, these re-regulation efforts in the Anglo-Saxon model may frequently end up in a watered-down, paradoxical de-re-regulation movement, which is readily observed in USA in the fragmentation of the Dodd-Frank Act and the birth of the Financial Choice Act in 2017. Aiming at 'freeing and liberating' the banking organizations subject to various 'unnecessary' regulatory burdens, the 2017 Financial Choice Act constrains greatly the powers of varied financial regulators in regulating business activities and behaviors by the banking industry (US Financial Choice Act 2017). These are best exemplified in the repeal of FDIC's Orderly Liquidation Authority (OLA) based on Title II of Dodd-Frank Act (which is replaced with a new sub-chapter in the Bankruptcy Code in addressing the failures of the large financial institutions), removal of the FDIC's supervisory role in reviewing and regulating the resolution plan, or the living will, of the governed financial institutions, and repeal of Financial Stability Oversight Council (FSOC) authority in designating non-bank financial institutions and related 'financial market utilities' as systemically important financial institutions (SIFIs) and rescind its designated SIFIs retroactively. Specifically, the bill prioritized weakening the roles and powers of the Consumer Financial Protection Bureau (CFPB), the most significant regulatory innovation by the Dodd-Frank Act in the aftermath of the 2008 global financial crisis, in disciplining and harnessing a great variety of business operations of the banking organizations. For instance, the bill changes CFPB's name to the 'Consumer Law Enforcement Agency,' strengthens the US President's control over its leadership, and limits greatly the agency's authority in bringing relevant enforcement actions and supervision over financial lending by specific financial institutions such as payday loans and vehicle loans, which may potentially pose risks to the less educated customers. Moreover, the deregulative gestures by the bill are manifested in loosening the current stress test regime, prolonging the Comprehensive Capital Analysis and Review ('CCAR') process from one to two years and confining further the Federal Reserve's power in intervening in the bank's planning for profits distribution under certain circumstances. Another drastic and bold deregulatory move by the bill is to repeal the Volker Rule, one of the most important creations by the Dodd-Frank Act which intends to control the overall risk exposures by the banking industry through prohibiting insured depository institutions from engaging in proprietary trading and investing in or sponsoring hedge funds and private equity funds. These financial reforms proposed by the bill can be construed as overthrow of the re-regulation framework by the Alabama government in addressing the 2008 global financial crisis and become a start of another round of potential financial deregulation in USA (US Financial Choice Act 2017).

3.2.4 Legal Intervention

Traditionally, legal intervention plays an important role in generic corporate governance in the Anglo-Saxon model countries. A similar instance can be observed in the context of corporate governance in banking organizations, despite bank's industrial specialty and demanding requirements for professional knowledge. First, the court may exert great influences on bank governance in many perspectives, typically with regard to the fiduciary duties by the board of directors and management, such as the duty of care, duty of loyalty, and duty of disclosure. Cyclically, the court may raise the standards of the fiduciary duty for the bank directors and impose stricter liabilities during or immediately after a wave of bank failures.

Secondly, the financial regulators can be pretty aggressive in legal interventions by initiating various actions against the banks, challenging their duty of compliance, and imposing major penalties. For instance, US Securities and Exchange Commission (SEC) has been proactively engaged in launching charges against the financial industry as well as collecting fines and compensations, which is particularly evident *ex-post* the 2007–2009 financial crises. As listed in Table 3.5, up to January 2013, there were altogether 153 entities and individuals in financial industry charged by

Table 3.5 Summary of charges by SEC against the financial industry and the collection of fines and compensation

Number of entities and individuals charged	153
Number of CEOs, CFOs, and other senior corporate officers charged	65
Number of individuals who have received officer and director bars, industry bars, or commission suspensions	36
Penalties ordered or agreed to	> $1. 53 billion
Disgorgement and prejudgment interest ordered or agreed to	> $756 million
Additional monetary relief obtained for harmed investors	$400 million[a]
Total penalties, disgorgement, and other monetary relief	$2.68 billion

[a]In settlements with Evergreen, J. P. Morgan, State Street, TD Ameritrade, and Claymore Advisors
Source US SEC, January 9, 2013

SEC, including 65 CEOs, CFOs, and other senior corporate officers and 36 individuals received officer and director bars, industry bars, or commission suspensions. The total penalties, disgorgement, and other monetary reliefs reached unprecedented high $2.68 billion. Meanwhile, the legal firms, by soliciting the aggrieved parties by the malpractice or breach of fiduciary duties by the bank, have been launching aggressive and voluminous civil actions.

Sometimes, the legal intervention in the Anglo-Saxon model may become so influential that it cannot only impact on how a bank practice, but actually determine what a bank does. And, the banks even have to hire ex-regulators to cope with the deluge of litigations in the context of chaotic laws and multiple litigants. For instance, as listed in Fig. 3.7, after the 2007–2009 financial crises, US banking industry was buried in increasing hills of judicial subpoenas, orders and claims and mountains of legal documents and paperwork, which resulted in excessively high legal costs (Economist, Oct 13, 2012).

3.2.5 *Implication of Legitimacy on Paradigm and Frame in Corporate Governance in Banking Organizations*

Discussed in Chap. 2, as the discourse at the background of cognition, the legitimacy may greatly influence the formation of the paradigm and frame. In the context of corporate governance in banking organizations in LME like USA and UK, this is manifested in the formation of the shareholder primacy model (the paradigm) and the specific governance structure of the bank (the frame). With less concerns for and constraints from the real economy, the bank in LME gradually sets up its own kingdom and is 'more individualized and freer' to pursue its own best interests, i.e., maximizing its profitability and bringing best returns to the investors, while frequently ignoring the interest of other stakeholders or the stability of the finan-

3.2 The Anglo-Saxon Model

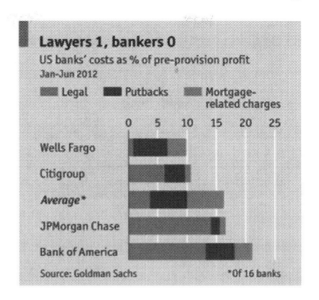

Fig. 3.7 US bank's legal costs 2012. *Source* The Economist, Oct 13, 2012

cial system. Such paradigm of the shareholder primacy is reinforced by the financial deregulation movements. With the conventional belief in self-discipline by the banks and reluctance to intervene in their operations, the regulator actually gives the banks wide discretions in pursuing their own interests, while imposing less pressure on them to either protect the interests of the various stakeholders or serve the real economy. Moreover, the increasingly competitive market environment, which financial deregulation intends to produce, further intensifies competitions within and beyond the banking industry. To survive the cutting-throat competitions, banks are forced to achieve the best performance (usually in short term, annually or even quarterly) and attract investors by providing maximized investment returns. Meanwhile, the active legal intervention further contributes to shaping the paradigm of shareholder primacy. By prescribing profound and detailed standards of the fiduciary duty on the board of directors and senior management, such as the duty of care, duty of loyalty, and duty of disclosure, the court actually provides an enhanced legal protection for the interests of the shareholders ex post. Though the latest round of financial reforms in UK and USA, in the form of financial re-regulation, apparently re-booted the bank's concerns for the key stakeholders, the clients mainly, they cannot fundamentally change the bank's paradigm as discussed. For example, there is a varied 'colorful' re-occurrence of bank scandals targeted at taking advantages of the banks' clients and customers of different kinds.

The legitimacy discourse of banks in LME may also influence the constitution of specific governance arrangements. For instance, the discourses of the bank's disintegration from the real economy and the financial deregulation may largely shape the orientation of the bank board, which is prioritized on the maximized profitability and bringing best returns to the investors, rather than the sustainable long-term development. The discourse of financial deregulation, on the prerequisite of a more independent and self-disciplined board of directors, can affect the composition of the bank board, exemplified by the requirement for a higher proportion of the outside directors, stricter criterions of independence, and more independent board committees. Meanwhile, the discourses of financial disintermediation of the bank and laxer regulation may influence the arrangement of risk management. With the banks' active engagement in 'gambling' on various financial derivatives like CDO and aggressive practice in securitization, they are subject to a higher risk appetite, difficulty in managing long-chained risks, and exposure to more complicated risks. The 'freestyle' financial regulation before the 2007–2009 financial crises, either caused by the regulator's reluctance or inadequate capability to intervene in banks' business operations, provided further discretions for the banks to take their chances and pull in excessive risks or even pursue illegal but highly profitable practice. The discourse of active legal interventions, on the other hand, may greatly impact on the formation of legal duties of the board of directors and management. For instance, by setting specific criterions on the duty of care in the context of banking industry, the court illustrates to the bank directors and managers what constitutes an adequate performance of their legal obligations. Meanwhile, legal actions and charges by financial regulators may further clarify the boundary of the duty of compliance expected of the bank.

3.3 The Continental Model and State-Affected Model

3.3.1 Continental Model

In what is labeled as the Continental model, or the CME capitalisms, corporate governance in banking organizations is legitimized in the bank's integration in the national economy, close relationship with the industry and enterprises, and contribution to economic growth. Meanwhile, the government regulates by coordinating the interests of the bank with those of the industrial sectors and legal intervention is seemingly less important compared with its counterpart in the Anglo-Saxon model.

A. Bank and economy

In the Continental model, the bank is said to be closely integrated into real economy, oriented toward the long-term financing for the industry, and play a significant role in corporate governance of non-financial firms. Considering the overwhelming dominance of the bank in the financial sectors, this model is also termed as the 'bank-based' model (Gerschenkron 1962; Allen and Gale 2002; Stulz 2002; Hardie and Howarth 2009; Hardie and Maxfield 2010), as in Table 3.2. In such a pattern of financial capitalism, there is observed a high degree of concentration in the financial industry. As illustrated in Fig. 3.1, the bank loans (the non-securitized) in Japan and West Europe (including Germany and France) takes 23% and 28%, respectively, in the whole financial sector, much higher compared with that of USA. Frequently, the bank provides the lion's share in the long-term external funding to enterprises, while takes in a large proportion of financial savings from the household in the form of deposits. And, there is observed a close relationship between the banks and non-financial enterprises, which leads to a relational bank relationship in contrast with the arm's length one in the capital market-based system. The capital market in this model has been traditionally limited in size and role for enterprise financing, which comprises a relatively small percentage of financial sector assets, involves fewer issuers and participants, and the trading volume is comparatively low. As observed in Fig. 3.1, in Japan and Western Europe (including Germany and France), the stock market capitalization takes only 16 and 17% in the whole financial sector, much lower compared with that of USA. These are caused by several factors. From the historical perspective, the banks in the Continental model were said to use their influence to prevent the growth of the stock market, as it may compete with the banks as the funding provider to the large enterprises and collectors of the household deposits. Moreover, the financial regulators, typically the central bank and finance ministry, intentionally held back the development of the stock market as they feared that a liberalized stock market might endanger its policy of monetary stability Fischer and Pfeil (2003). Though many drastic reforms have taken place and the capital market has been developing fast in the Continental model countries in the past decades, the bank still maintains its dominance in the financial sector.

Secondly, there has been a shared discourse among the bank managers, regulators, and the general public that the bank, private or public, bears a special responsibility to the national economy, the development of the enterprises, and the welfare of the society at large (Hackethal et al. 2006). For instance, the savings banks and cooperative banks in Germany, with a dominant status in German banking industry, claim to be designed for 'working for the public or mutual good rather than for shareholders' and argue to be 'well suited to the mixture of households and small companies (known as the Mittelstand) that they serve' (Economist, November 10, 2012). Under the austere economic situations in periods of 2007–2009 financial crises, for instance, these two pillar banks increased the medium- and long-term loans extensively and provided about two-thirds of all lending to Mittelstand companies and 43% of lending to all companies and households. Though the private big banks cut off their medium- and long-term lending, they greatly increased the short-term loans to the enterprises and the households. These contribute greatly to the recovery and good performance of the German economy in times of economic recession (Economist, Nov 10, 2012) (Fig. 3.8).

Thirdly, in contrast with the prevalent financial disintermediation of the bank in the Anglo-Saxon model, the bank in the Continental model mostly functions as a financial intermediary, which is mainly involved in providing financial liquidity and monitoring services. As a depository institution, the bank is engaged in providing depositors with liquidity insurance as liquidity providers. Specifically, the bank acts as the delegated monitor for investors and provides monitoring services, avoiding thereof the duplications monitoring costs which is caused by the informational asymmetry between the debtor firm and the creditor depositor. As a financial intermediary accepting deposits and extending loans, the bank in this model ensures the depositor

Fig. 3.8 Changes of bank loans by German banks from 2007 to 2012. *Source* The Economist, November 10, 2012

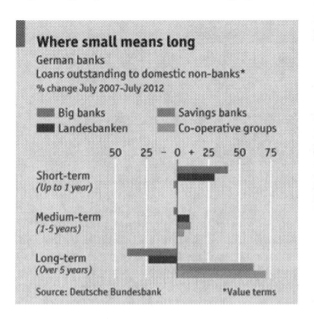

(the investor) better access to their funds and borrowers against the risks that the funding will be withdrawn prematurely (Diamond and Dybvig 1986).

Fourthly, the prevalent Hausebank or main bank system in the Continental model leads to an intimate relationship between the bank and the enterprises, typically represented in Germany and Japan. The Hausebank, or the main bank, takes a special place in the financing relation with the firm, exemplified by its premier status, a closer relationship, and privileged access to information with the firm. This distinguishes the Hausebank from other banks which also provide funding. However, the Hausebank also takes on extra responsibility. For instance, in times of economic difficulty and worsening financial situations by the firm, the Hausebank has to maintain or even increase its lending, though other banks may reduce their combined lending exposure (Elsas and Krahnen 1994, 1998). In this context, the bank actually provides the implicit liquidity insurance to its established long-term enterprise clients, which reinforces the bank's loans as the dominant external financing (Hackethal and Schmidt 2004).

Meanwhile, the inter-relationship between the bank and enterprise in the Continental model is strengthened by the bank's significant role in corporate governance of the enterprises (Deeg 1998; Vitols 2005). On one side, this results from the bank's historical role as the large shareholder in the firms. On the flip side, as the significant creditor the main bank or Hausebank of the firm, the bank obtains strong powers in corporate governance of the firms and their business operations, well observed in its presence on the supervisory board of the firms and access to privileged and valuable information (Schmidt 2003). Due to the large stake vested in the firms, either by shareholdings or financial lending, the bank has a strong incentive to monitor the

3.3 The Continental Model and State-Affected Model

firm (Shleifer and Vishny 1997) and may intervene directly when its client firms run to a financial distress (Lehmann and Neuberger 2001; Edwards and Fischer 1994).

B. Financial regulation and coordination

Though distinguished from the *laissez-faire* style of regulation in the Anglo-Saxon model, financial regulators in the Continental model generally take a comparatively liberal approach and rely considerably on self-discipline by the banking institutions. Traditionally, the banks in this model have significant 'say' in their business operations and financial activities and are less subject to intervention from the government. In Germany, for example, banks are 'universal' and can provide all kinds of financial services to their clients. The financial regulators mainly view their functions as supervising and monitoring a self-regulatory financial system. Meanwhile, the major financial reforms are frequently orchestrated and coordinated between the government and banking industry. For instance, the major reforms in the stock exchange and centralizing the stock activities in Frankfurt were agreed upon by major banks and the finance ministry in Germany (Vogel 1996; Allen and Gale 2002).

However, financial regulation in this model can also be restrictive, which is grounded in the protection of the bank's creditors and depositors, maintaining the viability of the banks, and the soundness of the overall financial sector. Financial regulators, such as the central bank, the financial ministry, and the bank supervisor, may be actively involved in promulgating guidelines and principles, supervising various business operations of the bank, or even intervening from time to time in the bank's financial activities. In Germany, for instance, the Federal Banking Supervisory Office (FBSO, Bundesaufsichtsamt für das Kreditwesen) has been actively engaged in a great variety of supervising activities and 'has far reaching rights to obtain information, intervene into management decisions, recall bank managers, impose moratoria and close a bank' (Fischer and Pfeil 2003, p. 11). The central bank, the Bundesbank, also takes an active stand in bank supervision by issuing guiding principles and rules and developing the process of ongoing supervision, prudential regulation, and auditing. Its intervening role was typically observed, historically, in obstructing the introduction of securitized money market instruments for monetary policy reasons and deterrence of entry by foreign banks in German financial market (Fischer and Pfeil 2003).

Specifically, regulatory restrictions and interventions in the Continental model are intended to maintain the stability and sustainability of the overall national financial system. In Germany, for instance, there used to be varied restrictions on entry into the banking business, restricting the competition in banking industry, protecting Germany's universal banks from 'invasion' of foreign banks, and constraints over the provision of competing financial services and products provided by nonbanking institutions (Fischer and Pfeil 2003). The latest examples are the passing of the financial transaction tax and the capped bonuses of the bank's executives. The former imposes a tax on the financial transactions on derivatives and intends to curb speculative financial trading which may adversely affect the stability of the financial market (Oliver 2008; EU, European Financial Stability and Integration Report 2013). The later, as a more intrusive policy, directly intervenes in the arrangement of the compensation package for the bank's management and constrains excessive risk-taking activities of the bank (EU, CRD IV 2013).

C. Implication for paradigm and specific governance structure in corporate governance in banking organizations

The legitimacy of bank governance in CME, represented by the bank's integration into the real economy, active financial support for industrial sectors and enterprises, and stricter financial regulation, highlights the formation of the paradigm of the stakeholder model in corporate governance in banking organizations. With strong orientations toward economic growth, industrial development, and growth of the enterprises, the bank in this model frequently pursues a long-term, sustainable profitability rather than short-run best economic performance. Specifically, serious concerns are given to the protection of the interests of various stakeholders of the bank, such as the clients, the employees, the depositors, and the society at large. The paradigm of the stakeholder model is reinforced by the discourse of stricter financial regulation. For instance, by coordinating the bank with the general economy and industrial development, the regulator orients the bank toward sustainable economic development, financial stability, and protection of the interests of different constituencies. By mandatory requirement, the financial regulator, in particular, demands the bank to consider the interests of the clients and the employees.

The legitimacy of bank governance also presents important implications for the development of specific governance structures of banks in CME. Considering the close connection between the bank and the real economy, the orientation of the bank board in CME, in contrast with its counterpart in LME, is targeted at promoting the interests of various stakeholders and economic development, rather than prioritizing solely the maximized profitability and best investment returns to the shareholders. By mandatory requirement on the presence of employee representatives on the bank's board (supervisory board), the regulator actually influences the composition of the bank board and its degree of independence. The latest regulatory cap on the banker's bonus, on the other hand, directly shapes the remuneration package and its composition for bank executives in CME. For risk management, the bank in CME seems to have moderate risk appetites and comparatively more manageable sets of risks due to its intertwining with the real economy, typically its 'real' and direct lending relationship with the corporate and individual clients. Specifically, the bank is in a better position to monitor and synchronize 'soft' information from its corporate clients due to its active role in corporate governance of the generic firms and status as the main bank or key creditor, which are missing in the context of LME. This is further reinforced by the stricter financial regulation on risk taking. Meanwhile, the limitation on competitions within the banking industry, and between the banks and the nonbanking organizations in CME, sets less pressure on the banks to take more risks (for the sake of higher returns) and snatch the short-term maximized profitability. However, the bank's close integration into the real economy and the regulator's coordination for financing the industries and enterprises may pose extra risks, typically the credit risks, considering the possibility of voluminous non-performing loans by the enterprises as a result of financing them in times of their financial difficulties.

3.3 The Continental Model and State-Affected Model

Frequently, such default and bad loans by the enterprises may result in great threats to the health of the banks in CME and in turn the whole financial system.

3.3.2 State-Affected Model Countries

For the State-affected model, or the SME capitalism, typically represented by France, the legitimacy of corporate governance in banking organizations is said to, over decades, build on the bank's proactive involvement in policy objectives, strong support for national economy, explicit or implicit dominance and active intervention by the state, and weak legal protection. Interestingly, though Japan is categorized frequently as the CME capitalism, it also exhibits strong characteristics of the State-affected model. With globalization and progression of market economy, however, the pure SME has been retreating and is said to change toward an alternative hybrid of CME and LME.

As a key player in real economy, banks in SME have long been positioned as 'credit instruments' and are oriented, or directed by the regulators, toward effectively and reliably allocating low cost funds to the industry, which are expected to promote long-term economic growth by means of transferring funds from the households to the corporate sector (Vogel 1996; Imai and Komiya 1994). Specifically, banks are restrained by the designed financial system which is biased toward bank lending, and hence, the government can easily control the flow of financial aid and direct them to prioritized sectors (Zysman 1983). For instance, in France, the government has traditionally controlled the financial flows by means of a national operation of a wide range of semi-public financial institutions, exerted great influence on the largest commercial banks, and actively participated on the board of most prominent investment banks. Meanwhile, private banks are indirectly controlled by being compulsorily organized into banking associations which institutionalizes a close tie with the regulators and the industry (Vogel 1996). In Japan, on the other hand, its Ministry of Finance (MoF) has used various means to maximize its controls over the financial system, facilitated major ministerial functions, and deployed the functional 'policy banks' to achieve designated policy objectives (Stephen 1990).

In return for the credit service and low-interest rate financial assistance, banks in the model are frequently awarded a large portion of the enterprises' borrowing business. Such interdependent relationship between banks and industries is believed to contribute to healthy development of the real economy. Meanwhile, the bank's dominant role in economy is strengthened by regulator's intentional restraints on the development and the size of the capital market, such as imposing stringent conditions, restrictive regulatory measures, and even active interventions which adversely affect the trading activities and volatility of the market. These regulatory measures largely constrain the financing function of the capital market and hinder its ability to provide adequate capital to the enterprises (Vogel 1996).

Characterized with a more centralized regulation style, financial regulators in SME countries have a closer control over the banking organizations. Historically, they can enjoy more decisive leadership and play an overwhelming role in financial activities, such as removing credit controls, creating new money markets, and liberalizing the interest rates. Not infrequently, the financial regulators are able to orchestrate the financial market and perform more of restructuring regulatory powers. In Japan, for instance, the MoF has been both a powerful bureaucracy and singular political institution which can integrate the political bargains into the financial policies, without being either independent from the financial institutions or captive to them. More importantly, the MoF officials always filter in some of their agenda in structuring these deals, such as their ideology for Japan, the financial system, and for the ministry itself (Vogel 1996). In the event of significant financial reforms, the financial regulators in Japan can easily take the lead, set the reform agenda, and shape the outcomes of the proposed reforms in their wide administrative discretion. Specifically, they may insert their own preferences into the policy outcomes and enhance their powers and jurisdictions. The appeals from financial institutions, however, are less likely to be considered by the regulators as they already decide which groups to favor and which to compensate and henceforth manipulate the deliberation to gain industrial acceptance. Though the regulators may be inspired by ideas from the financial institutions, with heavy regulation and a firm hand, they can always persuade the financial community, overcome their resistance, and resolve their conflicts (Vogel 1996).

Similar to CME, restrictive financial regulations for the sake of financial stability are prioritized in SME countries, such as limitations on entrance into the banking industry, restricting bank competitions and providing administrative measures for minimizing the risk of bank failures. Meanwhile, specific mechanisms are developed for better control over the management and practices in the financial institutions, such as timely intervention by means of close working relationship between the financial regulators and the financial institutions. In Japan, for example, the representatives of financial institutions frequently interact with the industry and stay informed of the latest development in the MoF (the so-called MoF-watchers). Such practice is welcomed by the MoF as the ministry believes the control over the financial system is a product of their close contact with the financial institution, and such cooperative relationship is deemed to further promote the effective policy implementations (Vogel 1996; Litt 1990). In France, on the other hand, the regulator may control the banks by delegating its officials as the directors of the bank board to avoid excessive risky decisions (Vogel 1996).

The legitimacy of bank governance in SME presents significant implications for the formation of the paradigm and frame discourses in corporate governance in banking organizations. For instance, under the close control by the state, banks are frequently engaged in promoting economic growth, funnelling funds to relevant industries and enterprises in accordance with policy objectives, and contributing to the achievement of national economic strategy. This may sometimes undermine, in the short run, the maximized profitability for the shareholders and best performance of the bank. Meanwhile, the legitimacy discourse may present an important implication for developing the bank's specific governance structure. Considering stricter financial regulation and bank's integration into the economy, the bank board in SME is more subject to the influences of the government policies and oriented toward promoting the bank economic growth and national development strategy. Meanwhile, the appointment of chairman or CEO may be prone to great political influences, and sometimes, delegates from the government will be assigned to the board of the bank and act as the board directors or supervisory board directors. Regarding the executive pay, financial regulators in this model may use more intervening measures and impose more stringent standards. As a result of the bank's intimate relationship with the real economy and restrictions on the competition, the bank in SME generally has a moderate risk appetite. However, there may be excessive risk exposures in the process of financing the development of industries and enterprises, typically the credit risk, which may result in voluminous bad loans. Meanwhile, weak legal intervention in SME may lead to the less detailed specifications of the legal obligations and limited judiciary protection for the private interests of the bank investors.

3.4 Conclusion

Exploring the kaleidoscope perspectives of corporate governance in banking organizations, the present chapter reviews the legitimacy of the bank's governance structure in varied institutional settings, which mainly elaborates on the sophisticated discursive discourses of the role of bank in the economy, the function of financial regulation, and the influence of the judicial system in LME, CME, and SME countries, all of which are argued to contribute to legitimizing the institutional grounds for the production and reproduction of corporate governance arrangement in banking organization around the world. The chapter provides a solid analytical basis for analyzing the legitimacy of corporate governance in Chinese banking organizations in Chapter 4 and prepares as well the study of paradigm and frame discourses in the bank governance system in the following chapters.

References

Acharya, V. V., & Yorulmazer, T. (2007). Too many to fail—an analysis of time-inconsistency in bank closure policies. *Journal of Financial Intermediation, 16,* 1–31.
Allen, F., & Gale, D. (2002). *Comparing financial systems.* Beijing: Ren Min University Press.
Antzoulatos, A. A., Thanopoulos, J., Tsoumas, C. (2008). Financial system structure and change—1986–2005: Evidence from OECD countries. *Journal of Economic Integration, 23,* 977–1001.
Bair, S. C. (2007). Presentation in Federal Deposit Insurance Corporation on possible responses to rising mortgage foreclosures before the committee on financial services, US House of Representatives, 17 April 2007. New York: Washington D.C.
Bauma, D. J., Palmiter, R. A., & Partnoy, F. (2007). *Corporations law and policy* (6th ed.). NY: West Publisher.

Bernanke, B. S. (2010). Causes of the recent financial and economic crisis. *Presentation Before the Financial Crisis Inquiry Commission*, 2 Sept 2010. New York: Washington, D.C. http://www.federalreserve.gov/newsevents/testimony/bernanke20100902a.htm. Accessed 05 Jan 2012.

Claessens, S., Keen, M., & Pazarbasioglu, C. (2010). Financial sector taxation: The IMF's report to the G-20 and background material. Washington: International Monetary Fund.

Deeg, R. (1998). What makes German banks different. *Small Business Economics, 10*(2), 93–101.

Diamond, D. W., and Dybvig, P. H. (1986). Banking theory, deposit insurance, and bank regulation, *The Journal of Business, 59*(1), 55–68.

Edwards, J., & Fischer, K. (1994). Banks, finance and investment in Germany. Cambridge: Cambridge University Press.

Elsas, R., & Krahnen, J. P. (1998). Is relationship lending special? Evidence from credit data in Germany. *Journal of Banking and Finance, 22,* 1283–1316.

Ergungor, O. E. (2004). Market-vs. bank-based financial systems: Do rights and regulations really matter?. *Journal of Banking & Finance, 28*(12), 2869–2887.

Ergungor, O. E. (2008). Financial system structure and economic development: structure matters. *International Review of Economics & Finance, 17*(2), 292–305.

European Union. (2013). *European parliament capital requirements directive (CRD IV)*. Brussels: Belgium.

Fischer, K. H., & Pfeil, C. (2003). Regulation and competition in German banking: An assessment (No. 2003/19). CFS Working Paper.

Gerschenkron, A. (1962). *Economic backwardness in historical perspective. A book of essays*. Cambridge, MA: Harvard University Press.

Hackethal, A., Schmidt, R. H., & Tyrell (2004). Financing patterns: Measurement concepts and empirical results (Working Paper No. 125). University of Frankfurt.

Hackethal, A., Schmidt, R. H., & Tyrell (2006) The transformation of the German financial system (Working Paper). Frankfurt: Main.

Haldane, A. G. (2009) Banking on the state. *Conference Paper in the Federal Reserve Bank of Chicago Twelfth Annual International Banking Conference on 'The International Financial Crisis: Have the Rules of Finance Changed?*, 25 September 2009. Chicago.

Hardie, I., & Howarth, D. (2009). Die Krise but not La Crise? The financial crisis and the transformation of German and French banking systems. *Journal of Cutaneous Medicine and Surgery: Incorporating Medical and Surgical Dermatology, 47*(5), 1017–1039.

Hardie, & Maxfield, S. (2010). What does the global financial crisis tell us about Anglo-Saxon financial capitalism? *Paper for Workshop on the Financial Crisis, EMU and the Stability of Currencies and the Financial System*, 2010.

Hellwig, M. (1991). Banking, financial intermediation, and corporate finance. In A. Giovanni & C. Mayer (Eds.). (1995). *European financial integration*. Cambridge: Cambridge University Press.

Imai, K., & Komiya, R. (Eds.). (1994). *Business enterprise in Japan—views of leading Japanese economists*. Massachusetts: Massachusetts Institute of Technology.

Kay, J. (2015). Finance is just another industry. BIS Papers No 84, Towards a "new normal" in financial markets? *14th BIS Annual Conference*, June 26, 2015. Switzerland: Basel Committee on Banking Supervision.

Lehmann, E., & Neuberger, D. (2001). Do lending relationships matter? Evidence from bank survey data in Germany. *Journal of Economic Behavior and Organization, 45*(4), 339–359.

Levine, R. (2002). Financial structure and economic growth: Cross-country comparisons of banks, markets, and development (Eds). Cambridge: MIT Press.

Litt, D. G., Macey, J. R., Miller, G. P., & Rubin, E. L. (1990). Politics, bureaucracies, and financial markets: Bank entry into commercial paper underwriting in the United States and Japan. *University of Pennsylvania Law Review, 139*(2), 369–453.

Mathiason, N., & Bessaoud, Y. (2011). Tory Party funding from City doubles under Cameron. *The Bureau of Investigative Journalism, 8*(11).

Mitchell, J. (2001). Too many to fail and regulatory response to banking crises (Working Paper) (2011).

References

Oliver, P. (2008). *A general financial transaction tax—source of finance and enhancement of financial stability*. Presentation at European Parliament, Brussels. Austrian: Austrian Institute of Economic Research.

Rajan, R. G. (1992). Insiders and outsiders: The choice between informed and arms length debt. *Journal of Finance, 47,* 1367–1400.

Reid, M. (1988). *All change in the city*. London: Macmillan.

Schmidt, V. A. (2003). French capitalism transformed yet still a third variety of capitalism. *Economy and Society, 32,* 526–554.

Shleifer, A., & Vishny, R. W. (1997). A survey of corporate governance. *Journal of Finance, 52*(2), 737–783.

Stephen, J. A. (1990). The political economy of Japanese saving: How postal savings and public pensions support high rates of household saving in Japan. *Journal of Japanese Studies 16*(1), 61–92.

Stulz, R. M. (2002). Financial structure, corporate finance, and economic growth. In K. A. Demirguc & R. Levine (Eds.), *Financial structure and economic growth: Cross-country comparisons of banks, markets, and development*. Cambridge: MIT Press.

Tyler, D. (2012). A record $2 trillion in deposits over loans—The Fed's Indirect Market Propping Pathway Exposed, December 26, 2012. New York: Zero Hedge.

Vitols, S. (2005). Changes in Germany's bank-based financial system: Implications for corporate governance. *Corporate Governance: An International Review, 13*(3), 386–396.

Vogel, S. K. (1996). *Free markets, more rules, regulatory reform in advanced industrial countries*. Ithaca and London: Cornell University Press.

Zysman, J. (1983). *Governments, markets, and growth: Financial systems and the politics of industrial change*. Ithaca and NY: Cornell University Press.

Chapter 4
Legitimacy of Corporate Governance in Chinese Banking Organizations

4.1 Introduction

Continuing the institutional analytical framework of discursive institutionalism and variety of capitalisms on the study of corporate governance in banking organizations, this chapter offers an in-depth analysis on the legitimacy discourses of bank governance in Chinese institutional context. In contrast to the existing categories of VoC, i.e., the LME model in Anglo-Saxon countries like USA and UK, the CME model in Continental countries like Germany, and SME model in countries like France and Japan, institutional settings in China are shown to take a hybrid form that may combine different ingredients of the CME, SME, and LME 'recipes.' In the context of legitimacy for corporate governance in Chinese banks, for instance, this hybridity is apparent in the discourses on banks' integration into the national economy, close relationships with industries, and intertwining with enterprises of different kinds. Regarding the discourses of financial regulation, running in parallel is continued close control and administration by the government and increasing orientation on opting for deregulation. In terms of legal intervention, meanwhile, Chinese courts are legitimated as playing a paradoxical role of passivism and activism, where strong policy orientation and consideration for social stability are frequently prioritized. Meanwhile, the discourse of international impact is increasingly significant in the legitimization of particular corporate governance arrangement in Chinese banking organizations, especially considering China's active presence in international economic organizations, intensified competition from foreign banks gaining their grounds in China, and the fast overseas expansion of Chinese banks.

As discussed in Chap. 2, there are mainly three typologies of capitalisms in VoC, namely LME, CME, and SME, which are the creation of western political economy. When applied in Asian context, there is a different picture due to the 'evident heterogeneity' of technology, products, and forms of organization, and 'plurality of institutional architectures' (Boyer 2005; Carney et al. 2009). On one side, some scholars endeavor to stereotype Asian capitalism into state capitalism or familial

© Springer Nature Singapore Pte Ltd. 2019
W. Zou, *Corporate Governance in the Banking Sector in China*, CSR, Sustainability,
Ethics & Governance, https://doi.org/10.1007/978-981-13-3510-5_4

capitalism, based on either its prominent characteristics of relational connections among politicians, state officials, and elite entrepreneurs (Krueger 1974), enduring interfirm networks (Fruin 1998; Weidenbaum and Hughes 1996), or its dominant role of the state in the progress of industrialization (henceforth the state capitalism) (Amsden 1989; Wade 1990; Kim 1998). On the flip side, other scholars stress on the varieties of Asian capitalisms, considering the different authority structures (Hamilton and Biggart 1988), the different economic stages (under the same umbrella of familial capitalism) (Kim 1998; Steier 2009), the various capitalist configurations (Orrù 1997), or even over-emphasis on national uniqueness and divergence (Whitley 1999).

Similar issues occur when the western VoC scholars attempt to categorize China into one of the existing groups of capitalisms. For instance, Richard Carney (2007) argues that growing reliance upon banks in Chinese development will 'turn China toward a CME style of capitalism.' In contrast, Szamosszegi and Kyle (2011), when analyzing the role of the state-owned enterprises (SOEs), argue that China is pursuing a state-guided capitalism. And, Witt (2010) concludes that China in many respects resembles a liberal market economy (LME). There are still other scholars who argue for the familial capitalism in Chinese context considering the significant status of the family-ruled enterprises (Tsui-Auch 2004; Kim 1998). Yeung's (2004, 2006), refusing the stereotyped single capitalism typology for China, tries to portray China as a hybridized capitalism for its 'institutional bricolage or recombination' (Crouch 2005), constant efforts to innovate 'creative' institutional solutions by selecting and recombining elements from the established models of capitalisms, henceforth resulting in new institutional settings with resemblance to the original models (Campbell 2004). Meanwhile, the so-called Chinese capitalism or ethnic Chinese capitalism is said to wield great influence on the constitution of the Asian capitalisms, especially the Southeast Asia capitalism (Hamilton 1996), as 'capitalism operates under a distinct logic in Southeast Asia and much of this is results from the specific functioning or social capital of Chinese business' (Crawford 2000, p. 73), and 'the flow of people and wealth - rooted in regional dialect and kinship - has provided a regional foundation for the socioeconomic networks that define capitalism in Southeast Asia today' (Crawford 2000, p. 78).

Though these literatures cover some of the institutional characteristics of the Chinese case, they do not adequately capture the complicated nature of Chinese political economy. Specifically, the aforesaid typology of capitalism, which is deeply embedded in Euro-American political economy, is not interested, welcomed, and accepted in China. By exhibiting some typical features of CME, SME, and LME, Chinese economy is better understood as a hybrid model which needs to be well 'blended' with 'Chinese specialties' for proper understanding of China's institutional settings (Table 4.1).

Viewed in this context, the discourses that legitimate corporate governance in banking organizations in China can be seen to refer to the followings, the bank's close ties with the macroeconomy, its intimate relationships with industries, intertwining with enterprises, and strong policy orientation and administrative governance (coupled with the increasing financial deregulation).

4.1 Introduction 77

Table 4.1 Discursive analysis of corporate governance in banking organizations in China

Model	Typology of ideas as discursive institutionalism		
	Legitimacy	Paradigms	Frames
Chinese model	Integration into the national economy and reform process, close connection to industrial sectors, intertwining with enterprises; Close control by the state, in parallel with financial deregulation and retreat of the state intervention; Paradoxical judicial activism and passivism, with concerns for public policy and social stability; And increasing influence from international discourse and financial globalization	A hybrid paradigm of the Continental model, the State-affected model, and the Anglo-Saxon model; The enhanced shareholder primacy theory, characterized with the state as the controlling shareholder and specific agency problem; And the diversified stakeholder theory with concerns for multiple constituencies	The organizations and behaviors of board of directors with focus on the orientation of the board of directors, its composition and size, and the independence of the board with various impediments; Regulation on executive pay focusing on the composition of the executive compensation, the regulatory measures, and the coordination process; Risk management on the formation of the risk framework, the risk appetite, and the specific risk management in Chinese context; And legal duties composed of the compliance duty and fiduciary duties, with strong regulatory influence

Meanwhile, there is a paradoxical legal intervention *ex ante* and increasing international influences. The chapter will address each of these elements in turn.

4.2 Bank and Economy

4.2.1 Bank and Economic Development

Traditionally and frequently legitimized as efficient financial intermediaries for raising and allocating financial resources, Chinese banking organizations, particularly the large-sized state-owned commercial banks and joint-equity commercial banks, are well integrated into the fabric of national economy. This is typically represented by the banks' active engagement in national economic planning, extending generous loans to prioritized sectors and industries on most favorable conditions, and financing the development and upgrading of state-owned enterprises as well as targeted regional development. Historically, Chinese banks have long been justified for 'serving the real economy' in their business strategies and enterprise cultures, which is best observed in the sampled banks. For instance, Bank B states that its business strategy and function are to 'earnestly carry out the macroeconomic policies of the State, consciously serve general interest of the national economy, highlight the due responsibilities of a large bank to support the sustainable development of the real economy,' which, in practice, focuses on innovations in economic restructuring, support for under-developed economic and social sectors, and financing for economic growth (Bank B 2012b, p. 25). Bank C, on the other hand, has 'Patriotism and Serving the People' as its 'soul,' which is themed upon 'pursuing the well-being for the public, and the wealth and great power for the state,' and sets the discourse of 'serving the public and improving the people's living' as the fundamental principles for its overall business operation and financial activities (Bank C 2012b, p. 9).

In this context, a great variety of financial instruments and credit policies are designed and developed by Chinese banking organizations to promote the sustainable economic development, which intends to echo, not infrequently, the long-term social and economic agenda set by the government. In Bank B, for example, its Shanxi branch prioritized massive investment to facilitate the development of key enterprises, projects, and industries in Shanxi Province based on directives in the *National Twelfth Five-Year Plan*. And, its Ningbo Branch provided strong financial assistance to the local economic development by implementing the 'Six Priorities' strategy, which extends to the upgraded manufacturing industry, modern service industry, marine economy, high-quality industrial technique reconstruction projects, demand of the economically affluent counties and towns to develop the economy, and small- and micro-sized enterprises. Meanwhile, the bank's Hebei Branch has been elaborating on step-up efforts for key strategic regions and county markets under the theme of 'One Circle, One Zone, One Region, and One Batch' (Bank B 2012b, p. 34–36).

Moreover, Chinese banks, on a continuous basis, state that they are obliged to contribute to economic development in different regions by optimizing the allocation of credit resources, and achieve henceforth the equilibrium and balanced regional economic growth. Bank B, for instance, differentiates its financing strategy toward varied regions, sets relevant priority policies, and provides extra credit support. These include in-depth development and exploration of the western region, facilitating the rise of the central region, and revitalization of the old industrial bases in the northeastern region. In 2011, the increase in newly issued loans to the central region, the western region, and the northeastern region amounted to 128.201 billion RMB, 169.105 billion RMB, and 54.305 billion RMB respectively which represented an annual increase of 13.94%, 14.81%, and 13.29% compared with 2010. Meanwhile, major credit was extended to key strategic regions, with newly extended corporate loans of 282.515 billion RMB and accounting for 54% of the newly issued corporate loans by the bank (Bank B 2012b).

And, in times of economic difficulties and social turbulence, especially during the 2007–2009 global financial crises, Chinese banks played critical roles in stabilizing the national economy. Typically, under the umbrella of the '40 Trillion Stimulus Package' in 2009, Chinese banking industry extended voluminous loans to crisis-

4.2 Bank and Economy

Table 4.2 Statistics on bank loans by Chinese banking industry and financial institutions in facilitating the Chinese National '40 Trillion Stimulus Package' in 2009 unit: billion RMB

Categories	Total of bank loans (2009)
Key national infrastructure projects	29,133.78
Reconstruction programs in Wei Chun *ex-post* 2008 earthquake	1766.82
Affordable accommodation projects for the low-income group	1144.42
Social engineering projects	3772.63
Independent technology innovation and adjustment in industrial structure projects	2337.10
Energy-saving, pollution control, and eco-construction projects	3096.47
Projects for social advancement	2078.82

Source CBA (2009)

related national projects, which embraced the improvement of the infrastructure facilities in urban and rural areas, upgrading of the existing railway system, launch of more environment-friendly projects, etc., as illustrated in Table 4.2. Such drastic move was not frequently found in either SME or CME model countries, and even less in LME ones.

In addition to the official views by Chinese banking industry, expressions of the discourses which position Chinese banks as crucial financial assistance to the national economy can also be found elsewhere. First and foremost, the regulatory discourse plays a significant role in the bank's integration into the national economy. For instance, after *2011 National Finance Conference* when the central government emphasized upon the role of Chinese banks in serving the economic development and social progress, typically their financial support for the real economy, the green industry, and rural financial reforms, active responses were observed from the banking organizations industrial-wide, whether state-owned or highly privatized (China, Premier Wen Jiabo Speech, January 7, 2012). For example, the chairman of the board of directors in Bank A stressed that Bank A would implement the guidance in 2011 *National Finance Conference* and *2011 Economic Working Conference by Chinese Central Government*, and integrate the macroeconomic coordination policies into the bank's mid- and long-term business strategy. In practice, the bank would be committed to the development of the real economy, the steady and sustainable economic growth, and social welfare projects (Bank A, Internal News, January 11, 2012). Similarly, the chairman of the board of directors in Bank B emphasized on Bank B's dedication and contribution to the national economy, and its mission to finance the policy-prioritized industries like agriculture and service sectors.

Secondly, the historical discourse on the specific role of the bank is in persistence and embedded in Chinese generic institutional configuration. In China's 'Single Bank' period before 1978, which was modeled upon the bank system from former Soviet Union, People's Bank of China (PBoC) was the only bank national-wide which multi-functioned as the central bank, financial regulator, and commercial bank, with branches extended all over China. And, the sampled banks were no more than departments of PBoC or relevant ministries and performed limited and designated functions set by the government. For instance, Bank A was responsible for funding key infrastructure projects, while Bank C was mainly engaged in international banking activities. In this context, Chinese banks were more administrative organizations than private financial institutions and delivered secondary and supplementary financing based on the state's needs and planning. From 1979, especially after the issuance of the grand *opening-up and reform* policy which changed drastically the political and economic landscape of China, Chinese banks started to spin off the PBoC and acquire, to some extent, their separate and independent financial identities. Nevertheless, positioned as industrial-specific banks, they were still closely bound to the real economy and served the industrial development, though with different focuses. For example, Bank D was responsible for extending credits to the agriculture industry, developing rural-focused financing, and setting up diversified cooperatives in the rural areas. Bank C continued its engagement in international banking and financial activities, such as trading in foreign currency and facilitating international trade and business. Bank B was designated for funding the development of manufacturing industries, promoting the commercial and economic activities at large, and supporting the growth of service industries, henceforth accelerating the progress of the *commodity economy* in China. And, Bank A was missioned in planning and managing voluminous loans to infrastructure projects and major construction programs developed by the state. With a strong tinge of public function, these giant banks were highly policy-oriented and served various industrial sectors in times of China's economic transition. Similar traces could be observed in other less or indirectly state-controlled banking organizations like the joint-equity commercial banks as well as the highly privatized banks, where the close ties with real economy were frequently the key tone due to strong government directives and the general financial environment (Wang and Guo 2008).

Thirdly, the dominance of banks in Chinese financial system is reinforced by the limited, suspended, and controlled development of the capital market. Chinese stock market did not take shape until the 1990s and has been playing comparatively limited role in funneling funding to the enterprises, considering its total value, economic power and influence, and national strategic importance. As illustrated in Fig. 6.1, up to the end of 2012, the total assets by financial institutions in Chinese banking industry amounted to 134 trillion RMB, which increased by 4.8 times compared by that before financial reforms in 2003 (CBRC 2013). In contrast, the total value of the Chinese capital market amounted to 23.9 trillion RMB in 2012, with Shanghai Stock Exchange of 16.49 trillion RMB and Shenzhen Stock Exchange of 7.41 trillion RMB (NetEase, January 8, 2013), which was sharply dwarfed by that of Chinese banking industry (Fig. 4.1).

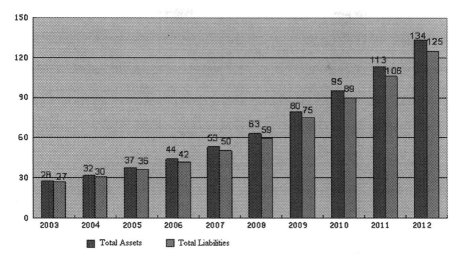

Fig. 4.1 2003–2012 total assets and total liabilities of Chinese banking industry unit: trillion RMB. *Source* CBRC (2013)

4.2.2 Bank and Industries

Under the strong orientation and coordination by the government, Chinese banks have developed a fairly close relationship with industrial sectors, which are manifested, traditionally, through massive financial lending to prioritized industries such as energy, telecommunications, and real estate (Lei 2009). And, responding to a series of reform efforts in generic economic structure by the state, Chinese banks have been prioritizing loans in new national projects and economic programs like communication, environmental protection, upgrading of industrial structure, and *new* manufacturing with national strategic significance (Bank A, Internal News, January 11, 2012). The latest example is the strengthened financial assistance to agriculture and rural economy, which is less popular in the past and most rare in the Anglo-Saxon model countries. In the context of the constant policy guidance and directives by the central government, such as *The Guidance on Promoting Innovation in Financial Products and Business Patterns for Rural Areas on Full Aspects* jointly issued by PBC, CBRC, and other financial regulators (CBRC 2010b), Chinese banking organization are fairly proactive in approving massive credits to the agricultural sector and finance a great variety of projects and programs in rural areas throughout China. For instance, Bank D initiated six key programs in 2011 in financing the overall rural development, which focused on the agricultural industrialization, rural urbanization, goods circulation, public service at the country level, etc. (Bank D 2012). Likewise, Bank B reinforced its lending policies to the rural regions, which prioritized on financing the rural infrastructure projects, manufacture of farming machinery, and reforms of the bank's sub-branches at the county level. Also, the bank renovated more accessible financial services tailed to the needs in different stages of agricultural production, processing, and circulation (Bank B 2012b).

In practice, various mechanisms are developed by Chinese banks for financing the rural areas and the agricultural sector. First and foremost, specific financial lending has been expanding rapidly in support of the 'Three Rural Issues' policy, i.e., the sustainable development of the agriculture, general progress in the rural areas, and better welfare for the peasant households. From 2009 to 2011, for instance, the balance of the rural-related loans in Bank A rose from 5, 895.21 to 10,499.12 billion RMB, increasing by around 78% (Bank A 2012, b). For the same period in Bank D, such loans increased from 12, 055 to 16,753 billion RMB, increasing by around 39% (Bank D 2012). Similar moves can be observed in Bank B and Bank C. Secondly, an extensive financial network has been set up in the rural regions around China, including the standard and simplified sub-branch of the banking organizations, POS machines and automatic teller machine (ATM), and mobile and internet financing services specifically targeted at the population in remote and impoverished areas. By the end of 2010, financial services by Chinese banks had well reached out to almost all the rural areas in every province and autonomous zone in China, though the coverage in the east and central regions was better than that of the west region. This is well evidenced in Bank D, which, by active financial technological innovation, had operated 'a total of 25,000 self-service banking devices such as ATMs and CRSs, 1.368 million payment transfer telephones and 201,000 POSs, and 76,000 withdrawal terminals for farmers in rural areas at or below county level, covering 38% of village administrative units nationwide,' and afforded better financial access to the farmers who can 'use their cards to withdraw and transfer money without leaving their village' (Bank D 2012, p. 35).

Thirdly, a great variety of programs and projects in the rural areas are sufficiently financed by Chinese banks to boost the agricultural economy. Bank D, for instance, prioritized investment in the agricultural industrialization process and aimed to accelerate 'the development of leading industrialized enterprises, increasing farmers' income share in the industry chain, and promoting the national strategy of industrialization, urbanization, and modernization of agriculture' (Bank D 2012, p. 36). By the end of 2011, the bank had increased its coverage for agriculture enterprises at the national and provincial level to 73% and 52%, respectively. And, varied financing strategies were designed to accommodate the needs and the local specialty of different regions. For example, Bank D's Xinjiang Branch capitalizes on the region's distinctive forestry and fruit resources, and provides strong financial assistance to the county-level fruit storage and processing enterprises and the local major fruit growers. By the end of 2011, a total balance of 2.086 billion RMB loans had been granted to the forestry and fruit industries (1.891 billion RMB in corporate loans and 195 million RMB in loans to individual fruit growers) (Bank D 2012). Bank B initiated as well many innovative measures for financing the development of rural economy and agriculture industry. Considering the needs and specialties of the local agricultural enterprises in different phases of procurement, production, and sales, the bank's Qingdao Branch specifically designed individualized financial products like 'Agro Financing Express,' which consolidated different production stages in the agricultural enterprises and intended to provide the 'commodity financing based on specialty agricultural products, supply chain financing products, and other business varieties' (Bank B 2012b, p. 44). Meanwhile, Bank B set up a strategic partnership (by its Heilongjiang Branch) with Heilongjiang Agricultural Reclamation Bureau and Beidahuang Group and initiated pilot programs of individual loans for modern farming machinery, which aimed to facilitate the process of agricultural mechanization and accelerate the development of the new rural areas (Bank B 2012b).

Moreover, financial innovations by Chinese banks are encouraged in accommodating the 'new' rural economy. For example, guided by *Notice on Experimental Rural Financial Reform in Lishui, Zhejiang Province* (PBC 2012), Chinese banks took great initiatives in test-water financial reforms in Zhejiang Province and provided 'venturous' financial assistance to the forestry in Lishui. These embodied the establishment of new medium- and small-sized community banks, employment of the innovative credit patterns, and expansion of the collateral categories. Such moves contributed further to developing the three-tier rural credit system, which is composed of the small sum and credit-based loans, collateral-dependent loans, and loans with sound guarantees. Particularly, with breakthrough in the traditional state ownership and marketability of the forest resources, the title to the forestry could be used as a new type of collateral. By 2012, bank loans based on ownership to forests had amounted to 51.61 billion RMB, with the outstanding balance of 26.35 billion RMB, which well met the needs of the local peasants engaged in forestry, the storage corporations, and relevant warehouses (Stock Times, May 18, 2012).

4.2.3 Bank and Enterprises, SOEs Versus SMEs

From a historical perspective, there has been observed an intimate relationship between banks and enterprises in China, especially the state-owned enterprises (SOEs), which is said to be the product of strong policy orientation, overlapping of the majority shareholders (the state), cultural homogeneity, and strong political connections. In transitional economies, SOEs frequently enjoy very strong politicalities which can bring them extra values and advantages (Fisman 2001; Johnson and Mitton 2003; Faccio 2006), such as favorable treatments by the government, lax taxation policies, and loosened regulations (Faccio 2006). Specifically, SOEs may gain easier accesses to loans by the state-owned banks on more preferential conditions (Charumilind et al. 2006), in particular the long-term loans where banks are reluctant to extend due to much higher cost of monitoring, stringent requirement upon collaterals, and information asymmetry (Diamond 1991, 1993). In Chinese context, SOEs enjoy similar political connections (Brandt and Li 2003; Cull and Xu 2005; Jiang and Li 2006) and better accesses to the long-term financial lending from the state-owned banking organizations (Ma 2001). Not infrequently, such loans are said to be better guaranteed, apparently, due to the implicit government salvation in times of financial difficulties (by the SOEs) which may mitigate or even eliminate default risks (Jiang and Li 2006). And, such intimate bank–enterprise relationship in China has been customized to the extent that massive credit to SOEs is widely accepted and normalized, while those to non-SOEs are less favored and subject to strict scrutiny (Ma 2001). For instance, over 50% of the overall outstanding bank loan in China is frequently allocated to the SOEs. Meanwhile, there is manifested a continuous interdependency between Chinese banks and the SOEs. On one side, the bank needs the borrowing business from SOEs to maintain a comparatively stable and safe interest income, maximize the profitability of its deposits, and achieve designated business objectives. On the flip side, the bank has to attract voluminous deposits from the profitable SOEs to retain an adequate capital pool. Such reliance on SOEs further strengthens the close connections between banks and the SOEs in Chinese institutional settings.

The aforesaid bank–enterprise relationship is also being fostered for small- and micro-sized enterprises (SMEs), though not without variances. Against the backdrop of strong and constant policy efforts for maintaining economic growth, creating more job opportunities, and accelerating the development of SMEs, as typified in *Notice on Support for Further Improvement on Financial Services by Commercial Banks to SMEs* (CBRC 2010c), Chinese banks are proactively financing this type of enterprises which were less favored in the past. For instance, Bank B has been continuously supporting and funding the expansion and growth of SMEs and places such practice on top of its business agenda (Bank B 2012b). Bank D, in 2011, launched various new business measures to 'help SMEs overcome financial difficulties and boost their real economic development, including reducing financing costs, eliminating unreasonable bank charges and helping to maintain their liquidity' (Bank D 2012, p. 67).

Firstly, there has been a sharp rise in bank loans to SMEs by Chinese banking industry. By the end of 2010, for example, the total loans from Chinese banks to the SMEs had amounted to 75,000 billion RMB, which was 9.4% higher than the increase of the averaged bank loans during the same period (CBA 2011). Such unprecedented bank lending significantly eased out the financial difficulties faced by many SMEs and efficiently facilitated their survival and business operations. And, by the end of 2011, the outstanding SMEs loans by Bank B had well amounted to 959.3 billion RMB, increased by 302.8 billion RMB or 46.1% over the beginning of the year (Bank B 2012b). Bank D, similarly, extended a total of 575.219 billion RMB in loans to 45,265 SMEs and further 110 billion RMB in personal business loans to hundreds of thousands of SMEs' owners as well as individually owned businesses (Bank D 2012). Secondly, special internal rules and mechanisms are designed and developed for financial lending to SMEs. For instance, Bank C formulated its own *Guidance for SMEs' Business* and *Management of Wholesaling for SME Clients* (Bank C 2012b). Bank B established new departments specifically responsible for bank loans to SMEs throughout the bank group, which involved the head office, 38 one-tier branches, and over 300 specialized sub-branches under the two-tier branches (Bank B 2012b).

Thirdly, innovative financial products and services, which are tailored to the needs and specialty of SMEs, are carefully elaborated and designed by Chinese banks. For instance, Bank D offers SMEs better access to bank financing and greatly simplifies for loan approval procedures, which include new financial products like 'Easy

Loan,' 'Self-service Revolving Factory Credit Facilities,' and 'Factory Loan,' as well as individualized trade financing products targeted at providing stable financial assistance to the industrial chains, supply chains, and logistics in SMEs' business activities. Meanwhile, taking into account regional variances, Bank D innovates financial products with distinctive local features like 'Overdraft Loans,' 'United Insurance and Credit,' and 'Loans for Government Procurement Bids,' along with other diversified financing options such as financial leasing, equity funds, and various flexible financing vehicles (Bank D 2012). Considering the uniqueness of the financial lending to SMEs, namely 'short, frequent, and urgent,' Bank B engineers specialized financial products, such as 'mid-term turnover loans, circular loans, trade financing, operational property loans, standard plant building mortgages,' and the 'E-loan Express' business which makes it easier for these small-sized enterprises to apply to, receive, and pay back loans through internet (Bank B 2012b, p. 55). Bank A, based on the multi-party agreement among the bank, the local government, and SMEs, develops *Helping and Guaranteed Financing Business* (Bank A 2012). Similar financial efforts are manifested at the industrial level by other banks, such as Xing Ye Bank's *Xing Ye Sesame Blossoming Loan Business* targeted at SMEs which are in preparation for going public, Beijing Commercial Bank's new financial products engaging SMEs in new industries like technology innovations, culture sectors, and environmental protection (CBA 2010).

Moreover, other drastic reforms are initiated regarding financial lending to SMEs by Chinese banking industry, which takes into account of the nature of such enterprises, their vulnerable economic situations, and the potential credit risk exposures. In *Notice on Support for Further Improvement on Financial Services by Commercial Banks to SMEs*, for instance, CBRC started to differentiate and encourage higher tolerance for nonperforming bank loans by SMEs, which considered inclusively varied credit risks, the cost of financing, and relevant viable financial settlements. This is best exemplified in *The Working Guidance on Financial Services for SMEs by Financial Institutions of the Banking Industry in Shenzhen*, which is said to purposely 'loosen' supervision over on the bank credit to SMEs, increase risk tolerance rate for nonperforming bank loans by SMEs from 1% to 5%, and in turn provide better financial assistance to boost fast development of these enterprises. Nevertheless, such financial deregulation is not a signal for unrestrained financing to SMEs, but a clarified policy orientation in addressing the banks' concerns, in particular their credit approval departments, on granting related SMEs loans more speedily (Xinhua Net, April 12, 2012).

4.3 Bank and Administrative Control, Governance and Financial Regulation

4.3.1 Financial Control and Administrative Governance

Traditionally, there has been a strict government control and restrictive financial regulation over Chinese banking organizations. On one side, this is the legacy of the highly concentrated financial system, when the identities of banks and government were overlapped, the government could directly intervene in banks' business operation and use banks as 'credit instruments' to channel financial resources to the needs of the planned national economy. On the flip side, the government is motivated to continue such intervention, though in a less and limited scale, in the context of uncertain economic transition, desire for rapid GDP growth, and pressure to deal with various financial hardships resulting from the paramount economic reforms.

First, at the macro level, the central government has been planning and monitoring on the total volume of the bank loan by Chinese banking industry on the annual basis, allocating 'the quota of credit' to different banks, while leaving to the banks the discretion on how to use their loans. At the regional level, the local government has been actively intervening in even directing the allocation of financial resources from varied banks, which is always successful considering its local dominance. For instance, to support the development of local SOEs and regional economy, the local government may frequently motivate or press the banks to provide generous long-term bank lending, even in cases of insufficient collaterals and high default risks.

Secondly, the selection of the board of directors and the senior management in many giant Chinese banks may be subject to great influence from the government. For instance, it is, not infrequently, the government that selects and appoints senior management in the large-sized state-owned banks, such as the chairman of the board of directors, the CEO, and the chairman of the supervisory board. In this context, the senior managers might be strongly politically oriented and pursue earnestly national policy objectives in the bank's business operations. Other senior managers, though not directly appointed by the government, are required to register with related financial regulators and subject to close regulatory supervision.

Thirdly, at the operation level, Chinese financial regulators may forge close regulations on various banking practices, their operation procedures, the financial innovations, and the development of new banking products or services. Meanwhile, the bank loans are heavily oriented by the government for the prioritized sectors, key industries, and national projects with strategic significance, as discussed in the relationship between bank and economy. And, by frequent informal meetings, policy guidance ('window-guiding'), and annual on-site inspections, the regulator can reinforce its influence on the bank's business practice and its governance structure. In closely monitoring the varied business lines by the bank, for instance, the regulator can efficiently restrict and call off financial products and banking activities which are deemed as excessively risky. A typical example was the issuance of the *New Rules for Bank Loan* (The New Rules) by CRBC in 2010, or termed as *The Three Regulation Ordinances and One Guidance,* which imposed constraints upon many of the major banking business in Chinese banking industry. They embrace *The Temporary Regulation for Liquidity Cash Loans* (CBRC, No. 1 2010a), *The Temporary Regulation for Individual Loans* (CBRC, No. 2 2010a), *The Temporary Regulation for Loans for Fixed Assets and Guidance for Project Financing Business* (CBRC, No. 2 2009), and *Guidance for Project Financing Business* (CBRC, No. 71 2009). These New Rules intended for setting up better mechanisms in managing the bank's loans, facilitating the sustainable development of the national economy, guiding the banks in efficiently using and allocating their financial resources for the real economy, and preventing against the credit risks.

4.3.2 Deregulation

In parallel with the close financial regulation, however, there has been increasing opt for deregulation in Chinese banking industry. The *opening-up and reform policy* from the 1980s has gradually constrained the government's overall intervention in Chinese banks, while market-oriented regulation started to take place, especially after the significant financial reform in 2003. In this new scenario, direct government control is losing colors and gives away to more liberal economic and legal mechanisms as best exemplified by the modern financial regulation and supervision. First, the regulatory style by Chinese financial authorities has changed from the past bureaucratic and tight control to the present more market-oriented and participant-friendly coordination. Typically, the regulators 'walk out of their kingdom' and go to the 'factory floor' for better understanding of the specific banking business, the needs of banking organizations, and the problems to be resolved timely. For instance, a periodical research project has been set up by CBRC for its officials to conduct on-site research programs in Chinese banks, such as the arrangement of risk management, internal control, and the credit policy. Instead of directing the business activities of the banks, such research projects are only intended for better discernment and update of information on various aspects in Chinese banking industry and provide henceforth empirical reference for regulation-making.

Secondly, in preparing and issuing new policy guidance, principles, and regulations, Chinese financial regulators increasingly stress upon transparency and actively consult opinions from a wide range of sources, such as the banking industry, academia, and public. In the process of 'importing' international principles of BIS I, II, and III into Chinese regulatory jurisdiction, for instance, the financial regulators coordinated with Chinese banks on the key terms of these international discourses and related implementation process. For example, regarding liquidity risk management based on BIS III, CBRC has arranged a wide range of discussions, negotiations, and seminars with representatives from key Chinese banking organizations, and integrated their needs and wishes into the final policy documents, such as the quantitative risk management models, risk measurement, and relevant risk indicators. Similar practices can be observed in the principle on corporate governance of commercial banks in China, when CBRC actively consulted opinions from the banking industry, organized seminars and discussions on specific governance issues, and informed banks of relevant revisions.

Thirdly, a standardized corporate governance structure has been established in Chinese banks, where the board of directors and senior management, rather than the government's officials, run the bank and make significant business decisions. Typically, the selection and appointment of the bank directors and senior executives are increasingly based on their professional expertise, experience, and skills rather than the conventional political qualification and loyalty. And, Chinese banks have also more *say* in decision making with regard to significant investments and are less subject to the government command and intervention (CBA 2010). Meanwhile, financial deregulation, as an extensive move by different Chinese financial regulators, extends to many new fields, which embrace acquiescing for nonbanking institutions' engagement in certain banking business, granting more freedom to Chinese banks regarding their expansions into insurance and mutual funds business, and loosening control over the interest rates.

However, financial deregulation is ever never an easy job in China and it takes decades to achieve the present comparatively laxer financial environment. The first round of financial deregulation for Chinese banking organizations started in the 1980s. In 1985, the PBoC, relevant ministries, and departments of the central government jointly drafted the blueprint for the financial reform in Chinese banking industry, which particularly clarified the status of certain key large-sized state-owned banks as independent market players. That implies that these banks would be free from controls by the government, independent in their decision making, and fully responsible for their business activities. In practice, the reform also pertained to the management of the bank's capital, the allocation and changes in the bank's profits, and accountability of the head of the bank.

The second round of deregulation took place in the 1990s. In 1993, with the issuance of *The Decision on the Reform of the Financial System*, the large-sized state-owned banks were restructured further from the traditional industrial-specific financial institutions into independent commercial banks. Specifically, the government loosened the banks' bondages from their respective industries, transferred their policy financing functions to the newly established policy banks, expanded the banks' business scope, and promoted free competition in the financial market. These deregulative moves were further codified through the promulgation of *The Chinese Commercial Bank Law* in 1995, which recognized the independent identity of the state-owned commercial banks and expedited their transformation. In general, the second round of financial regulation can be summarized as:

4.3 Bank and Administrative Control, Governance ...

(i) The establishment of the independent identity of the commercial bank, centralized management in using and allocating the bank's loans, and issuance of relevant regulation in managing the bank's capital;

(ii) The establishment of internal control system, the emphasis on the balance of the bank's assets and liabilities, and the enhanced management over the bank's risk exposures;

(iii) Improvement in the bank's corporate governance structure in accordance with *Chinese Corporate Law* and *Chinese Commercial Bank Law*, division of powers and responsibilities among the board of directors, the senior management and the supervisory board, and clarification of their separate functions,

and optimizing the bank's organizational structure, restructuring the networks of branches and subsidiaries in different localities.

The latest round financial deregulation was initiated in 2003, which actually greatly reshaped the landscape of corporate governance in banking organizations in China. In contrast to the past financial reforms, this round financial move was more drastic and purported to establish a market-oriented financial system. First, most of the solely state-owned large-sized banks went public and became listed shareholding commercial banks, with Bank C and Bank A as the first group in 2004. By the end of 2006, 13 giant public commercial banks had become listed corporations. And up to 2010, all the sampled banks had turned into listed financial institutions. Secondly, there was observed a drastic reform on the ownership structure of Chinese banks. On one side, with its establishment in 2002, Central Huijin Investment Ltd. (CHI), on behalf of the state, became the majority shareholder of the key large-sized state-owned Chinese banks. By appointing representatives to the banks' board of directors and supervisory board, CHI can efficiently monitor the performance of the banks and fundamentally change the scenario of insufficient shareholder supervision in state-owned banks. On the flip side, as required by CBRC, many of the large-sized commercial banks introduced the 'strategic' foreign investors and hired foreigners as the board members, which partially internationalized the shareholding structure. Thirdly, a standard corporate governance framework, by referring to international practice, was set in place and widely accepted by Chinese banking organizations. These embody the collective decision-making process by the shareholder's general meeting, the board of directors, the senior management and the supervisory board, the enhanced internal control system, and the strengthened risk management mechanisms. Further financial deregulation can be observed in the relaxation on market entrance into Chinese banking industry, increasing privatizations of the medium- and small-sized banks, less restrictions and government interventions, and promotion for free market competition (Wang and Guo 2008).

4.4 Bank and Legal Influences

Categorized mainly as the Continental legal system, China shares a family resemblance with the Continental law countries like Germany, France, and Japan, such as the codification of laws, the inquisitive role by the judges, and limited influence of the precedents (the decisions of the prior cases). Regarding corporate governance in banking organizations, these are represented by less legal intervention, a passive gesture by the court, and strict application of the laws. On the other hand, however, there is observed increasing judicial activism in China which results from strong political influences, regulatory orientations, and pursuit for balance between legal justice and overall social stability. For instance, the Supreme People's Court of the People's Republic of China (SPCPRC) explicitly manifested, in its *Reform Blueprint of the People's Court for the Third Five-year Plan from 2009* to *2013 in China* (SPCPRC 2009a), such paradigm by emphasizing the balance among 'legal effects, political effects, and social effects' in Chinese judiciary system. Meanwhile, a complementary legal guidance further stresses upon Chinese court's role in achieving the CCP's mission, the overall interests of the people and the paramount authority of Chinese Constitution and statutes (SPCPRC 2009a).

4.4.1 Judicial Passivism

Similar to its counterpart in the Continental law countries, Chinese court frequently takes a passive stand in hearing the financial cases due to the strict reading, interpretation and application of the law, significant influences from the public policy and regulatory orientation, and concerns for overall social stability. First, the existence of the specific institution in Chinese judiciary system, the Committee on Political and Legal Affair (CPLA), may potentially constrain the discretion of the court and bring about certain political influences. Delegated by the CCP, the CPLA is responsible for formulating policies on the legal affairs, reviewing court decisions on cases with significant social and economic significance, and supervising the performance of the judiciary officials and judges at varied levels and localities (Lv 2010). However, due to its composition and strong political discourses, the CPLA may possibly bring hindrance to the court and impact henceforth its independence. Specifically, the CPLA may wield overwhelming influences on the major decisions by the court, especially when it performs its coordination functions on the complicated or new cases with significant social impacts, and intervenes directly as part of its supervision authority (Yin 2012).

Secondly, there are certain legislative impediments on initiating legal actions in China, which may constrain the plaintiff from pursuing adequate relief against corporate malpractices in the financial market. As stimulated in *Several Rules on Civil Compensations Cases for Misstatement Allegation in the Stock Market* (Chinese Supreme Court 2002), for instance, the civil actions against malpractices by the listed companies in Chinese stock market can be divided into the several or joint action, but do not specify the category of the general class action. This largely encumbers the recourse for the injured parties, considering the higher costs and expenses for the joint actions, inconsistent court decisions, and unequal compensation for the losses. Meanwhile, it restrains the court's motivation and power in shaping the practice of the listed corporations, such as sufficient information disclosure, proper performance of the fiduciary duties by the corporate board directors and senior managers, etc. Another barrier to the court's intervention arises from some specific, prerequisite legal procedures for civil actions. For instance, the injured investors are not entitled to start a valid civil action unless there is an existing administrative penalty or criminal charge imposed on the listed corporations. However, such an arrangement is generally not economically feasible for the plaintiff as the charged listed corporations may have run out of funds after paying the administrative penalties. These legislation deficiencies may largely constrain the court from exerting sound influence on the practice and governance structure of the listed corporations (Yang 2010). Thirdly, the academic background, knowledge, and experience of the judges may also confine the court's competence in intervening in financial cases. Increasingly, judges in present China largely graduate from law schools of known universities, frequently hold a JD or master's degree in law, and are educated with some economic courses. However, compared with judges in the Anglo-Saxon law countries who have generally practiced laws for years as lawyers and are specialized in economic and financial cases, Chinese judges may be comparatively less equipped in hearing highly technical financial cases. Meanwhile, the comparative insignificance of the legal precedent and its rare application in Chinese judicial system may further weaken the judges' ability in handling fairly sophisticated litigations in banking and finance.

In practice, these may bring extra difficulty in proper interpretation of the laws and effective legal enforcement on financial cases. In *Notice on Foreclosure, Detainment and Freezing of the Assets in the Execution by the People's Court* (Chinese Supreme Court 2004), for instance, though the court can foreclose the real estate by the debtor of the bank who defaults in repaying the bank loans, it cannot put such estate on auction, for sale, or as payment for repaying the debts if such real estate is the fundamental living necessity for the debtor and his dependent family member. This barricades efficient legal enforcement on the disputed real estate and hinders the bank from collecting nonperforming mortgage loans from the defaulting individuals. Another case of judicial pessimism is represented in the court's attitude toward the transfer of credit right to the nonperforming financial obligations owned by large-sized SOEs, as observed in *Summaries of Working Seminars on Cases of Transference of Non-Performing Rights to Financial Related Liabilities* (Chinese Supreme Court 2009b). Legally, transfer of the credit right to nonperforming liabilities to a new creditor falls into the private realm, which is completed by the private agreement between contracting parties. Only in exceptional cases where there is significant violation of social policies will the court intervene. However, the Chinese Supreme Court sets fairly restrictive criteria upon the validity of the contract regarding the transfer of such credit right. It specifies not only additional procedures such as the application for approval, official registration, and submission for official record, but also the substantive scrutiny of the fairness regarding the valuation of transferred credits and related assets. Such extrajudicial requirements bring about more barricades to the new creditors in claiming due repayment for the debts through judicial means. Meanwhile, the indebted large-sized SOEs can counterclaim against the new creditors by challenging the validity of the contract on the credit transfer, which may lead to burdensome lengthy litigations, unexpected high costs and expenses, and delayed clearance of the credits. Nevertheless, this controversial judicial interpretation justifies itself in considering the specialty of Chinese transitional economy, where the settlement of financial debts of over 1 billion RMB by SOEs is differentiated from the generic settlement of debts between private contracting parties, and involves the transfer of voluminous state assets and re-allocation of economic interests. 'Whether such transfer can be achieved in transparent, fair and justified procedures impacts upon the overall interests of the people and the state, and the effectiveness in the management of the state assets. In this context, it is inadequate in evaluating the transfer of the credit to such nonperforming financial debts in accordance with the general contract principle of free will and protection of the private rights' (China, Supreme Court 2009b, p. 3).

4.4.2 Judicial Activism

On the other hand, Chinese courts are fairly active in guiding, orienting, and participating in a great variety of financial activities by Chinese banking organizations through different means, which embrace significant court decisions, judicial guidance and advice. For instance, in 2009, the Supreme Court of Guangdong Province issued judicial advice to key regional financial regulators, such as the Guangzhou Branch of PBoC, the Guangzhou Bureau of CBRC, and the Administrative Office on Financial Services of Guangdong Province, and instructed the banks should assure that their loan/lending business cope with the latest changes in the legislation. Specifically, the court advised that the bank scrutinize the adequacy of collaterals for bank loans, control and prevent credit risks caused by the void or invalid collaterals, and monitor closely the performance of duty of care by relevant bank employees. The Second Intermediate Appellate Court in Shanghai, on the other hand, provided specific judicial advice to Shanghai Bureau of CBRC regarding illegal investment in stock markets by Shanghai Branch of Guangda Bank, which amounted to 25 billion RMB. The court advised the Shanghai Bureau of CBRC to take timing and efficient measures to ensure that Guangda Bank immediately rectifies its illegal practice and mitigates relevant credit risk exposures (NetEase, July 25, 2005). The Shanghai Supreme Court, on the other hand, issued a series of judicial advice in 2007 for preventing substantial risks in voluminous stock transactions by Chinese banks, such as illegal stock trading by using the 'sensitive and delicate' investment, the deficient information disclosure and misstatement, and legal risks accrued from delegated wealth management. In this scenario, the Chinese court, as a complementary to the financial regulators, actually plays the role of the 'backup financial supervisor' and facilitates the implementation of many key financial policies.

Meanwhile, the court's activism can be found in its positive role in promoting key financial reforms. For instance, against the backdrop of drastic and innovative financial reforms in Wenzhou in 2012, the local appellate court timely promulgated *Several Opinions on Judicial Support on Establishing the Experimental Region for Comprehensive Financial Reform in Wenzhou,* which well boosted the development of many private banking and loan businesses (Stock Times, May 22, 2012). The court's opinions purposely clarified and legitimized new patterns of private financing and investment in the region, and designed a creative registration process which required, procedurally, the official registration and record of the private borrowing from the bank that could be used as valid evidence in case of default or non-repayment. Moreover, the court reinforced the protection for the private investors, their legitimate rights, and their investment in new types of financial institutions, such as banks established at the county or village levels, micro loan companies, and rural financial cooperatives. In addition, restrictions over private shareholdings in these financial institutions were to be loosened. In parallel, the court also stressed upon the balance between the financial innovation and prevention of financial risks, and avoided major financial failures which might adversely impact on the overall financial reform (Stock Times, May 22, 2012).

4.5 Bank and International Influence

Increasingly, international influences of various kinds, as another set of institutional embedment, come to shape and reshape the discourse of corporate governance in Chinese banking organizations. These pertain to China's extensive memberships in varied international economic and financial organizations, further opening up to foreign financial institutions, and active participation in global financial markets and mounting overseas investment. By participating in, negotiating, and co-drafting the principles, rules and frameworks in key international financial organizations, Chinese financial regulators increasingly 'import' the international financial discourses into the governance structure of Chinese banking organizations. Up to 2013, for example, CBRC had integrated almost all the key principles and guidance by BIS regarding risk management in banking institutions, which covered the capital adequacy, credit risk, liquidity risk, market risk, legal risk, etc. Based on BIS I, II, and III, CBRC, for example, specifically modified *Guideline on Regulation of Liquidity Risk of Commercial Banks* (CBRC 2009) and drafted *Principles on Regulation of Liquidity Risk by Commercial Banks* (CBRC 2010d). As one of the most significant guidance on risk management for Chinese banking industry, these guidelines and principles adopted Basel's latest liquidity risk management framework and reinforced the use of mixed qualitative and quantitative methods in identifying, assessing, monitoring, and controlling liquidity risks on all key aspects of the business activities by Chinese banks.

Secondly, the increasing presence of foreign banks in China, deregulation upon their market entrance and business activities, and intensified competition brought by these international banks also exert great influence on bank governance in China. Up to September 2011, for instance, more than 47 countries and regions had established banking agency in China and become engaged in a great variety of banking activities, such as financing for the SMEs, investment in agriculture, airlines and transportations, wealth management, and international financial settlement. This embraces 39 registered foreign banks (with 247 branches and affiliates), one foreign financial and accounting firm, 93 branches, and 207 offices of foreign banks (CBRC 2011). Among these 39 registered foreign banks, the total asset for the top five banking institutions had well exceeded one thousand billion RMB. Benefiting from China's national treatment policy, foreign banks enjoy equal authorization as Chinese domestic banks with regard to the banking business either in RMB or in foreign currency, and are subject to the same financial regulations upon the capital adequacy, constraint over credit concentration, liquidity, etc. (CBRC 2011). With the fast expansion of their networks, foreign banks have established their business operations in 48 big cities in China, covering almost all the provinces and municipalities except Tibet Autonomous Zone, Gansu Province, Qinghai Province, and Ningxia Province. Up to September 2011, the total asset of foreign banking organizations in China had reached 2.06 trillion RMB, with a compound annual growth rate of 19% since 2001. Meanwhile, foreign banks had developed more than 240 different financial products in China, ranging from individual loans like 'Happy Loan' and 'Modern Loan,' the wealth management products, to consulting service for Chinese enterprises intending for international expansion. Moreover, foreign banks are proactively engaged in the financial derivative markets and take up around 34.6% of the total transactions (CBRC 2011).

The increasing presence of foreign banks in China brings about fierce competitions to Chinese banks in key economic regions and major banking business. The former focuses mainly on developed regions like Yangtze Triangular Zone, Zhujiang Triangular Zone, and the economic belt along Bohai Sea. The latter involves financial business in trade financing, financial lending to the real estate sector and SMEs, individual loans, and wealth management products. For instance, foreign banks are expanding fairly fast in coastal and metropolitan cities, merging and acquiring foreign and Chinese enterprises and financial institutions with great growth potentials, and competing aggressively for brokerage and investment banking business. Meanwhile, foreign banks are taking advantages of the domestic banks by attracting their experienced employees with higher pay. These actually set great pressures on Chinese banking industry and motivate Chinese banks to enhance their corporate governance for better performance and competitiveness, which focuses on more efficient ownership structures, better compensation and incentive mechanisms for excellent personnel, and sound risk management and internal control system. Meanwhile,

4.5 Bank and International Influence

Table 4.3 2011 international business expansion by the sampled bank (including Hong Kong, Macau, and Taiwan), unit: billion USD

Bank	The number of overseas branches and subsidiaries	The coverage of overseas countries and regions	Overseas total assets Unit: billion USD	Percentage of the overseas total assets in the total assets of the banking group (%)	Increased percentage compared with last year %
Bank B	239	33	1,247.29	5.1	64.7%,
Bank C	Not known	32	4,086	21.76	26.15%
Bank A	71	13	[a]4,212.12	3.61	[a]67.74%
Bank D	7	7	1,247.03	1.07	Not known

[a]Is the total of overseas operational business assets, and the increase rate against last is also based on such category of assets. The overseas total assets by Bank A in 2011 is 4,431.88 billion USD

Source Annual reports of the sampled banks, 2012

advanced financial technology, financial innovations, and new financial products are also actively developed and promoted industrial-wide (Wang and Cao 2005).

Another international impact on the discourse of bank governance comes from the rapid overseas expansion and financial globalization by Chinese banking organizations, which aim to provide financing to Chinese companies operating overseas and facilitate trading by foreign investors interested in exposure to Chinese RMB. As illustrated in Table 4.3, Bank C, based on its extensive international networks and long history of international banking and finance, has prioritized global expansion as its key business strategy. Up to 2011, its overseas branches had covered 32 countries and regions outside the mainland of China, and the total overseas asset reached to 4,086 billion USD and took 21.76% in its total asset (Bank C 2012a). Bank B, stressing on the significance of international business in its strategic development planning, has been expanding its global operation at an unprecedented pace in the past few years. And up to 2011, its overseas branches had risen to 239, covering 33 countries and regions. Meanwhile, its overseas total asset reached 1,247.29 billion USD, increasing by 64.7% compared with 2010, and took 5.1% in the total asset of the bank group (Bank B 2012a).

In this internationalization process, however Chinese banks are frequently subject to various investigations and stricter requirements on enhancing corporate governance by the host country. For instance, in gaining access to US financial markets, whether it involves acquisition of the established financial institution or setting up new branches or subsidiaries, Chinese banking organizations are subject to strict review on their corporate governance structures by officials and specialists from relevant US financial regulators like SEC and Federal Reserve. For instance, before Bank B was approved to acquire 80% stake in the US subsidiary of Bank of East Asia (a Hong Kong Company with 13 branches in New York and California), or Bank D was allowed to set up its branch in New York City and Bank C to set up its branch in Chicago, they underwent a series of strict tests on their governance arrangements. Meanwhile, Bank M, a large-sized highly privatized Chinese commercial bank, was refused by US Federal Reserve on buying into UCBH Holdings, Inc. (the holding company for United Commercial Bank) because of deficiencies in the bank's, corporate governance, risk management system, and anti-money laundering procedures (Wall Street Journal, May 12, 2012).

Other international influences on corporate governance in Chinese banks may result from the appointment of foreigners or professionals with strong international background as the bank's board directors and senior managers, customary overseas training and exchange programs with foreign banks, and recruitment of new employees with overseas academic background or working experience. For instance, as to be discussed in Chap. 7, hiring of the board directors international background is popular in the sampled Chinese banks, with each having over 20% of the board directors from the outside of mainland of China. Meanwhile, Chinese banks have developed long-term overseas training or exchange programs to enrich international experience of their managers and employees. For instance, Bank A has established strategic partnership with JPMorgan Chase and periodically sent its middle-ranked managers to USA for around 6 months training and on-job learning.

4.6 Implication for Paradigm and Specific Governance Structure

The legitimacy of corporate governance in Chinese banks, summarized as the bank's proactive role in real economy, strict financial regulation and control by the state, paradoxical legal intervention, and increasing international influence, poses strong influence on the formation of the next-level discourse, the paradigm. For instance, the paradigm of the governance arrangement in Chinese banks presents a hybrid nature due to the 'blended' legitimacy discourses which integrate some of the specific features from CME, SME, and LME. With the banks' integration into the real economy and active financing for the development of industrial sectors and the enterprises of various kinds (SOEs and SMEs), Chinese banking organizations frequently pursue a long-term, sustainable profitability rather than short-run best performance. And, serious concerns are given to the protection of the interests of a wide range of stakeholders, such as the sustainable economy, the bank's creditors and depositors, the financial regulators, the employees, and the local community and society at large. Such paradigm of the stakeholder model is reinforced by the strong regulatory discourse in China through close and strict financial regulation. By policy orientations, regulatory guidance, and working conferences, Chinese financial regulators may efficiently coordinate Chinese banks with sustainable economic development, financial stability, and protection of the interests of various constituencies. Meanwhile, though to a limited extent, the paradigm of the stakeholder model is strengthened by the court's intervention *ex ante*. By stressing upon the significance of the social stability

4.6 Implication for Paradigm and Specific Governance Structure

and financial sustainability, the court actively orients the bank toward the protection of the interests of different interest groups, even those of the bank's debtors. Moreover, a parallel paradigm of the state-affected model may be present in China due to the discourse of a more intervening role by the financial regulator, especially in cases of financial uncertainty and implementation of key national development strategies. For instance, in accordance with relevant financial regulations and directives, Chinese banks are directed toward issuing voluminous loans to the prioritized industrial sectors, key infrastructure projects, and most underdeveloped regions, though such investment, apparently, is less profitable in the short term. On the other hand, however, the discourse of financial deregulation movements and international influence promotes the paradigm of the shareholder primacy. For instance, with the progressing financial deregulation, Chinese banks lay specific emphasis on enhancing profitability and best performance in the marketplace. Meanwhile, with intensive competitions within the banking industry and from other nonbanking financial institutions such as stockbrokers and trust corporations, Chinese banks are now under greater pressure to compete, maximize their profits, and bring better investment returns to the shareholders. The international influence, either caused by the competitions from foreign banks investing in China or Chinese banks' global expansion, also reinforces the paradigm of the shareholder primacy in corporate governance in Chinese banking organizations.

Moreover, the aforesaid legitimacy provides important implications for the frame of specific governance structure in Chinese banking organizations. For instance, with the close connection between the bank and the real economy and strong impacts by the regulatory discourse, the bank board in China is, to some extent, more oriented toward serving the economic development, promoting the interests of various stakeholders, rather than maximizing the profitability of the bank and the best investment returns to the shareholders in the short run. And, the intensive financial regulatory framework may also influence the arrangement of governance structure in Chinese banks. For instance, the financial regulator may direct the composition of the compensation package, specific ratio of different variable pays, and an implicit cap on the total remuneration for bank board directors and senior managers. Regarding risk management, Chinese banks generally present a moderate risk appetite, specific concerns on certain credit risk exposures, and more direct lending relationships with the corporate and individual clients. For instance, Chinese banks are somehow less motivated to take more risks (for the sake of higher returns) to achieve short-term maximized profitability against the backdrop of certain legal constraints on competitions within and beyond the banking industry and paramount regulatory orientation for the long-term profitability and overall financial stability. On the flip side, however, the bank's close integration into the real economy and the regulator's guidance for financing the economic development may bring about extra risks, such as potential massive credit risk exposures from the borrowing local governments, enterprises, or industrial sectors. And, the strong financial regulation also finds its way into the production and reproduction of legal obligations in Chinese banking organizations, such as the specific legal compliance criterion, the measurement, and evaluation.

4.7 Conclusion

Focusing on the specific institutional setting in Chinese context, this chapter explores the legitimacy discourses of corporate governance in banking organizations in China. Against the backdrop of a hybrid nature of CME, SME, and LME model countries, Chinese banks gain the legitimacy from their integration into the national economy, close connections with major industries, and the intertwining relationship with SOEs and SMEs. For financial regulations, a paralleled discourse of close control and deregulation is present which greatly influences bank governance in many aspects. Though Chinese court apparently plays a limited role in shaping the discourse of governance structure of Chinese banks, it is proactive in intervening *ex ante* in the bank's business operation by various judiciary measures. And, with the increasing involvement in financial globalization, whether by means of Chinese banks' international expansion or increasing presence of foreign banks in China, international influence shows great strength in reshaping the governance structure of Chinese banking organizations. In sum, as the discourse at the background of the cognition, the legitimacy provides significant implications for the paradigm and frame of bank governance in Chinese context, which will be discussed in the following chapters.

References

Amsden, A. (1989). *Asia's next giant: South Korea and late industrialization*. New York and Oxford: Oxford University Press.

Bank A. (2012). 2011 CSR Report of Bank A, Bank A. Retrieved May 25, 2012, from http://www.BankA.com.

Bank B. (2012a). 2011 Annual Report of Bank B, Bank B. Retrieved May 25, 2012, from http://www.BankB.com.

Bank B. (2012b). 2011 CSR Report of Bank B, Bank B. Retrieved May 25, 2012, from http://www.BankB.com.

Bank C. (2012a). 2011 Annual Report of Bank C, Bank C. Retrieved May 25, 2012, from http://www.BankC.com.

Bank C. (2012b). 2011 CSR Report of Bank C, Bank C. Retrieved May 25, 2012, from http://www.BankC.com.

Bank D. (2012). 2011 CSR Report of Bank D, Bank D. Retrieved May 25, 2012, from http://www.BankD.com.

Boyer, R. (2005). Coherence, diversity, and the evolution of capitalisms—the institutional complementarity hypothesis. *Evolutionary and Institutional Economics Review, 2*(1), 43–80.

Brandt, L., & Li, H. (2003). Bank discrimination in transition economies: Ideology, information, or incentives? *Journal of Comparative Economics, 31*(3), 387–413.

Campbell, J. L. (2004). *Institutional change and globalization*. Princeton: Princeton University Press.

Carney, R. (2007). Contested capitalism: Financial politics and implications for China, GARNET working paper no. 15/07, Nanyang Technological University.

Carney, M., Gedajlovic, E., & Yang, X. (2009). Varieties of Asian capitalism: Toward an institutional theory of Asian enterprise. *Asia Pacific Journal of Management, 26*(3), 361–380.

Charumilind, C., Kali, R., & Wiwattanakantang, Y. (2006). Connected lending: Thailand before the financial crisis. *The Journal of Business, 79*(1), 181–218.

References

China Banking Association. (2009). *The Self-discipline convention of the banking industry of China.* Beijing: China Banking Association.

China Banking Association. (2010). 2009 CSR Report of Chinese banking industry, China banking association. Retrieved July 26, 2012, from http://www.china-cba.net.

China Banking Association. (2011). 2010 CSR Report of Chinese Banking Industry, China Banking Association, Retrieved July 28, 2012, from http://www.china-cba.net.

China Banking Regulatory Commission. (2009). *Guidance for Project Financing Business, no. 71,* Beijing: China Banking Regulatory Commission.

China Banking Regulatory Commission. (2010a). *The Temporary Regulation for Individual Loans, no. 2,* Beijing: China Banking Regulatory Commission.

China Banking Regulatory Commission. (2010b). *The guidance on promoting innovation in financial products and business patterns for rural areas on full aspects, no. 198.* Beijing: China Banking Regulatory Commission.

China Banking Regulatory Commission. (2010c). *Notice on support for further improvement on financial services by commercial banks to SMEs.* Beijing: China Banking Regulatory Commission.

China Banking Regulatory Commission. (2010d). *Principles on Regulation of Liquidity Risk by Commercial Banks.* Beijing: China Banking Regulatory Commission.

China Banking Regulatory Commission. (2011). *WTO report: 10 Year opening-up of Chinese banking industry and supervision over foreign banks since China's entrance into WTO.* Beijing: China Banking Regulatory Commission.

China Banking Regulatory Commission. (2013). Diagram of total assets and liabilities of Chinese banking industry, Jan, 28th, 2013. Beijing: China Banking Regulatory Commission. Retrieved March 22, 2013, from http://www.cbrc.gov.cn/chinese/home/docView/4E26991646BF4E9D860F8F671380B85A.html.

Crawford, D. (2000). Chinese capitalism: Cultures, the Southeast Asian region and economic globalization. *Third World Quarterly, 21*(1), 69–86.

Crouch, C. (2005). *Capitalist diversity and change: Recombinant governance and institutional entrepreneurs.* OUP Oxford.

Crouch, C., Streeck, W., Boyer, R., Amable, B., Hall, P. A., & Jackson, G. (2005). Dialogue on 'Institutional complementarity and political economy'. *Socio-Economic Review, 3*(2), 359–382.

Cull, R., & Xu, L. C. (2005). Institutions, ownership, and finance: the determinants of profit reinvestment among Chinese firms. *Journal of Financial Economics, 77*(1), 117–146.

Diamond, D. W. (1991). Monitoring and reputation: The choice between bank loans and directly placed debt. *Journal of Political Economy, 99*(4), 689–721.

Diamond, D. W. (1993). Seniority and maturity of debt contracts. *Journal of Financial Economics, 33*(3), 341–368.

Faccio, M. (2006). Politically connected firms. *American Economic Review, 96*(1), 369–386.

Fisman, R. (2001). Estimating the value of political connections. *American Economic Review, 91*(4), 1095–1102.

Fruin, W. M. (Ed.). (1998). *Networks, markets, and the pacific rim: Studies in strategy.* Oxford University Press on Demand.

Hamilton, J. D. (1996). This is what happened to the oil price-macroeconomy relationship. *Journal of Monetary Economics, 38*(2), 215–220.

Hamilton, G. G., & Biggart, N. W. (1988). Market, culture, and authority: A comparative analysis of management and organization in the Far East. *American journal of Sociology, 94,* S52–S94.

Jiang, W., & Li, B. (2006). Institutional settings, the state ownership, and the differentiated loans by banks. *Journal of Financial Research, 11,* 116–126.

Johnson, S., & Mitton, T. (2003). Cronyism and capital controls: evidence from Malaysia. *Journal of Financial Economics, 67*(2), 351–382.

Kim, B. W. (1998). Family, social relations, and Asia capitalism. *Journal of International and Area Studies, 5*(1), 65–79.

Krueger, A. O. (1974). The political economy of the rent-seeking society. *The American economic review, 64*(3), 291–303.

Lei, C. (2009). Analysis of the reform of state-owned commercial banks: A political economy perspective. *Journal of Central University of Finance & Economics, vol, 2.*

Lv, Z. (2010). The Political and Legal Committee through the lens of the legal-social science-legal views on the Political and Legal Committee in China. *Forward Position, 8.*

Ma, D. (2001). Profits maximization should be prioritized by state-owned commercial banks–An analysis of the relationship between the pursuit for profitability and implementation of economic policy objectives by state-owned commercial banks. *Journal of Financial Research, 1.*

NetEase. (2005). Judicial advice reveals illegal trading in stocks by G bank, July 25th, 2005, Beijing: Netease. Retrieved November 05, 2011, from http://biz.163.com/05/0725/10/1PGIP7L600020QEV.html.

NetEase. (2013). Total market value of Shang Hai and Shen Zhen Stock Exchanges exceeded 23 trillion RMB last year, January 8th 2013, Beijing: Netease. Retrieved April 15, 2013, from http://news.163.com/13/0108/08/8KMCPKRC00014JB5.html.

Orrù, M. (1997). Dirigiste Capitalism in France and South Korea. *The economic organization of East Asian capitalism*, 368-382.

People's Bank of China. (2012). *Notice on Experimental Rural Financial Reform in Lishui*. Zhejiang Province, Beijing: People's Bank of China.

Steier, L. P. (2009). Familial capitalism in global institutional contexts: Implications for corporate governance and entrepreneurship in East Asia. *Asia Pacific Journal of Management, 26*(3), 513.

Stock Times. (2012). Financial reforms in Lishui, May 18, 2012, Beijing: Stock Times

Szamosszegi, A., & Kyle, C. (2011). An analysis of state-owned enterprises and state capitalism in China. Working paper, U.S.-China Economic and Security Review Commission, October 26, 2011.

The Supreme People's Court of the People's Republic of China. (2002). *Several rules on civil compensations cases for mis-statement allegation in the stock market*. Beijing: The Supreme People's Court of the People's Republic of China.

The Supreme People's Court of the People's Republic of China. (2004). *Notice on foreclosure, detainment and freezing of the assets in the execution by the People's Court*. Beijing: The Supreme People's Court of the People's Republic of China.

The Supreme People's Court of the People's Republic of China. (2009a), *Reform blueprint of the people's court for the third five-year plan from 2009–2013 in China, no. 14*. Beijing: The Supreme People's Court of the People's Republic of China.

The Supreme People's Court of the People's Republic of China. (2009b). *Summaries of working seminars on cases of transference of non-performing rights to financial related liabilities*. Beijing: The Supreme People's Court of the People's Republic of China.

Tsui-Auch, L. S. (2004). The professionally managed family-ruled enterprise: ethnic Chinese business in Singapore. *Journal of Management Studies, 41*(4), 693–723.

Wade, R. (1990). Industrial policy in East Asia: Does it lead or follow the market. *Manufacturing Miracles: Paths of Industrialization in Latin America and East Asia,* 231–266.

Wall Street Journal (Asia). (2012). Overseas acquisitions by Chinese banks in USA, May 12 th, 2012. New York: Wall Street Journal.

Wang, P., & Cao, T. (2005). Influences by foreign-invested banks to China and relevant solutions—Analysis based on international experience. *Research on Economics and Management, 9,* 46–50.

Wang, G., & Guo, T. (Eds.). (2008) *30 years of Chinese economic reform- the volume of financial reform.* Chong Qing: Chong Qing University Press.

Weidenbaum, M. L., & Hughes, S. (1996). *The bamboo network: How expatriate Chinese entrepreneurs are creating a new economic superpower in Asia.* Simon and Schuster.

Whitley, R. (1999). *Divergent capitalisms: The social structuring and change of business systems.* OUP Oxford.

Witt, A. M. (2010), China: What variety of capitalism? Faculty and research working paper, 2010/88/EPS.

References

Xinhua Net. (2012). Tolerance for default loans by small and micro enterprises is raised to 5% in Shenzhen, April 12th, 2012, Beijing: Xinhua Net. Retrieved July 25, 2012, from http://news.xinhuanet.com/fortune/2012-04/12/c_122969583.htm.

Yang, L. (2010). Deficiencies in civil liability legislations in securities related cases and proposed improvement. *Guide to Business, 8.*

Yeung, H. W. C. (2004). *Chinese capitalism in a global era: Towards a hybrid capitalism.* Routledge.

Yeung, H. W. (2006). Change and continuity in Southeast Asian ethnic Chinese business. *Asia Pacific Journal of Management, 23*(3), 229–254.

Yin, X. (2012). Review of the functions by the Political and Legal Committee of Chinese Communist Party in political and legal relations. *Law Science, 6,* 3–11.

Part III
Corporate Governance in Banking Organizations: Paradigm

Chapter 5
Paradigm Discourses on Corporate Governance in Banking Organizations

5.1 Introduction

Continuing the discursive analysis on corporate governance in banking organizations, this chapter explores the production of bank governance at the paradigmatic level, namely the models. Constantly argued in generic corporate governance literatures, several models of corporate governance can be distinguished based on varied orientations and relationship between multiple participants, which resonates with the telescope view of corporate governance. Traditionally, the Anglo-Saxon model and the Continental model of corporate governance have been dominating this field, although other models have been identified to some extent, such as the state-affected model, family group control model (in some East Asia countries), and insider control model (in countries of transitional periods). And, in the context of corporate governance in banking organizations, some variances are observed for these models due to the industrial specialty. For instance, the shareholder primacy model in bank governance is distinguished by the acuteness of agency problems, intensive conflict of interests between the residual claimants and fixed claimants, and the short-term stand taken by the investors and bank management. For the stakeholder model, referring to the specific concept of social responsibilities of the bank as a financial institution, protection for various stakeholders comes into the analytical picture. And, for the state-affected model, as a hybrid of the shareholder primacy model and stakeholder model, the paradigm discourse is marked by the state's positioning of the bank as playing an active role in support of national economic development. Meanwhile, the paradigms of these different models are found to well represent the varied legitimacy discourses as discussed in Chap. 3.

© Springer Nature Singapore Pte Ltd. 2019
W. Zou, *Corporate Governance in the Banking Sector in China*, CSR, Sustainability, Ethics & Governance, https://doi.org/10.1007/978-981-13-3510-5_5

5.2 General Models of Corporate Governance Around the World

5.2.1 The Anglo-Saxon Model

The Anglo-Saxon model, also known as the shareholder primacy model (Jensen and Meckling 1976; Shleifer and Vishny 1997; Barca and Becht 2002), originates in America and Britain and is followed by Canada, Australia, and some other common law countries. It is oriented toward maximizing shareholders' rights and interests while subordinating other stakeholders' claims. This theory is grounded on the status of the investor as the owner of the corporation, whose private property rights and interests are entitled to protection. Alternatively, the shareholder is taken as the residual claimant who takes the final residual risk in the event of corporate failures (Alchian and Demsetz 1972; Fama and Jesnen 1983). Meanwhile, the maximization of shareholder values is viewed as propelling the superior economic performance of the corporation and the economy as a whole (Fama and Jensen 1983).

The major concern in the Anglo-Saxon model is the agency problem, also known as the principal–agent problem, which arises from the separation of ownership from control of the corporation, with the investors owning the corporation while the managers controlling it (Berle and Means 1932; Jensen Meckling 1976; Shleifer and Vishny 1997; Demsetz and Lehn 1985; Eisenhardt 1989). It is said to occur when 'one or more persons (the principal(s)) engage another person (the agent) to perform some service on their behalf which involves delegating some decision-making authority to the agent.' In addition, 'if both parties to the relationship are utility maximizers, there is good reason to believe that the agent will not always act in the best interests of the principal' (Jensen Meckling 1976, p. 334). This is further aggravated by the differing preferences of the owners and the managers, information asymmetry in the corporation, and different time horizons and risk appetites (Eisenhardt 1989).

Many solutions are proposed for mitigating such agency problem. Some scholars favor general contracts between the investors and the management, the incentive contract for the management's compensation, and the disciplinary reputation mechanism (Shleifer and Vishny 1997; La Porta 1996, 1999, 2000). Other scholars believe in the discipline of efficient market and design relevant market mechanisms to constrain the agency problem, such as strict monitoring, efficient market for corporate control and management labor, and better transparency (Learmount 2002). Though these delicately designed mechanisms can alleviate the agency problem to some extent, they cannot totally eliminate this corporate *syndrome* (Shleifer and Vishny 1997).

Although a concern with the agency problem dominates in corporate governance in the so-called Anglo-Saxon model, a subset of competing theories is developed based on the management homogeneity, typically represented by the stewardship theory. Instead of focusing on the conflict of interests between the management (the agent) and the owner (the principal), the stewardship theory contends that the managers should be positioned as good stewards, and in pursuing the best performance of the enterprise, they can both maximize the shareholders' interests and bring satisfaction to other stakeholders. 'A steward protects and maximizes shareholder's wealth through firm performance, because, by so doing, the steward's utility functions are maximized.' And 'a steward who successfully improves the performance of the organization generally satisfies most groups, because most stakeholder groups having interests that are well served by increasing organization wealth' (Davis et al. 1997, p25; Donaldson and Davis 1991).

5.2.2 The Continental Model

In contrast, the Continental model of corporate governance, also known as the stakeholder model (Cochran and Wartick 1988), is typically said with the extant literature to broadly reflect German corporate governance mechanism. This model is also argued to characterize corporate governance in Japan, Austria, and other European countries with variances. Alongside the shareholders' benefits, the stakeholder model specifically takes into account the stakeholders' interests and often balances them in case of conflicts.

At the paradigmatic level, the stakeholder theory argues that the corporation is an organization composed of different groups of stakeholders and its purpose is to manage their interests, needs, and viewpoints (Freeman 1984, Freeman and Evan 1990; Donaldson and Preston 1995, Clarkson 1995, Clarke and Clegg 2000). The stakeholder is classically defined as any group or individual who can affect or be affected by the achievement of the organization's objectives (Freeman 1984). And, the management is expected to manage the corporation for the benefits of its stakeholders and promote their rights and participation in the decision-making process (Donaldson and Preston 1995). This implies that the managers, apart from acting as the shareholders' agent to ensure the survival and prosperity of the firm, have to safeguard the long-term stakes of each interest group. In this context, the management is expected to integrate various relationships and the interests of the shareholders and different stakeholders in a way that guarantees the long-term success of the firm (Freeman 1984).

Another significant feature of the Continental model of corporate governance is the existence of the large and controlling shareholders, who are either banks or other corporations by way of cross-holding or block-holding (Barclay et al. 1993; Becht and RNoell 1999; Bebchuk et al. 2000). As large shareholders are motivated to collect information on the corporation, monitor the managers closely, and impose great pressure upon the management regarding significant decisions, the agency problem, popular in the Anglo-Saxon model, is said to be less significant in the stakeholder model. The existence of large investors provides other merits as well, such as the more effective governing system, better performance by the managers, and less dependence on judicial systems. However, the control by such major shareholders causes another problem in corporate governance, namely the principal–principal problem (Shleifer and Vishny 1997). In contrast with the traditional principal–agent conflict in the Anglo-Saxon model, inherent in the Continental model of corporate governance is a principal–principal conflict, which mainly arises between majority (controlling shareholders) and minority shareholders because of the existence of the large and controlling shareholdings (Shleifer and Vishny 1997). Such concentrated ownership may frequently lead to imbalanced powers in the corporation, as best exemplified by the appointment and control of the directors and management, bias in significant business policies (such as investment opportunities, dividend pay-out police), and insider transactions, which results in undesirable expropriation issues much resembling that in the principal–agent conflict (Young et al. 2008). Typically, such problem can be seen as a product of the concentrated ownership and control by the business groups, state, or family structure, where legal protection for minority shareholders is most weak and even of 'out of place'.

5.2.3 Other Models and Relevant Theories

Apart from the aforesaid models, other types of corporate governance paradigms are identified by the extant literature. These include the state-affected model (such in France), family group control model in (as in Southeast Asian countries), and models in transitional economies typified in former Soviet Union countries. These models, though less influential in academic debate in the extant theories than the shareholder or stakeholder model, have their distinctive forms and specific features.

For instance, the state-affected model of corporate governance, which is said to be typically prevalent in France and many transitional economies, presents a unique governance arrangement which is by nature a 'hybrid' model, though close to the 'stakeholders' approach (Blazy et al. 2012). Instead of arguing for the merits of the shareholder primacy or the protection of the stakeholder interests, this model is frequently concerned with the state as the majority shareholder of the corporation, which pursues economic policy objectives and specified national development strategies (Schmidt 2003; Kang 2006). Interestingly, both principal–agent and principal–principal problems can be found in this model due to the existence of government as the owner and majority shareholder of the corporation. Though it may have merits in coordinating and facilitating the growth and development of national economy in certain periods of time, this model may limit corporate capacity for effectively responding to the dynamics of the global market competition.

The family control model, meanwhile, is characterized by the main owner's (family) active and decisive role in the key decision makings of the firm (Daily and Dollinger 1992; Melin and Nordqvist 2000), and the governance structure is primarily targeted at facilitating the owner of the firm to realize their particular vision, goals, and objectives (Melin and Nordqvist 2000). This model is said to overcome agency costs due to the duality of the manager and owner (Randøy & Goel 2003; Schulze 2003) and is held to provide for long-term perspective of the firm (Cadbury 2000) and altruistic behavior and trust (Van den Berghe & Carchon, 2003; De Paola and Scoppa 2001). On the flip side, however, the family control model is associated with costs and inefficiencies, such as prioritizing family interests over the firm's interests due to family loyalty (Randøy & Goel 2003; Schulze 2003), more significant monitoring costs (Van den Berghe & Carchon, 2003), and opportunistic behaviors by the non-family members (Baldridge and Schulze 1999).

5.3 Paradigm Discourses in Corporate Governance in Banking Organizations

5.3.1 The Anglo-Saxon Model: The Shareholder Primacy Theory Refined

When applied in corporate governance in banking organizations, the aforesaid generic models, somehow, may be reshaped and reproduced to accommodate the needs and specialty of the banks as distinguished from the general firms, which leads to the production of new paradigmatic discourses on bank governance in varied model countries.

As discussed, generic corporate governance in the Anglo-Saxon model is characterized with the shareholder primacy theory which focuses upon maximizing investors' interests, pursuing best performance of the corporation, and mitigating the agency cost (Jensen and Meckling 1976). Similar paradigm of the shareholder primacy can be observed in corporate governance in banking organizations in this model, but with variances. On one side, the general shareholder primacy theory applies as banks in this model frequently take the form of bank holding corporations/groups and are treated no different from general corporations (Adams and Mehran 2003). In the context of increasing financial disintermediation, cyclical deregulation, and fierce competition, there is immense pressure on the bank to procure best profitability and maximized return to the investors (always assessed in the short term) while ignoring its industrial specialty. On the flip side, due to the uniqueness of the banking industry, the shareholder primacy theory in corporate governance in banking organizations takes on some new characters, exemplified with excessive pursuit of profit maximization, acute agency problems, and intensive conflicts of interests between the shareholders and the stakeholders.

A. The primacy of the shareholders' interests

As the priority of the priorities, bank managers in the Anglo-Saxon model have been committed to pursuing the best performance and maximization of the bank's profitability. And, it has long been the culture of the Wall Street and London financial center to bring in as much and fast profits as possible from every channel. Such orientation toward profitability even becomes the motto and the only criterion to evaluate the success, value, and meaning of the existence of the bank and its employees (Smith 2012). Sometimes, however, the desire for maximized investment returns can stretch so far as to derail the bank off the track and henceforth subordinate the interests of the bank stakeholders and the public at large. These are readily observed in series of notorious bank scandals before and after the global financial crisis, like the LIBOR manipulation, London Whale Gambling, mis-selling of financial products like payment protection insurance in UK, money laundering by couples of large multinational banks, when the banking organizations are willingly and intentionally engaged in excessive risky or illegal financial transactions to harvest a windfall without any care for its legitimacy and legality (USA Today, July 18, 2012; The New York Times, June 28, 2012; The Guardian, June 29, 2012).

To better achieve the shareholder primacy in the context of bank governance, there has been increasing emphasis on the protection of the shareholders' interests in the Anglo-Saxon model. Progressively, a bank, not different from a generic firm, is expected to 'build long-term sustainable growth in shareholder value' and 'accountable to shareholders for its performance in achieving this objective,' specifically the long-term success of the bank on its stewardship (US New York Stock Exchange 2009 UK, Financial Reporting Council 2012). For this end, active engagement and involvement by the shareholders, especially the institutional investors, are reinforced and more shareholder rights are legitimized in corporate governance, business operation, and major business decision making in the Anglo-Saxon banking organizations. In UK, for instance, the investors are playing an increasingly important role as the stewardship and may hold the board of directors of the bank accountable for various responsibilities. In practice, the shareholder's role goes beyond the traditional voting and embraces 'monitoring and engaging with companies on matters such as strategy, performance, risk, capital structure, and corporate governance, including culture and remuneration. Engagement is purposeful dialogue with companies on these matters as well as on issues that are the immediate subject of votes at general meetings' (UK, Financial Reporting Council 2012, p. 10). Meanwhile, the shareholders are exerting more influence regarding the arrangement of the executive remuneration by means of advisory vote or even binding vote, the so-called say on pay, and henceforth better control the extortions by the management in the form of excessive compensation (UK 2013; US 2010). Additional mechanisms are also developed by banking organizations, such as relational bank directors who are specifically responsible for better communication with the investors and providing sound transparency.

For the shareholder primacy discourse in bank governance in the Anglo-Saxon model, meanwhile, there is paralleled intentional neglect over the interests of the stakeholders. Though protection for the interests of the bank's constituency is mentioned by the banks, such as funding the small enterprises and protection for the clients, it is frequently weakly implemented and gives away to the pursuit of maximized profitability. In even worse cases, which were prevalent in the 2007–2009 financial crises, the bank managers intentionally took advantages of the stakeholders and prospered at their expenses. These are typically exemplified by the general practice of treating the customers as 'muppets,' mis-selling 'toxic' financial products, conducting fraudulent transactions with the bank's clients, and 'ripping their clients off,' which becomes the rule of thumb for maximizing bank's profits in US and UK banking industry (Greg 2012; Securities and Exchange Commission 2010). And in the aftermath of the global financial crisis, the subordination of the stakeholders' interests by the Anglo-Saxon banking organizations is not less observed.

5.3 Paradigm Discourses in Corporate Governance …

On the other hand, however, the paradigm of the shareholder primacy does not totally exclude concerns for the stakeholders, as banks in the Anglo-Saxon model are increasingly aware of the significance of protecting the interests of relevant constituencies in their performance of good citizenship, such as the bank's suppliers, the communities and consumers, the neighborhood and regional welfare, the employees, and the environmental sustainability (Citi Group 2011). The concerns for the bank's stakeholders, especially the clients and taxpayers at large, are further reinforced *ex-post* 2007–2009 financial crisis, when the regulatory discourse strengthens and mandates the protection of the bank stakeholders' interests through a new round of financial re-regulation and reforms. In USA, for instance, the Dodd-Frank Act explicitly states the discourse to 'promote the financial stability,' 'to protect the American taxpayer by ending bailouts, and to protect consumers from abusive financial services practices' (US 2010). And, such regulatory discourse is echoed in the new orientation of the bank's paradigm which presents serious concerns for the its constituencies. For instance, in USA, a bank is 'guided at all times by the best interests of the client, taking into account the broader needs of society and the environment' (Citi Group 2011, p. 1), and with emphasis on 'responsible finance,' the bank is more oriented toward 'responsible lending—providing capital to support customers of all economic backgrounds and projects that serve the public' (Citi Group 2011, p. 1). Goldman Sachs, in its *2013 Business Standard Committee Impact Report*, explicitly states that '(the bank's) Our clients' interests always come first' and the bank's business standards committee will ensure that the bank will 'meet or exceed the expectations of our clients, other stakeholders and regulators' and 'contribute to overall financial stability and economic opportunity' (Goldman Sachs 2013, p. 1). Specifically, the bank combines the protection of the clients' interests with the employees' remuneration by stressing upon 'individual accountability for clients in our annual employee performance review process and, for senior client relationship professionals, in compensation determinations' (Goldman Sachs 2013, p. 3). Nevertheless, it is always challenging for the Anglo-Saxon banks to find a sound balance between the over-emphasized shareholder primacy focusing on maximized profitability and due protection for the interests of the banks' multiple constituency.

B. An acute agency problem

As discussed at the beginning of the chapter, the key concern for general corporate governance in the Anglo-Saxon model is the principal–agent problem or agency problem, which is found to dominate in banking organizations as well. However, due to the specialties of the banking industry, such as the high-leverage capital structure, opaqueness in financial information, and strict financial regulation, there are some deviations from the generic model. These are characterized with the acuteness of agency problems, aggregated conflicts of interests between shareholders and other stakeholders, and less efficient monitoring due to deposit insurance system.

First and foremost is the acuteness of agency problem in banking organizations, which largely results from the short-term stand taken by the bank management. Frequently, the bank managers take a short-range horizon which motivates them to cash in their compensation, including both the equity-based stocks and options and bonuses, far before the final consequences of their business decisions are realized, especially those with long-term duration like merger and acquisition, stabling new lines of business, etc. (Bebchuk and Fried 2003, 2004, 2005). In this context, the bank management may focus excessively on short-term results while less concerned on the adverse effects of the risk taking upon the long-term shareholder value. This is typically represented in the 2007–2009 financial crisis (Blankfein 2009), when the bank executives' pay was tightly connected to the highly leveraged bets on the value of the bank' assets and the bank management ignored any losses that risk taking could impose on other key stakeholders, such as the creditors, depositors, and taxpayers at large (Bebchuk et al. 2010).

Another contributory factor to the acuter agency problem in banks is the fundamental change in the relationship between the shareholders (the residual claimant) and creditors (as the fixed claimant), and the laxer monitoring over riskier activities by the bank management. Due to the higher debt-to-equity ratio in banks, with the shareholders contributing only around less than 10% of the total asset, the conflict between the fixed claimants (creditors and depositors) and the shareholders is exuberated in contrast with generic corporations. This leads to reinforced 'wealth transferring effects' from the fixed claimants to the residual claimants, frequently in the form of excessive risks taken by banks for the sake of higher investment returns. Meanwhile, distinguished from generic firms where the fixed claimants and other stakeholders control the risks more closely by means of contracts or other devices, monitoring by fixed claimants in banking organizations is laxer due to more serious free-rider problems. Moreover, the presence of deposit insurance system and potential bailouts by the government, in either explicit or implicit form, largely removes the fixed claimants' incentives to monitor the bank. In the absence of adequate monitoring by the fixed claimants, the shareholders of the bank and the management may 'conspire' and assume higher risks for higher returns in the short run, while transferring most of the losses to the depositors in cases of investment failures, especially when the bank is near or already in the period of insolvency (Bebchuk et al. 2010).

This is well evidenced in the re-occurrence of moral hazards in the banking industry in the Anglo-Saxon model, such as frauds, self-dealings, and excessive shirking by the bank management. For instance, early in the 1980s in USA, frauds and self-dealing transactions were found around one-thirds of today's bank failures. And between 1990 and 1994, insider lending contributed to over half of 286 bank failures. In addition, as large portions of the bank's assets were held in the form of illiquid forms, such violations were even harder to be detected (Bebchuk and Fried 2003). More evidence is readily observed in 2007–2009 financial crisis and its aftermath, where there is an innovative toxic 'cocktail' of various violating and illegal practices by banking management ringing overall over the world, from malpractices in sub-prime mortgage to London Whale gambling and notorious LIBOR scandal.

C. Implication of paradigm over the formation of governance structure of the bank

The paradigm of the shareholder primacy presents great influences on constituting specific governance structures in banking organizations in the Anglo-Saxon model. For instance, the (shareholder primacy) discourse effectively impacts on the orientation of the bank board, which focuses on the maximized profitability and best investment returns to the shareholders in the short run. Meanwhile, such discourse largely decides the composition of the bank board, as best represented by higher independence of the board of directors and the varied board committees. These are targeted at providing stronger monitoring on the bank managers, mitigating the agency problem, and protecting the interests of the shareholders. The paradigm of the shareholder primacy also shapes, to some extent, the regulation on the executive pay, especially the composition of the banker's remuneration package. Frequently, shareholders in this model prefer to use options or vest of shareholdings as key part of the executive's compensation, which is presumed to better align the interests of the bank's management with those of the investors and henceforth provide effective incentives for the managers to achieve better performance. Meanwhile, though there are various constraining mechanisms like the shareholders' 'say on pay,' the investors are not reluctant to grant generous remuneration to the bank executives so long as their pay is adequately correlated to the bank's profitability and investment returns. For risk management, due to the high-leverage capital structure of the bank, shareholders in this model may prefer higher risks for higher returns, which further amplifies the bank's risk appetite and encourages bank managers to pursue excessive risks for abnormally higher earnings. Furthermore, the paradigm may influence the constitution of the legal obligations by the board of directors and management, typically their fiduciary duty, which are purported to provide strong protection for the bank's shareholders.

5.3.2 The Continental Model and the State-Affected Model

A. Stakeholder theory in bank governance

In contrast, the paradigm for corporate governance in banking organizations in the Continental model is featured with the stakeholder theory, which emphasizes the protection of the interests of various stakeholders. Banks in this model are purported to be 'responsible for independently managing the enterprise in the interest of the enterprise, thus taking into account the interests of the shareholders, its employees and other stakeholders, with the objective of sustainable creation of value' (German Government Commission 2012, p. 15), and firmly 'believe that the best way for us (the bank) to create sustainable value for our shareholders, is by committing ourselves to all the constituencies around us who have a stake in our success' (Deutsche Bank 2012, p. 6). In practice, various measures are taken to accommodate the needs of different categories of stakeholders, including but not limited to the clients, employees, government, communities, regulators, along with environmental sustainability and economic stability.

First and foremost, banks in this model stress upon expanding sustainable products and financial services for the private and corporate clients (Commerz Bank 2012). Specifically, a series of mechanisms are employed to assess and enhance the customers' banking experience, such as periodical surveys, analysis of the degree of the customers' satisfaction, and timely responses to the customers' complaints. And, the benchmark of the customer's satisfaction is frequently used as a variable in determining the compensation for the bank executives. Meanwhile, customer-oriented programs such as 'Market Leadership Course' are proactively promoted to improve the quality standard (Commerz Bank 2012).

Secondly, employees are carefully and well treated in the Continental banks. For example, a comprehensive range of professional development and self-advancement opportunities are provided to the bank employees to enhance their skills and expertise, and a wide range of training programs is henceforth designed and developed. Considering the prevalent stress and tension problems in the banking industry, tailored heathcare programs are initiated for the bank employees, such as periodical health checks and anti-stress treatment (DZ BANK Group 2012). Meanwhile, there are various options for flexible working hours, part-time working models, or other employment arrangements, which are purposed to achieve the balance of work and life for the employees. Further measures pertain to the diversification and gender equality in the workforce and varied benefits designed for the employees' families (DZ BANK Group 2012).

Thirdly, the Continental banks embrace the government and regulator as special stakeholders. Theoretically, banks, in contrast with the generic firm, own massive accountability to the government as a significant stakeholder in the economic sense. This can be readily observed in the bank's unique access to the government financial safety net (by means of explicit or implicit deposit insurance or other forms of government guarantees) in the event of financial difficulties or nearing insolvency, which is rare or impossible for generic corporations. The government is indeed a potential owner, though disguised, in the form of less concerned stakeholder in more 'peaceful' times (Usui 2003). For instance, when there are bank failures, especially the large ones, the government always chooses to bail out the collapsed banks and injects voluminous funding from the taxpayers. In this scenario, the bank bears a significant responsibility to the state, the overall economy, and the public at large, especially considering its designated economic function. 'The presence of an effective corporate governance system, within an individual company or group and across an economy as a whole, helps to provide a degree of confidence that is necessary for the proper functioning of a market economy'(BIS 2010, p. 6). Such accountability is impeding especially in the event of the domino effects caused by the 'bank run' and the follow-up financial contagion, which in turn leads to the collapse of the financial system and then the avalanche of the whole social system. In this context, including the government and regulator as important stakeholders, banks in the Continental model actively implement their responsibility of compliance with the legal and supervisory requirements and prevent money laundering and the financing of terrorism. In practice, these pertain to better transparency in business relationships and financial transactions, verification, and documentation of the client's identity, and clarification of the origin of the assets employed in the business relationship or transaction (Commerzbank 2012).

5.3 Paradigm Discourses in Corporate Governance … 115

Another stakeholder of the bank, though frequently invisible, is the environment. In the Continental model, the banks' concerns for the environment mainly focus upon environmental protection and energy saving. These are observed in the bank's financing and investment in energy and resource efficiency projects, promoting activities on energy and environmental sustainability, and reducing its own impacts on the environment. For these ends, specific organizations and mechanisms are developed, such as the environmental steering committee, environmental and social reputation risk framework, and certified sustainability management system (Deutsche Bank 2012). In practice, these embrace innovation and marketing of various sustainable financial products and projects, emission trading, and advisory services for clean technology business (DZ BANK Group 2012).

Moreover, banks in the Continental model extend the concept and category of the stakeholders to a wider sense. For instance, to improve the welfare of the community and society at large, various philanthropic actions are taken by the banking organizations, including but not limited to charitable donations, financial assistance to talented but poverty-stricken students to continue their study and their way into universities, and promoting employment by financing socially beneficial enterprises. Meanwhile, there has been an increase in micro-finance by the banks to help needed people set up their small businesses (DZ BANK Group 2012; Commerzbank 2012).

The paradigm of the stakeholder theory in the Continental model plays a significant role in producing specific corporate governance in the banking organizations. For instance, the discourse largely decides on some key aspects of the organization of the bank board, such as the board's orientation and composition. With a higher proportion of employee representatives in the supervisory board of the bank, the bank has to afford serious concerns for the interests of the employees as the key stakeholder. The two-tier board structure and inclusion of different kinds of directors (in the supervisory board mainly), meanwhile, also lead to a large-sized bank board in the Continental model. Regarding the regulation on executive pay, as the large shareholders and the supervisory board can have a close control and effective monitoring over the bank management, the use of shareholding as incentive is less popular compared with its counterpart in the Anglo-Saxon model (though this is being changed by the latest CRD IV by the European Parliament considering the risk taking by the banks). The paradigm of the stakeholder theory also sheds lights on the formation of risk management in banking organizations. For instance, the banks generally have a comparatively less risky appetite due to concerns for various stakeholders, such as their long-term clients, the employees, the economic development, and the overall financial stability.

B. State-affected model—a hybrid of models

Theoretically, the paradigm for corporate governance in banking organizations in the State-affected model takes on a hybrid of the shareholder primacy model and stakeholder model. On one side, better performance of the bank and maximized investment returns for the shareholders are emphasized in this model, presenting a paradigmatic resemblance of the shareholder primacy in the Anglo-Saxon model. And, 'Regardless of its membership or how it is organized, the Board of Directors is and must remain a collegial body representing all shareholders collectively. It is required to act at all times in the interests of the company' (France 2015, p. 5). On the flip side, similar to the Continental model, the interests of various stakeholders are taken into account under the umbrella of corporate social responsibility. In France, for instance, the banks use various indicators to assess the implementation of the bank's social responsibility, such as the business indicator, social indicator, and environmental indicator. For the business indicator, it embraces the bank's compliance practice, social and environmental evaluation of the counterparties and projects, products and services oriented toward sustainable development, customer satisfaction, and contribution to local development. And for the social indicator, it covers the welfare and benefits of the employees, skills and career development programs, working hours, and health and safety. And regarding the environment indicator, it embraces environmental management system, environmental awareness, etc. (Societe Generale Group 2012; Credit Agricole S.A. 2012). Meanwhile, there is observed a paradigmatic specialty in the State-affected model where the banks are responsible for financing the economy. French banks, for instance, explicitly state their roles in real economy and claim 'we are the leading financial partner of the economy and we intend to carry on fulfilling this role,—because we know that the lending of today produces the jobs and growth of tomorrow' (Crédit Agricole 2012, p. 35). And 'supporting the growth of the French economy is a priority for the bank. In 2011, it (the bank) played a major role in the French effort to support businesses, associations and individual' (Societe Generale Group 2012, p. 35). Such discourse is represented in the increase of the outstanding loans by French banks in the turmoil of financial crisis and economic recession, when the banks are generally reluctant to issue loans (as well observed in the Anglo-Saxon model countries). For instance, in 2011, there was an increase in outstanding loan of 4.6% by Crédit Agricole, 4.4% by Societe Generale, 5.1% by BNP Paribas (BNP Paribas 2012; Societe Generale 2012; Crédit Agricole 2012). Meanwhile, the banks are actively engaged in financing the strategic customers and large corporations, with the purpose of financing the real economy. The regional banks, on the other hand, are committed to financial support for the major projects by various sectors and local authorities and support the local economy by a wide range of tailored banking services (BNP Paribas 2012).

The paradigm of corporate governance in banking organizations in the Sate-affected model leads to the constitution of some specific governance arrangement for the banks. For instance, the bank board is frequently oriented toward financing the economic development and granting generous credit to industrial sectors and enterprises, rather than solely maximizing the interests of the shareholders. The composition of executive pay, presenting the hybrid of the shareholder primacy and stakeholder model, uses both high ratio shareholdings as efficient incentives, and adequate fixed salary and performance-related bonus as the long-termism remuneration for the bank managers. With regard to risk management, banks in this model have frequently moderate risk appetites and the risks come mainly from financing the real economy. Typically, the deterioration of certain industry and collapse of the large enterprises may bring about much higher risk exposures. With comparatively less emphasis on the protection of private investors, the legal duties of the bank are limited, which are represented by fewer specifications of the fiduciary duties imposed upon the bank's board of directors and senior management.

5.4 Conclusion

Exploring the *telescope* perspectives of corporate governance in banking organizations, the present chapter reviews the paradigm discourses. Based on the study on different models in generic corporate governance, the chapter explores and develops the new paradigm analysis on corporate governance arrangement in banking organizations, which summarizes dominant orientations prevalent in various models of bank governance across countries, namely the refined shareholder primacy theory, the more inclusive stakeholder theory, and the hybrid state-affected theory. These guiding discourses, at the paradigmatic level, are found to be closed connected with, shaped by, and represent as well the legitimacy discourses with regard to the role of bank in the economy, the function of financial regulation, and the influence of the judicial system in varied institutional settings such as LME, CME, and SME. This context provides a solid ground for study on the specific paradigm discourses in corporate governance system in banking organizations in Chinese institutions and a sound basis on analyzing varied specific governance practices, the frame, in the upcoming chapters.

References

Adams, R., & Mehran, H. (2003). Is corporate governance different for bank holding companies? *Economic Policy Review, 9,* 123–142.

Alchian, A. A., & Demsetz, H. (1972). Production, information costs, and economic organization. *The American economic review, 62*(5), 777–795.

Baldridge, D. C., & Schulze, W. S. (1999, August). FAIRNESS IN FAMILY FIRMS: AN ORGANIZATIONAL JUSTICE PERSPECTIVE ON AGENCY PROBLEMS. In Academy of Management Proceedings (Vol. 1999, No. 1, pp. C1-C6). Briarcliff Manor, NY 10510: Academy of Management.

Barca, F., & Becht, M. (2002). *The control of corporate Europe.* Oxford University Press.

Barclay, M., Holderness, C. G., & Pontiff, J. (1993). Private benefits from block ownership and discounts on closed-end finds. *Journal of Financial Economics, 33,* 263–291.

Bebchuk, L. A., & Fried, J. M. (2003). Executive compensation as an agency problem. *Journal of Economic Perspectives, 17,* 71–92.

Bebchuk, L. A., & Fried, J. M. (2004). *Pay without performance-The unfulfilled promise of executive compensation.* Harvard: Harvard University Press.

Bebchuk, L. A., & Fried, J. M. (2005). Pay without performance: Overview of the issues. *Journal of Applied Corporate Finance, 17*(4), 8–23.

Bebchuk, L. A., Kraakman, R., & Triantis, G. (2000). Stock pyramids, cross-ownership, and dual class equity: the mechanisms and agency costs of separating control from cash-flow rights. In *Concentrated corporate ownership* (pp. 295–318). University of Chicago Press.

Bebchuk, L. A., Cohen, A., & Spamann, H. (2010). The wages of failure: Executive compensation at Bear Stearns and Lehman 2000–2008. Yale J. on Reg., 27, 257.

Becht, M., & Rnoell, A. (1999). Blockholdings in Europe: An international comparison. *European Economic Review, 43,* 1049–1056.

Berle, A. A., & Means, G. C. (1932). *The modern corporation and private property.* New Brunswick, N.J.: Transaction Publishers.

BIS. (2010). *Principles for enhancing corporate governance.* Switzerland: Basel Committee on Banking Supervision.

Blankfein, L. (2009). I'm doing God's Work, Meet Mr Goldman Sachs, interviewed by John Alridge in The Sunday Times, London.

Blazy, R., Boughanmi, A., Deffains, B., & Guigou, J. D. (2012). Corporate governance and financial development: a study of the French case. *European Journal of Law and Economics, 33*(2), 399–445.

BNP Paribas. (2012). 2011 Annual Report of BNP Paribas. http://www.bnpparibas.com. Accessed 11 Oct 2012.

Cadbury, S. A. (2000). The corporate governance agenda. *Corporate Governance: An International Review, 8*(1), 7–15.

Citi Group. (2012). 2011. Annual Report of Citi Group. http://www.Citigroup.com. Accessed 15 Oct 2012.

Clarkson, M. E. (1995). A stakeholder framework for analyzing and evaluating corporate social performance. *Academy of management review, 20*(1), 92–117.

Clarke, T., & Clegg, S. (2000). Management paradigms for the new millennium. *International Journal of Management Reviews, 2*(1), 45–64.

Cochran, P. L., & Wartick, S. L. (1988). *Corporate governance: A review of the literature.* Financial Executives Research Foundation.

Commerzbank. (2012). 2011. Annual Report of Commerzbank. http://www.commerzbank.com. Accessed 15 Oct 2012.

Crédit Agricole S.A. (2012). 2011. Annual Report of Crédit Agricole S.A. http://www.credit-agricole.com. Accessed 11 Dec 2012.

Daily, C. M., & Dollinger, M. J. (1992). An empirical examination of ownership structure in family and professionally managed firms. *Family business review, 5*(2), 117–136.

Davis, J. H., Schoorman, F. D., & Donaldson, L. (1997). Toward a stewardship theory of management. *Academy of Management review, 22*(1), 20–47.

Demsetz, H., & Lehn, K. (1985). The structure of corporate ownership: Causes and consequences. *Journal of political economy, 93*(6), 1155–1177.

De Paola, M., & Scoppa, V. (2001). The role of family ties in the labour market. An interpretation based on efficiency wage theory. *Labour, 15*(4), 603–623.

Deutsche Bank. (2012). 2011. Annual Review of Deutsche Bank. http://www.db.com. Accessed 17 Oct 2012.

Donaldson, L., & Davis, J. H. (1991). Stewardship theory or agency theory: CEO governance and shareholder returns. *Australian Journal of management, 16*(1), 49–64.

Donaldson, T., & Preston, L. E. (1995). The stakeholder theory of the corporation: Concepts, evidence, and implications. *Academy of Management Review, 20,* 65–91.

DZ BANK Group (2012). 2011 Annual Report of DZ BANK Group, DZ BANK Group 2012. Available at: http://www.dzbank.com. Accessed 15 October 2012.

Eisenhardt, K. M. (1989). Building theory from case study research. *Academy of Management Review, 14*(4), 532–550.

Fama, E. F., & Jensen, M. C. (1983). Separation of ownership and control. *The journal of law and Economics, 26*(2), 301–325.

France (2015). Corporate governance code of listed corporations, Association Française des Entreprises Privées (Afep), Paris: Association Française des Entreprises Privées

Freeman, R. E. (1984). *Strategic management: A stakeholder approach.* Boston: Pitman.

References

Freeman, R. E., & Evan, W. M. (1990). Corporate governance: A stakeholder interpretation. *Journal of behavioral economics, 19*(4), 337–359.

Jensen, M., & Meckling, W. H. (1976). Theory of firm-managerial behavior, agency costs and ownership structure. *Journal of Financial Economics, 3*, 4, 305–360.

German Government Commission (2012), German Corporate Governance Code, Berlin: German Government Commission

Kang, N. (2006). A critique of the "varieties of capitalism" approach, research paper series. Nottingham University. http://www.nottingham.ac.uk/business/ICCSR. Accessed 26 Jun 2011.

La Porta, R., Lopez-De-Silane, F., Shleifer, A., & Vishny, R. W. (1996). Trust in large organizations (No. w5864). National Bureau of Economic Research.

La Porta, R., Lopez-de-Silanes, F., & Shleifer, A. (1999). Corporate ownership around the world. *The journal of finance, 54*(2), 471–517.

La Porta, R., Lopez-de-Silanes, F., Shleifer, A., & Vishny, R. W. (2000). Agency problems and dividend policies around the world. *The journal of finance, 55*(1), 1–33.

Learmount, S. (2002). Corporate Governance: what can be learned from Japan? OUP Oxford.

Melin, L., & Nordqsvist, M. (2000). Corporate governance processes in family firms. The role of influential actors and the strategic arena. In *ICSB World Conference* (pp. 42–65).

Randøy, T., & Goel, S. (2003). Ownership structure, founder leadership, and performance in Norwegian SMEs: implications for financing entrepreneurial opportunities. *Journal of business venturing, 18*(5), 619–637.

Securities and Exchange Commission. (2010). Securities and exchange commission v. goldman, sachs co. and fabrice tourre.

Sachs, G. (2013). Business Standards Committee Impact Report. http://www.goldmansachs.com. Accessed 15 Jun 2013.

Schmidt, V. A. (2003). French capitalism transformed yet still a third variety of capitalism. *Economy and Society, 32,* 526–554.

Shleifer, A., & Vishny, R. W. (1997). A survey of corporate governance. *Journal of Finance, 52*(2), 737–783.

Schulze, W. S., Lubatkin, M. H., & Dino, R. N. (2003). Toward a theory of agency and altruism in family firms. *Journal of business venturing, 18*(4), 473–490.

Smith, G. (2012). *Why I left goldman sachs- a wall street story*. New York: Grand Central.

Smith, Greg (2012). Why i am leaving goldman sachs. *The New York Times*, March 14, 2012, 14, A27.

Societe Generale Group. (2012). 2011. Annual Report of Societe Generale Group. http://www.societegenerale.com. Accessed 23 Oct 2012.

The New York Times. (2012). JPMorgan trading loss may reach $9 billion, June 28, 2012, New York: The New York Times, Available at: http://dealbook.nytimes.com/2012/06/28/jpmorgan-trading-loss-may-reach-9-billion/?_r=0. Accessed 30 July 2012.

The Guardian. (2012). High street banks agree to payouts for mis-selling financial products, June 29, 2012, London: The Guardian, Available at: http://www.theguardian.com/business/2012/jun/29/banks-fsa-review-compensation-payouts. Accessed 20 June 2012.

UK Financial Reporting Council. (2012). *The UK Corporate Governance Code*, September 2012 London: Financial Reporting Council.

UK (2013), Enterprise and Regulatory Reform Bill 2012–2013.

US (2010), Wall Street Reform and Consumer Protection Act of 2010 (Dodd Frank Act).

USA Today (2012), 'Libor scandal explained and what rate-rigging means to you', July 18, 2012, New York: US Today. Available at: http://usatoday30.usatoday.com/money/perfi/credit/story/2012-07-18/libor-interest-rate-scandal/56322230/1. Accessed 25 Nov 2012.

US New York Stock Exchange (2009), Report of the New York Stock Exchange Commission on Corporate Governance, New York: New York Stock Exchange.

Usui, T. (2003). Corporate governance of banking organizations in the United States and in Japan. *Delaware Journal of Corporative Law, 28.*

Van den Berghe, L., & Carchon, S. (2003). Redefining the role and content of corporate governance from the perspective of business in society and corporate social responsibility. In *Corporate governance and capital flows in a global economy* (pp. 481–490). Oxford University Press.

Young, M. N., Peng, M. W., Ahlstrom, D., Bruton, G. D., & Jiang, Y. (2008). Corporate governance in emerging economies: A review of the principal–principal perspective. *Journal of Management Studies, 45*(1), 196–220.

Chapter 6
The Paradigmatic Analysis on Corporate Governance in Banking Organizations in China

6.1 Introduction

Following the previous chapters on the legitimacy analysis in corporate governance of Chinese banking organizations and the discourse study on generic banking organizations around the world, Chap. 6 considers in particular the paradigmatic discourses which are at work in constituting the key orientations of bank governance in Chinese context. On initial examination, the paradigm of corporate governance in Chinese banking industry is a hybrid in nature, which draws upon elements of both the shareholder primacy and stakeholder model. However, in order to understand the specific form taken by this hybridity, it is necessary to explore the ways in which the broader discourses and institutions that legitimate banking practices in China function to produce uniquely Chinese characteristics. By examining these discourses and institutions, it will be shown that an enhanced shareholder primacy model has been developed. With the state as a majority shareholder of many large-sized Chinese banks, the desire to balance the maximization of shareholder interests with stakeholders' interests has emerged as a core paradigm. The diversified stakeholder discourse, on the other hand, highlights bank's serious concerns for interests of a great variety of constituencies, from the general economy to the individual employees, from the regulators to the clients, and from the environmental protection to the social welfare at large.

6.2 The Enhanced Shareholder Primacy Theory in China

6.2.1 The Paradigm of the Enhanced Shareholder Primacy

As discussed in the previous chapter, the shareholder primacy discourse of corporate governance, typically found in the Anglo-Saxon model countries, is best character-

---

© Springer Nature Singapore Pte Ltd. 2019
W. Zou, *Corporate Governance in the Banking Sector in China*, CSR, Sustainability, Ethics & Governance, https://doi.org/10.1007/978-981-13-3510-5_6

ized by the maximization of the shareholder's interests, subordination of the stakeholders' rights, and mitigation in the agency costs (Jensen and Meckling 1976). But due to many specialties of the banking industry like high-leverage capital structure, opaqueness in financial information and strict financial regulation, the paradigm of the shareholder primacy deviates in corporate governance in banking organizations, which are characterized with the acuteness of the agency problem, the aggregated conflict of interests between the shareholders and other stakeholder, typically the fixed claimants like the depositors, and lack of efficient monitoring over the bank's management.

The paradigmatic discourse of the shareholder primacy in corporate governance in Chinese banking organizations, in contrast with the Anglo-Saxon model, takes on a hybrid specialty, especially considering the presence of the state as the controlling or majority shareholder, directly or indirectly. On one side, as the key investment contributors and residual claimants for final losses, the bank's shareholders are entitled to the protection of their interests and proper returns for their investment (Zhang 1996), which results from the paradigm of the generic shareholder primacy. This is reinforced by the fact that many large-sized commercial banks in China, even if they are owned by the state, are listed corporations and subject to strong market discipline and monitoring. For instance, Bank B announces its objective of 'creating value as an outstanding company and rewarding our shareholders with a steady growth' (Bank B 2012, pp. 12–13). Bank D emphasizes 'further reinforcement on increasing the bank's value, — and sustainable growth for the shareholders' (Bank D 2012). And, Bank A 'is greatly concerned with the overall interests of the shareholders, particularly the interests and claims by minority shareholders.' Meanwhile, it aims to 'provide equal treatment to all shareholders, consider the opinions and advice by the investors to enhance the bank's management and operation, and protect henceforth the shareholders' interests' (Bank A 2012, p. 20).

On the flip side, however, major variance can also be found in the paradigm of the shareholder primacy in Chinese banks. Specifically, serious concerns are voiced by the banks with regard to the large stakes held by the state, the state's implicit and unlimited liability as the *special* shareholder, and the bank's overwhelming role in the overall financial system. In this context, the shareholder primacy discourse in China can be said to have developed into an *enhanced shareholder primacy* paradigm that is distinguished from the Anglo-Saxon model. For instance, most of the Chinese major banking organizations, in particular the sampled banks, stress upon the sustainable profitability, the long-term development, and continuous growth for the shareholders' value instead of the short-term maximized profits (Bank B 2012; Bank A 2012). Meanwhile, there is a special emphasis on the protection of the investment by the state. For instance, Bank C emphasizes in particular its orientation in 'the preservation and increase of the value of the state assets' (Bank C 2012, p. 22).

The enhanced shareholder primacy in Chinese bank governance is found to largely attribute to the presence of the state as the controlling or largest shareholder. First, as the majority shareholder and major residual claimant, the state is entitled to and claims for protection of its economic interests and proper investment returns. This is reinforced by the implicit restrictions upon the transferability of the state's share-

6.2 The Enhanced Shareholder Primacy Theory in China

Table 6.1 Investment in large-sized sampled banking organizations by CHI on behalf of the state in 2012, unit: billion

Bank	Nature	Total shareholding	Shareholding by CHI	Percentage of the shareholding by CHI (%)
Bank A	State-owned, Joint-equity Commercial Bank	2500.11	1428.36	57.13
Bank B	State-owned Joint-equity Commercial Bank	3490.83	1236.94	35.43
Bank C	State-owned Joint-equity Commercial Bank	2791.47	1887.01	67.60
Bank D	State-owned Joint-equity Commercial Bank	3247.94	1303.10	40.12

Source CHI Web site, 2012

holding, which locks it up as the key and long-term investor. Meanwhile, in times of economic uncertainties or financial crisis, the state may even increase its investment in major banks. As illustrated in Table 6.1, a large investment is vested by the state in some of the largest Chinese commercial banks. And even for banks which are not directly owned by the state, many of the large shareholders are SOEs or local governments, which lead to the potential or 'indirect' ownership of the state.

Secondly, the enhanced shareholder primacy in China draws on further importance considering the specialized status of the state as the controlling shareholder. Distinguished from other general shareholders of the bank, the state frequently acts as the implicit and unlimited-liability investor and provides, in time of needs, 'deposit insurance' for the invested banks (though the deposit insurance system is officially set in place by Chinese government). More than often, the creditors and depositors, in their understanding of the banking organizations in China, base their transactions on the state credit instead of the creditability of a specific individual bank, though most of the Chinese banks are now independent legal entities and subject to Chinese bankruptcy law as generic corporations. And, in the events of voluminous non-performing loans, financial hardship, or nearing insolvency by Chinese banks, the state, as the majority shareholder, may frequently inject extra capital, set up specific mechanisms to deal with the bad assets, and maintain the resilience and continuity of the bank. In this context, the enhanced shareholder primacy takes on extra significance in bank governance in China, as the maximization of the shareholders' interests and the sustainable profitability of the bank will not only affect the welfare of the investors, but the systematic financial stability, national economy, and in due course even the state solvency.

6.2.2 The Agency Problem

As discussed in Chap. 5, the agency problem in corporate governance arises from the separation of ownership from control of the corporation, with the investors owning the corporation while the managers controlling it (Berle and Means 1932; Jensen and Meckling 1976; Eisenhardt 1989). The management, as an 'economically rational person,' may always maximize his own interests by expropriating shareholders (Jensen and Meckling 1976). The agency problem in corporate governance of banking organizations is further aggravated and characterized with acuteness, the aggregated conflict of interests between the shareholders and other stakeholder, and less efficient monitoring.

Regarding the agency problem in corporate governance in Chinese banking organizations, specialties are present due to the existence of the controlling state ownership, best represented by the long-chain of delegation, the lack of efficient monitoring, and the involvement of multiple agents. Theoretically and legally, Chinese state-owned banks are owned by the people in general. However, due to the impossibility for the public to practically own and manage the bank, the power to manage the bank, as well as its legal ownership, is delegated to the state as the public's agent, who further re-delegates such power to certain specified legal entities, such as the government departments or CHI. This necessarily leads to a long and multi-facet chain of the agency relationship, from the people at large as the principal, to the state, and in turn the specific agency or department in the government, the CHI, and finally to the board of directors and senior management of the bank. The participation of varied agents in this complicated process further amplifies the agency problem. For instance, as the agent of the state, CHI is not liable for the losses by the invested banks and cannot 'feel the pain' as the true owner in case of the banks' insolvency. In the absence of the true owner and lack of efficient monitoring, the banks' management can easily run the bank at their own will and maximize their interests at the owner's costs. Meanwhile, the agency problem of another kind may take place within the bank. Legally, the head office of the bank acts as the legal person and takes ultimate responsibility to the shareholders. And, in the context of the bank's wide geographic coverage, it has to delegate the powers downward to various branches at different levels and in various localities. However, the losses incurred by these branches are to be born by the head office due to its independent legal entity status. In this sense, the relationship between the head office and the branches of the bank resembles that of the traditional principal–agent scenario.

6.3 The Diversified Stakeholder Theory

6.3.1 General Theory on Stakeholders

In parallel with the enhanced shareholder primacy theory, there is a paradigm of the diversified stakeholder discourse in corporate governance in Chinese banks. As discussed in Chap. 5, the dominant theory in general corporate governance in Continental model countries like Germany and Japan is the stakeholder theory, which focuses upon equal protection for corporate stakeholders, and the accountability of the management in implementing a balanced business strategy to achieve a long-term growth of the corporation (Freeman 1984). In the context of corporate governance in banking organizations, the paradigm of the stakeholder theory takes on more importance due to the specialty of the banking industry, such as the extra high debt-to-equity ratio, the exuberated conflict of interests between the fixed claimants (creditors and depositors) and shareholders, and less effective monitoring by the investors or deposit insurance agencies. The immense economic and social impacts by the banks, coupled with their unique role in the domestic and international financial system which is readily observable in the 2007–2009 financial crises, make these financial institutions more accountable to the public, the government, and the economy.

The paradigm of the stakeholder theory in the context of corporate governance in Chinese banks, considering the legitimacy discourses of bank governance as discussed in Chap. 4, is found to be a more diversified discourse. First and foremost, such discourse is well coordinated with the enhanced shareholder primacy theory where, for many large-sized commercial banks in China, the majority shareholder is the state which does care about the welfares of varying stakeholders. Secondly, it pertains to a great variety of constituencies and promotes their interests by various means, such as facilitating their participation in bank governance, responding to their concerns and demands, and helping produce a sustainable, harmonious, and win-win situation. These can be readily observed in sampled banks. Bank B, for instance, explicitly illustrates the demands by different stakeholders and the bank's due responses, as illustrated in Table 6.2. Meanwhile, Chinese banking organizations actively initiate the CSR Exchange Programs with relevant stakeholders, such as regulators, enterprises, and non-profit organizations (NPOs), which are illustrated in Table 6.3.

The paradigm of the stakeholder theory in Chinese banks is further manifested in the independent opinions by external auditing or consulting firms, who monitor and advise upon the performance of CSR by Chinese banking organizations. For instance, PricewaterhouseCoopers (PwC), in evaluating the delivery of CSR by Bank C in 2011, stated 'the Bank (Bank C) identifies the key stakeholders and understands their demands and concerns. In addition, in forming the development strategy, formulating

Table 6.2 2011 Bank B CSR report on protection for different stakeholders

Expectation and needs		Responses of ICBC
Government	Enhance sustainable and sound development of the economy Facilitate the public fiscal plan and serve the development objectives of the government	Earnestly carry out macroeconomic polities, optimize resource allocation function and support the sustainable development of the real economy, support the financial development, stable tax growth and provision of job opportunities for SMEs, agriculture, rural areas and farmers, and ethnic minority regions
Regulatory authorities	Operate in a compliant manner and conduct lair competition Maintain stability of the financial system	Strengthen compliance management, creditworthy operation Improve corporate governance, strengthen development of internal control, and promote the implementation of the New Basel Capital Accord
Shareholders	Gain satisfactory returns and market value Fully understand the operating status of the bank	Sustain healthy and stable operations, enhance profitability Strengthen investor relation management and ensure timely disclosure of information
Customers	Convenient and efficient financial products and services Comfortable business environment	Develop E-banking, optimize transaction process and innovate products and services Improve service quality, focus on customer experiences, upgrade and restructure branches
Partners	Fair procurement Honesty and mutual benefits	Adopt a fair and transparent procurement mechanism Stick to the principle of equality, mutual benefits and harmony
Employees	Good career planning and development opportunities Complete protection of rights and interests	Carry out human resources enhancement project, optimize employees training system Improve remuneration and incentive, insurance and benefits systems
Communities	Pay attention to community development Safe and healthy living environment	Conduct voluntary activities, help vulnerable groups, participate in social welfare undertakings Ensure safe operation, promote financial knowledge and environmental protection publicity
Environment	Pay dose attention to dimatic change and support low-carbon economy Advocate energy conservation and emission reduction Establish a conservation-minded society	Promote green credit, E-banking, and green financing channels Advocate green office, green procurement, carry out environmental protection, and public benefit activities

Source Bank B (2012)

6.3 The Diversified Stakeholder Theory

Table 6.3 2011 Bank B CSR exchange programs with stakeholders

Responsibility exchanges

Time	Sponsor	Conference
January	Ministry of Environmental Protection, etc.	2011 China Low-Carbon Economy Forum
March	Ministry of Environmental Protection	Discussion on green credit guide for steel, papermaking and coal industries
April	World Wide Fund for Nature	Finance, Environment, and Development Forum
May	China Beijing International High-tech Expo	2011 Summit Forum on Finance
May	CBRC	Discussion on 'International Comparative Study on Green Credit'
September	Global Reporting Initiative	Press Conference on Sustainable Development Reporting Guidelines (G3.1)
September	Ministry of Environmental Protection	Launching Meeting and Symposium on Assessment Project for Evidence-based Green Credit Policy
October	China Banking Association	Social Responsibility Training and Working Meeting
October	United Nations Environment Programme	'Summit Forum on Global Sustainable Finance' and trainings on social and environmental risks
November	CBRC	Seminar on 'Green Credit Guidelines'
December	ICBC	Experts from the Ministry of Environmental Protection, Development Research Center of the State Council, industry associations and universities were invited to provide lectures or have discussions in ICBC on green credit in steel, nonferrous metal, coal, cement, papermaking, and service industries

Source Bank B (2012)

business policies and delivering daily operations, Bank C takes into account the expectations of the stakeholders and the bank's influence's upon them' (Bank C 2012, p. 155). Also, in evaluating the responsiveness of the Bank C to the needs of the stakeholders, PwC stated 'considering the special business characteristics, relevant departments in Bank C have set up diversified communication channels for better communication between the internal and external stakeholders to reinforce corporate governance, enhancement in risk management, product innovation and optimization of the business procedures, which well respond to the main demands by the stakeholders' (Bank C 2012, p. 148).

Deloitte, in providing the third party's opinion upon CSR by Bank D in 2011, stated that 'based upon the extent of influence and significance, Bank D identifies the relevant stakeholders by various communication mechanisms, sort out their expectations.

Considering the influence from the bank's business operation and management upon the decision making by the stakeholders, Bank D figures out the substantive issues and responses actively to relevant stakeholders' (Bank D 2012, p. 152). Furthermore, Deloitte pointed out that 'the Bank has adopted good preparation procedures for its CSR report, collected relevant information in supporting the disclosure of its CSR performance in economic, social and environmental fields' (Bank D 2012, p. 152). Similar assurance opinions by external auditing or consulting firms can be observed in CSR reports by other sampled banks (Bank A 2012; Bank B 2012).

However, it is sometimes a challenge for Chinese banks to coordinate the competing interests among varied stakeholders. For instance, the state may focus upon the healthy and sustainable economic development, overall social progress, and long-term national prosperity. The regulators may demand adequate legal compliance by the banking organizations, prevention against various risks, and maintenance of a sound financial system. The clients, at the top of the security of their deposits, may pursue profitable and sustainable financial products and services, timely responses to their claims, and continuous improvement in the bank's services. The employees may care more for better welfares, career advancement, and professional opportunities. The society at large may look forward to a better social environment, more charitable donations, and social harmony. And the concerns for the environment extend to environmental protection, energy saving, and promotion of green finance (Bank A 2012). In this context, the paradigm of the stakeholder theory in Chinese banks is frequently manifested under the harmonious umbrella of corporate social responsibility (CSR), which is a much wider concept and integrated into the banks' business agenda, strategic development, and daily operations.

6.3.2 Stakeholders of Different Kinds

A. State and regulator as the stakeholders

When the state is treated as a key stakeholder, Chinese banks are largely involved in national economic planning, strategic development, and economic coordination, which color the banks with a strong mark of public interests. This is rare in the Anglo-Saxon model countries like USA and UK where financial disintermediation dominates, but similar to the State-affected model countries like France and Japan, and the CME model countries like Germany, where banks largely perform the financial intermediary functions and are actively involved in the national economy. As discussed in Chap. 4, Chinese banks are frequently oriented toward implementing macroeconomic policies, facilitating the industrial development, and actively supporting the development of the real economy. These can be readily read in the bank's active posture in financing the development of the industries, provide funding to SOEs, and developing specific financial assistance to SMEs (CBA 2011). Another stakeholder of Chinese banks, though seemingly less visible, is the financial regulator, such as CBRC, PBoC, and the Ministry of Finance. Representing the state and

6.3 The Diversified Stakeholder Theory

public at large, these special stakeholders are primarily responsible for the overall financial stability, preventing against financial risks of various kinds, and ensuring the bank's compliance with laws, principles, and rules at different levels. In practice, Chinese banks mainly implement their responsibility to the financial regulators by complying business operations, anti-money laundering, and anti-corruption, which will be further explored in Chap. 9.

B. Protection of the employees' interests

As one of the key stakeholders in Chinese banks, employees take a significant place in the paradigm of corporate governance in banking organizations in China. Based upon applicable Chinese laws and rules, such as labor law, labor contract law, and the bank's internal principles and guidance, a framework is developed in Chinese banks for the protection of the employees' rights and interests, which embraces the general meeting of the employees' representatives intended for the employees' effective involvement in the bank's operation and management, the establishment of a fair and efficient compensation system, and the 'career ladder' for the employees' professional advancement, etc (CBA 2011).

First and foremost, the 'voice' of the employees is expected to be 'heard' by the bank's board of directors and senior management. By means of the general meeting of the employees' representatives who are legitimately elected by all the employees, Chinese banks actively facilitate the employees' participation in managing the bank, better access to related information, and monitoring over the bank's key business activities. In Bank C, for example, around 61.76% of its branches have set up the collective negotiation mechanism, and 'One-to-One' liaison arrangement which effectively facilitates communication between the management and the employees. And, 'Reception Day' by the head of the branch and 'Forum' by the employees' representatives also contribute to enhancing the bank's democracy settings. (Bank C 2011). Bank A, on the other hand, has established three-tier general meetings of the employees at the levels of the head office, the branch, and the sub-branch. In 2010 annual meeting, for example, around 365 employee representatives and other special representatives were invited to review the progress of the stock option plan for the employees, the bank's pension arrangement, and the report on the mutual funds among the employees. Some internal rules were also examined such as the *Rules for Penalizing the Violation of Duties by Bank A Employees (Revision)* and the *Rules of Mutual Funds by Bank A Employees (Revision)*. Meanwhile, up to 125 proposals from the employees had been collected (Bank A 2011b).

Secondly, Chinese banks have been continuously improving the compensation mechanism for their employees, such as the contracts tailored for different posts and various welfare packages like complementary social insurance, enterprise pension, and extra medical care insurance. Meanwhile, a set of carefully designed periodical medical examinations, vocational leaves, and standardized working place safety is implemented for the sake of the employees' health and security (CBA 2011). Bank B, for instance, develops a mature and effective annual medical examination system for all its employees, promotes the individualized lifestyle based on health survey, and plans vaccination programs against seasonal epidemics. Meanwhile, taking into

Table 6.4 2009–2010 training sessions for employees in Chinese Banks

Year	No. of training sessions (Unit: Ten Thousand)	Attendance (Unit: Ten Thousand)	Costs and expenses (Unit: Ten Thousand RMB)	Person/day
2009	23.94	1036.60	0.17	7.01
2010	28.85	1243.00	0.21	9.24
Increased by	20.50	19.71	20.45	31.80

Source CBA (2011)

account the mental stress caused by intensive banking workload, Bank B holds periodical seminars targeted at the employees' mental health (Bank B 2012). Moreover, a diversified framework for the employees' career advancement is set in place. For instance, Bank C has categorized three different groups of posts for the employees, which includes management, banking practice and technical support, and well orients the employees' career advancement based on the needs by the bank and the individual specialties. And, an interpretative *Implementation Guidance for Qualified Post Training* is issued for further guidance (Bank C 2012).

Meanwhile, a great variety of training programs are initiated in Chinese banking organizations to update the employees' financial knowledge, improve their skills and expertise, and enhance their competence for increasingly complicated banking business. For instance, Bank C issues its *Internal Plan for 2009–2012 Training and Development Programs*, which designs a 'step-by-step' training program for the bank employees in different departments. Online courses and distance learning programs covering 300 different subjects are also provided throughout the bank group (Bank C 2012). As illustrated in Table 6.4, in 2010, Chinese banking industry held over 2,885,000 training programs and sessions at different levels, with attendance by over 12,430,000 bank employees.

Other mechanisms, for the benefits of the employees, are also developed in Chinese banking industry, such as humanity care programs, happiness survey, and mutual assistance fund. For example, in Bank A, a wide range of survey on young employees was conducted in 2010 at the head office as well as its 15 key branches, which focused upon the employees' tolerance for stress, degree of happiness, and their cognition about the bank. The survey intended for a better understanding of the needs of the young employees and developed henceforth efficient solutions (Bank A 2011). And, in most of Chinese banks, an internal mutual assistance system, such as mutual funding, is established to create a humanitarian and harmonious working environment for the employees. In Jiangsu Branch of Bank A, for instance, a 'Five Caring' project was set up to provide special care for troubled employees and their families, which pertained to the health conditions of the employees' children and family members, family economic situations, and accommodations (Bank A 2011).

6.3 The Diversified Stakeholder Theory

In 2010, mutual funding programs of such kind, for employees in Chinese banking industry, amounted to around 20.17 billion RMB (CBA 2011).

C. Customers as the key stakeholder

Purported to contribute to the sustainable economic development and social advancement, corporate governance in Chinese banks lays specific emphasis on protecting the interests of the bank's clients, specifically the creditors and depositors. From 2010, for instance, Chinese banking industry had launched industrial-wide campaigns and made a commitment of 'Fair Dealing' with customers to develop 'credible and friendly' banking practices, which was targeted at protecting the customers' rights and interests, enhancing the public's awareness of various financial risks, and performing the bank's CSR in due course (CBA 2011). These embraced reinforced self-discipline and internal regulations, strict legal compliance, and integrating 'premium service' into the bank's business strategy and daily operation. Meanwhile, a series of norms and rules are issued by CBA at the industrial level, such as *Norms for Retail Business Services in Chinese Banking Industry*, *Model Illustrations for Banking Financial Products*, and *Six Consensus on Reinforcing Self-regulation of Banking Fees*, etc.

Secondly, Chinese banks are actively engaged in promoting financial literacy to the banks' customers. The fast economic development, the complicated financial innovations, and the varying banking products and services have posed increasing risks to the bank's clients, most of whom have limited financial knowledge. In this context, Chinese banks take various measures to disseminate the basics of financial investment and educate the public on the general banking business and possible risk exposures. For instance, the banks integrate the financial essentials into their daily operations, such as the wealth management, identification of the fake currency, and awareness about money laundering, which enable the customers to better understand the general banking business, identify exposures to relevant financial risks, and henceforth select proper financial products and services (CBA 2011). Bank B, for example, developed a program of 'Knowledge Popularization on Investment and Wealth Management through Ten Thousand Kilometers' in 2010, which aimed to educate the public on private investment. And up to the end of 2010, such events and programs had reached around 20,000 in total and were attended by over 1 million customers (Bank B 2011).

Meanwhile, financial literacy by the public is reinforced by the regulatory discourses. For instance, sponsored by CRBC and assisted by CBA, a wide range of specific education programs were launched in Beijing in 2010, which was purported to disseminate the general financial knowledge to the public, help the public understand, identify and prevent relevant financial risks, and promote the healthy and sustainable development of the banking industry and a harmonious society (CBA 2011). Themed on 'Harmonious Finance and Better Life,' representatives from the members of CBA, typically the large-sized state-owned commercial banks, promised the banks' commitment in engaging the public for financial education, providing necessary training events, and protecting the customers' interests. And, around 1.4 million bank employees and 180,000 different bank branches and sub-branches were involved in this process (CBA 2011). Further moves by the banks pertain to tailored radio and television programs, Internet forums and wealth management seminars, and consulting outlets placed in the community on the periodical basis (CBA 2011).

Thirdly, better transparency and sufficient information disclosure are required on Chinese banks for effective protection of the bank's clients. For instance, in designing and marketing the financial products, Chinese banks are mandated to disclose adequate information and reinforce transparency on possible risk exposures through proper channels. Bank B, for example, specifically stresses upon its business principle of 'suitable products tailored to the customers' and 'calculable cost, controllable risk and full information disclosure,' and is specially concerned with the bank's 'credibility related to wealth management business in terms of strict permission of products, improved risk assessment, full disclosure of risks and enhanced personnel management' (Bank B 2012, p. 93). Almost in all materials, files and documentations related to a specific financial product or service, like the contracts, product manuals, and legal documents, Bank B uses clear and simple language to describe fully related risks, varied investment returns in different scenarios, and relevant risk exposures under various circumstances. Meanwhile, Bank B develops a specialized management system and 'if the risk asset of customer does not match with the selected financial product, the system will issue risk alert to the customer, execute control over the transaction, and disclose fully the risks of financial products and services' (Bank B 2012, p. 94).

Fourthly, Chinese banks gradually produce a friendly, intelligent, and efficient responsive system for customer services. At the industrial level, CBA issued the *Standards for the Operation of Customers' Service Center in Chinese Banking Industry* in 2010, which provided self-regulations and discipline upon the service quality, crisis management, and complaint resolutions by Chinese banks. And *Rules for Joint Meeting by Customer Service Centers*, on the other hand, was issued to standardize the practices of the customer's centers in the banks (CBA 2010). In this context, most of Chinese banking organizations update and renovate their call center services, which change from the traditional passive support service pattern to a more interactive, diversified, and client-focused service system that covers marketing, sales and customer relationship activities (CBA 2011). Meanwhile, an efficient responsive mechanism is set in place to address the customers' complaints, improve the service quality, and enhance the customers' banking experience, such as scheduled procedures for complaints' registration, procession, resolution, and review. For instance, in Bank B, the customer service and complaint solution system is designed to synchronize and update the processing of the customer's complaint, its solution, and related feedback. This includes periodical analysis on the customers' complaints, traceable monitoring and review, and timely services through the call centers and Web sites. Moreover, a complementary supervision system is developed to accommodate efficiently the significant and emergent issues and send briefings of the bank's oversight upon the customers' complaints on a daily basis. By the end of 2010, successful settlement of the customers' complaints in Bank B had reached a satisfactory 100% (Bank B 2012). Moreover, a survey mechanism on the customers' satisfaction

6.3 The Diversified Stakeholder Theory 133

is widely established in Chinese banking industry for better understanding of the customers' needs and personal banking experience, which is designed to facilitate an independent and objective assessment of the service quality, sort out the hidden problems, and make timely rectifications (CBA 2011).

D. Green credit and sustainable economy

Another 'invisibly visible' stakeholder of the bank is the environment. By integrating green credit into the banks' strategic planning, business activities, and daily operation, Chinese banks are increasingly engaged in promoting sustainable economic development, supporting the low-carbon economy, and improving the environmental conditions. In practice, these pertain to the formation of internal green credit policies, identification and prevention of the environmental risks, upgrading of the industrial structure (by expanding credits to new energy and environmental protection industries), and compliance with the environmental protocols and standards at both national and international levels. Moreover, Chinese banking organizations have been actively implementing the low-carbon financing strategy and repressing credits to the 'Highly Polluting, Highly Energy Consuming, and Over-Capacity' industries (CBA 2011). As illustrated in Table 6.1, there has been a continuous increase of bank loans approved to the energy saving and environmental protection programs in China, covering more major green credit projects and qualified corporate clients.

First, the regulatory discourses on environmental protection pose great influences on the paradigm of green credit by Chinese banking organizations. Financial regulators, typically CBRC, have issued various guidance and regulations on the green economy, such as *Opinions on Guiding the Credit Extension regarding Energy Saving and Pollution Reduction* (CBRC 2007), *Guidance on Green Credit* (CBRC, No. 4 2012), which are well echoed by Chinese banks in formulating their own green credit policies. For instance, Bank B formulated in 2011 its *Outline for the Implementation of Green Credit* which set the basic discourses, principles, and implementation guidance for the bank's green credit strategy. In practice, these include the establishment of the green credit system in the bank's financial lending strategy, the list management on the clients, and related sustainable financial innovations. Meanwhile, specific internal principles related to environmental protection, energy conservation, and emission reduction are developed, such as *Notice on Optimizing and Improving the Green Credit Classification of Corporate Customers*, *Notice on Printing and Distributing the Post-credit Management Procedure for Environmental Protection Industries under Key Attention*, and *Notice on Strengthening the Risk Control on Enterprises with Outdated Capacities* (Bank B 2012) (Table 6.5).

Secondly, at the operational level, various measures are implemented by Chinese banks to strengthen green financing and responsible investment. For instance, Bank B stresses upon financial support for national strategic projects involving energy saving, environmental protection, reconstruction, and upgrading programs with new advanced energy-saving and environment-friendly technologies. Moreover, the bank prioritizes its lending to corporate clients engaged in environmental projects including new energy, energy saving, environmental protection, and comprehensive resource utilization, as illustrated in Table 6.6. Meanwhile, various green

134   6 The Paradigmatic Analysis on Corporate Governance …

Table 6.5 Statistics for energy-saving and environmental protection programs by financial institutions in Chinese banking industry 2007–2010

Year	The total amount of energy-saving and environmental protection programs (RMB 100 million)	The percentage of energy saving and environmental protection programs in total outstanding loan (%)	The number of energy-saving and environmental protection programs	The number or clients for energy-saving and environmental protection programs
2007	3,411.00	2.70	2,715	3,505
2008	3,710.16	3.11	2,983	3,615
2009	8,560.46	8.93	6,412	4,099

And in 2010, according to incomplete statistics, the total loans for energy-saving and environmental protection programs increase by 1.71% than 2009, with the balance of the loan increasing by 18.07% and the number of clients increasing by 11.2%

Source CBA (2011)

Table 6.6 Statistics on loans to green economic areas by Bank B (2011), Unit RMB 100 million

Area	Loan balance at the end of the reporting period
Energy saving and emission reduction	1,696
Clean energy development and utilization	2,082
Ecology, historical, and cultural conservation	1,398
Comprehensive resource utilization	728
Total green economic areas	5,904

Source Bank B (2012)

credit products are innovated by Bank B related to the carbon emission, energy saving, and related fields (Bank B 2012). Bank D, on the other hand, eagerly supports the development of the green industry, green agriculture, and tertiary industries. It specifically focuses on environmentally friendly projects like recycling, energy saving, and sewage disposal. By the end of 2011, targeted at its goal specified in the 'Eleventh Five-Year Plan,' a total of 88.168 billion RMB had been granted by Bank D to 599 energy-saving and environmental protection projects (Bank D 2012). Meanwhile, Bank D continues promoting its consultancy business on Clean Development Mechanism (CDM), and since 2008, it has provided sufficient financial support to 18 CDM projects which extend to water power, wind power, and bio-electricity (Bank D 2012).

Thirdly, for better understanding and timely implementation of the green credit policy, Chinese banks integrate into their business operations a great variety of environmental standards and protocols. And, a wide range of collaboration is initiated between Chinese banking industry, related government agencies and environmental organizations. At the same time, mission-specific training programs are promoted industrial-wide, which are subjected to the credit guidance, industrial policies, credit approval procedures, and international standards. For instance, as an active partic-

6.3 The Diversified Stakeholder Theory

ipant in various forums, conferences, and workshops by regulatory authorities and environmental protection organizations, Bank B promotes the practice of green credit and enhances its employees' awareness of low-carbon economy. In 2011, for example, Bank B participated in the 'Finance, Environment and Development Forum,' the '2011 China Low-carbon Economy Forum,' and the 'Global Sustainable Finance Summit' sponsored by CBRC, the Ministry of Science and Technology and the United Nations Environment Program (Bank B 2012).

Fourthly, green credit practice in Chinese banks also pertains to repression of financial lending to industries classified as 'Highly Polluting, Highly Energy Consuming and Over Capacity,' such as list management and biased pricing on bank loans based upon differentiated environmental risks. For instance, Bank B, by improving the classification system for green credit, reinforces its monitoring upon environmental risk exposures, such as close control over investment in corporate clients from industries with serious environmental concerns. And, the green credit standard is further enhanced and a one-vote veto credit policy is applied accordingly, which aims to scrutinize the projects and prohibit those which fail the set environmental standards. By the end of 2011, loans extended to over-capacity industries had been reduced by approximately 0.4 percentage (Bank B 2012). In Bank D, similar measures are developed, such as intensive management over the credit line, centralized credit approval, and strict list management. And the bank's overall green credit policies basically cover all the industries categorized as 'Highly Polluting, Highly Energy Consuming and Over Capacity,' such as polysilicon, plate glass, and wind power equipment. Meanwhile, the bank also sets up the one-vote veto mechanism and in 2011, and a total of 106 credit applications amounting to 4.157 billion RMB were rejected due to non-compliance with environmental standards. Furthermore, 1,099 clients in the aforesaid industries were delisted in 2011 with a repayment of 44.427 billion RMB in total loans (Bank D 2012). Further environmental moves by Chinese banking industry can be observed in the bank's efforts to create a green operational environment, such as the increase in self-service banking business, Internet and mobile banking which well reduces the workload at the counters. Meanwhile, Chinese banks are increasingly stressing on green business operation and low-carbon working environment, and have issued relevant guidance, principles or notices to forge a green working environment and promote a sustainable development culture throughout the bank group (CBA 2011).

E. Philanthropic mission and Charitable donation

Taking the society as a large stakeholder, Chinese banking organizations have been actively engaged in a great variety of philanthropic and charitable missions, such as generous financial assistance during and ex-post the natural disasters, efforts in the elimination of poverty, and continuous volunteering and charitable donations, which aim to deliver their citizenship and help with the establishment of a harmonious society. First, Chinese banks have issued general principles regarding the charitable mission, which are well integrated into their business operation. For instance, Bank B specifies the principle of 'Rooted in Society, Rewarding Society, and Serving Society,' which covers a wide range of philanthropic activities to enhance the public welfare, including but not limited to disaster and poverty reliefs, culture and education events, and community services (Bank B 2012). Bank A, on the other hand, articulates its mission as 'being concerned with social needs and participating in charitable missions' and labels its CSR performance as 'Sharing,' which represents the bank's orientation on philanthropic commitment (Bank A 2012, p. 52).

Secondly, Chinese banks employ various financial means in relieving the losses in the periods of natural disasters and financing the follow-up recovery programs and reconstruction projects. These pertain to timely charitable donations, emergent financing services, special credit expansion, and tailored fast channels for transferring of charitable donations from the public. For instance, immediately after the 2008 unprecedented earthquake in Wenchun, Sichuan Province, Bank B set up temporary mobile banks, such as 'Tenet bank,' 'Mobile van bank,' and 'Movable plank house bank' to expedite the transfer of varied charitable contributions (Bank B 2009), and emergency channels were established to process charitable funding free of charge, such as the 'Green Donation Channel' for donations from home and abroad (Bank C 2009; Bank B 2009). Help desks at the bank's outlets were also installed to advise on services concerning disaster relief remittance (Bank B 2009). For better efficiency, special mechanisms are initiated within the bank for expedited credit approval and disbursement, which facilitated timely financial assistance to the distressed regions and people and alleviated further adverse influences (Bank B 2009). And, extra bank loans were also issued for relevant disaster relief programs, such as financial lending to recovery, rebuilding and rehabilitation projects in the disaster-stricken areas. Meanwhile, Chinese banks helped underwrite and issue special bonds to provide extra funding to the affected areas from wider sources (Bank C 2009). Regarding the non-performing corporate or individual loans of different kinds issued before the disaster in the disaster-affected areas, a 'Four No' policy by the financial regulator was implemented by Chinese banks, which embraced no penalty on interests for the overdue payment, no bad official records for the default credits, no adverse effects on the corporate or individual clients applying for other financial support targeted at the disaster area, and no penalty for delayed collection on repayment of debts or fees (CBA 2009).

Thirdly, poverty reduction in underdeveloped areas frequently stands on the top of the CSR agenda in Chinese banking organizations, which includes extensive financial support for the local economy, charitable donations to education, and commitment to philanthropic medical care. By allocating peculiar financial resources, providing intelligence support, and developing tailored financial services, Chinese banking industry constantly contributes to the economic development in China's poor and remote regions. For instance, Bank B has designed a comprehensive mechanism to help the penurious area develop its local economy, which embraces the special project financing, intelligence support, hygiene improvement, technology facilitation, and financial assistance in case of natural calamity. Up to 2011, for instance, an aggregate of 7.64 million RMB had been invested by the bank for biogas green energy development in Linjia Village, Changchi Town, Nanjiang County and Chaya Township, Wanyuan City of Sichuan Province, which greatly improved the living standards and sanitary conditions of the local community. For developing a viable

6.3 The Diversified Stakeholder Theory

green economy, 660,000 RMB was further donated by Bank B to the edible tree fungus cultivation project in Chenhe Township, Tongjiang County, Sichuan Province (Bank B 2012). Bank C, from 2002 to 2010, invested continuously around 28.19 million RMB in designated undeveloped areas of Yongchun, Changwu, Gouyi, and Chunhua in Xianyang City of Shanxi Province, which pertained to school buildings, hygiene and water power projects, and rehabilitation programs (Bank C 2012).

Meanwhile, Chinese banks have been initiating a great variety of charitable donations, financial assistance, and special bank loans to educations at different levels in the underdeveloped areas. For instance, Bank A develops a set of charitable programs targeted at the poverty-stricken families in the poor areas. From 1996 to 2011, 7.80 million RMB was donated for building primary schools under the Hope Project, covering 38 primary schools, 73 libraries and playgrounds. And from 2007 to 2013, a total of 1.2 billion RMB was planned for assisting senior high school students from poor households to continue their study. Meanwhile, a total of 60 million RMB is planned, from 2009 to 2014, for donation to assist university students from needy families in the minority ethnic regions, with 22 million RMB dispatched and 7,833 students benefited (Bank A 2012). Bank B, up to 2011, had invested 3.77 million RMB in aggregate to improve education conditions in poor areas, which include massive financial assistance to rural teachers and university students from poverty-stricken households, rebuilding schools, and renovating local education facilities and infrastructures (Bank B 2012). Bank C, specifically, develops a wide range of financial products and services to students from destitute households for their university study. By the end of 2011, an aggregate of 170 billion RMB loans had been issued, benefiting 1.3 million university students from 476 universities and higher education institutions (Bank C 2012). Moreover, charitable medical programs of various kinds are also facilitated by Chinese banks to the underdeveloped areas. From 2007 to 2011, Bank B donated aggregately 9.1 million RMB in eyesight recovery treatment and over 3,300 cataract patients in poverty received such medical operations (Bank B 2012). And in 2011, 7 million RMB was donated by Bank A under the 'Health Care Mobile Van' project targeted at physical examination, medical treatment, and healthcare services for women in poor areas in Gansu Province, Qinghai Province, and Xinjiang Autonomous Zone (Bank A 2012).

In sum, the paralleled paradigmatic discourses of the enhanced shareholder primacy and diversified stakeholder orientation provide significant implications on developing specific governance structure in Chinese banking organizations. For instance, the enhanced shareholder primacy influences greatly the composition of the bank board and its orientation, especially in large-sized state-owned banking organizations. Due to the existence of the state as the majority shareholder, the non-executive directors representing the state may take a higher percentage in the bank board, which is thus more oriented toward long-term sustainable profitability and concerns for national economic development. Meanwhile, the enhanced shareholder primacy also greatly shapes risk management in Chinese banks. On one side, the discourse on protecting the sustainable interests of the shareholders, maintaining and increasing the value of the national assets of the state (as invested in the bank) requires the bank to take a moderate risk appetite. On the flip side, however, strong orientation toward boosting economic development, with the paramount influences from the state as the majority shareholder, may potentially result in excessive risk exposures in the process of financing certain industries and local governments. Moreover, the paradigm of the diversified stakeholder theory may also affect the arrangement of specific governance arrangements in Chinese banks. For instance, the stakeholder discourse frequently impacts on the composition of the supervisory board of directors by requiring the presence of certain ratio of employee representatives, directs the bank board to take into careful consideration, when setting the bank's business strategy, the interests of various stakeholders such as serving the real economy and expanding the green credit. Regarding risk management, Chinese banks generally have a lower risk tolerance due to concerns for a wide range of constituencies, such as the banks' long-term clients, the employees, national economic development, and the overall financial stability. Meanwhile, the paradigm of the stakeholder theory, with its emphasis on the bank's responsibility to the regulator, may influence the legal obligations of the bank typified by the duty of legal compliance which will be further explored in following chapters.

6.4 Conclusion

Echoing the hybrid nature of the legitimacy discussed in Chap. 4, the paradigm of corporate governance in Chinese banks exhibits a paralleled discourse of the enhanced shareholder primacy model and diversified stakeholder model. On one side, Chinese banks are oriented toward achieving sustainable profitability and bringing adequate investment returns to the shareholders. Specifically, the banks' performance is measured with maintaining and increasing the value of the national assets (in the form of investment in the banks) by the state, largely due to the presence of the state as the majority shareholder, directly or indirectly. On the other hand, Chinese banks are guided by the discourse of performing a wide range of CSR, which aims to protect the interests of various stakeholders, such as the economic development, the regulator, the employees, the clients, and the society at large. With the presence of the state as the controlling shareholder, these two paradigms can be well coordinated to some extent. The paradigm of corporate governance in Chinese banks may exert great influences on various aspects of the specific governance structure in Chinese banking industry, which will be explored in the following chapters.

Continuing the discursive institutional analysis of corporate governance in banking organizations, Chaps. 7, 8, 9, and 10 explore the discourse at the level of frames, i.e., the specific governance structure in practice, in banks across different models and then in China. The discursive frames pertain to four pivotal sets of subjects, namely the organization and behavior of the board of directors in the bank, regulation on executive pay, risk management, and legal duty. As the manifestation of the varied discourses of legitimacy and paradigm discussed in the following chapters, frames are analyzed in terms of how they contribute to the constitution and development of specific corporate governance structures in banks in different national institutional

6.4 Conclusion

settings and models. The discussion of the board of the bank illustrates how different paradigm and legitimacy discourses are represented in the orientation of the board of directors, the board size, and its independence. The regulation on executive pay, on the other hand, presents the implication of varied paradigms and legitimacies on the composition of the executive remuneration and differentiated regulative measures. The analysis of risk management, as the pivotal issue in the banking industry, manifests how divergent national legitimacy and paradigm co-function to constitute the conceptions of different risks, the overall risk management framework, and the specific risk management mechanism. And, the legal duties of the bank, mainly the compliance duty and fiduciary duty, represent the influence of different paradigm and legitimacy discourses in shaping the boundary of the responsibilities and the liabilities by the bank board directors and management.

References

Bank B. (2009). 2008 Annual Report of Bank B, Bank B. Retrieved May 25, 2012 from http://www.BankB.com.

Bank C. (2009). 2008 Annual Report of Bank C, Bank C. Retrieved May 25, 2012 from http://www.BankC.com.

Bank A. (2011). 2010 Annual Report of Bank A, Bank A. Retrieved May 25, 2012 from http://www.BankA.com.

Bank B. (2011). 2010 Annual Report of Bank B, Bank B. Retrieved May 25, 2012 from http://www.BankB.com.

Bank A. (2012). 2011 CSR Report of Bank A, Bank A. Retrieved May 25, 2012 from http://www.BankA.com.

Bank B. (2012). 2011 CSR Report of Bank B, Bank B. Retrieved May 25, 2012 from http://www.Bank B.com.

Bank C. (2011). 2010 Annual Report of Bank C. Retrieved May 25, 2012 from http://www.BankC.com.

Bank C. (2012). 2011 CSR Report of Bank C, Bank C. Retrieved May 25, 2012 from http://www.BankC.com.

Bank D. (2012). 2011 CSR Report of Bank D, Bank D. Retrieved May 25, 2012 from http://www.BankD.com.

Berle, A. A., & Means, G. C. (1932). *The modern corporation and private property*. New Brunswick, N.J.: Transaction Publishers.

China Banking Association. (2009). *The self-discipline convention of the banking industry of China*. Beijing: China Banking Association.

China Banking Association. (2010). 2009 CSR Report of Chinese Banking Industry, China Banking Association. Retrieved July 26, 2012 from http://www.china-cba.net.

China Banking Association. (2011). 2010 CSR Report of Chinese Banking Industry, China Banking Association. Retrieved July 28, 2012 from http://www.china-cba.net.

China Banking Regulatory Commission. (2012). *Regulation on qualifications of directors and management in banking financial institutions (consultative document)*. Beijing: China Banking Regulatory Commission.

Eisenhardt, K. M. (1989). Building theory from case study research. *Academy of Management Review, 14*(4), 532–550.

Freeman, R. E. (1984). *Strategic management: A stakeholder approach*. Boston: Pitman.

Jensen, M. C. & Meckling, W. H. (1976). Theory of firm - managerial behavior, agency costs and ownership structure. *Journal of Financial Economics, 3*(4), 305–360.

Weiying, Z. (1996). The ownership structure, corporate governance and principal-agent relationship - comments on views by Cui Zhiyuan and Zhou Qiren. *Economic Research Journal 9*.

Part IV
Corporate Governance in Banking Organizations: Frame

Chapter 7
The Board of Directors in Bank Governance in China

7.1 Introduction

Putting together the puzzles from all the previous chapters, this chapter starts to explore and explain how the discourses of legitimacy and paradigm, as discussed in Chaps. 3, 4, 5, and 6, are manifested in the specific governance structure in Chinese banks. Reflecting on the production of the board of director in generic corporations then banking organizations, the chapter studies specifically the organization and behavior of the board of directors in Chinese banks, which embraces the orientation of the bank board, its composition, the board size and its independence. Illustrating the hybrid nature of the paradigm discourses of the enhanced shareholder primacy and diversified stakeholder theory and relevant legitimacy discourses, the board of directors in Chinese banks are observed to be heavily guided toward sustainable profitability to the shareholders, active support for economic development, and balance of interests of various stakeholders. Similar representation of discourses of legitimacy and paradigm is demonstrated in the board composition, the board size, and the board independence in Chinese banking industry.

7.2 Study on Board of Directors in Generic Corporate Governance Arrangement

7.2.1 The Organization and Behavior of Board of Directors

As the 'tone at the top,' the board of directors decides 'to be or not to be' questions of the corporation, the enterprise culture and value, and the features of the corporate governance (OECD 2004, 2015). In this context, the organization and behavior of the board of directors take on special significance in the framework

---

© Springer Nature Singapore Pte Ltd. 2019

W. Zou, *Corporate Governance in the Banking Sector in China*, CSR, Sustainability, Ethics & Governance, https://doi.org/10.1007/978-981-13-3510-5_7

143

of corporate governance, such as the board structure, the board composition, and the board independence (OECD 2004, 2015).

The board structure varies in different models. Traditionally, a one-tier board structure dominates in the Anglo-Saxon model countries, which is said to help improve efficiency in business making process due to its more centralized characteristics. This board model entrusts both management and control powers to the board of directors, which enable it to possess the 'universal powers' within the corporation (Hopt and Leyens 2004). For the sake of detailed or specific corporate management, the managerial power is further delegated to the committees or individuals under the board level in larger companies. Meanwhile, for the check and balance of powers, a distinction has to be made between the executive or inside directors who are employed as management and the non-executive/outside directors not involved in day-to-day business. The non-executive directors perform both monitoring and strategic advising functions, which are functionally distinctive from the management responsibilities. In addition, as the non-executive directors are entitled to participate in decision-making process, they enjoy better monitoring powers than the supervisory board in the Continental model who can only make post-decision approvals (Hopt and Leyens 2004; UK, Combined Code 2003).

In contrast, a two-tier board model is widely used in the Continental countries like Germany, Japan, Netherlands, and the coordination arrangement is frequently mandatory for public corporations regardless of its size or listing (Hopt 1998). This board structure stresses upon the organizational division of management and control functions in corporate governance settings. The management board is responsible for running day-to-day business and implement corporate business strategies and policies. The supervisory board is mainly engaged in wide-ranged control functions, which include 'hard' functions of appointing, supervising, and removing members of the management board, and 'soft' ones of networking with shareholders, business partners to balance the interests within the corporation. Though in a large degree the supervisory board can control the management and monitor its compliance with law and the article of incorporation as well as the business strategies, it is not eligible in managing the corporations unless stipulated in the article of incorporation or according to their legitimate discretion (Hopt and Leyens 2004). Other types of board structures, though different in formality, are more or less connected to the aforesaid two patterns, either as a hybrid or derivative form. For instance, some countries like France, Italy, and Japan allow the corporation to choose from different models of board structures.

As a key feature of the board of directors, the board composition embraces mainly the source of the directors, the proportion of outside directors, the labor participation, and the board diversity. Firstly, the outside directors are playing an increasingly important role in corporate governance and the proportion of outsiders in the boardroom has been rising dramatically, though this is more or less an Anglo-Saxon model phenomenon (UK, Cadbury Report, 1992; UK, Code of Corporate Governance, 2010; US, Sarbanes–Oxley Act 2002). The proponents of such movement contend that more outside directors will lead to better board decisions and hence enhanced corporate performance (Rosenstein and Wyatt 1990, 1997), enhancement in corporate governance (Dahya 2002), increased value for shareholders (Dahya and McConnell 2005), reduced levels of earnings management (Benkel et al. 2006), and more efficient monitoring on the management (Weir and Laing 2000). However, other scholars doubt about the merits of the outside directors by challenging the correlation between corporate performance and the proportion of the outside directors (Agrawal and Knoeber 1996, 2001), their causal relationship and interaction (Bhagat and Black 2002), indispensable specialties of varied firms (Duchina et al. 2010), and the endogenous nature of the board composition (Lehn et al. 2004). Meanwhile, there may be a maneuvered increase of outside directors in periods of poor performance (Hermalin and Weisbach 2003) and biased study focusing on US board which is long dominated by the outside directors. In contrast, the outside board directors are less prevalent in the Continental model unless in the instances of the hybrid board pattern where outside directors are recognized and required. Instead, such 'outside' directors in the Continental model are mainly the directors of the supervisory board, who may play comparatively limited function of independence due to their comparatively lower ratio in the total board of directors (Germany, Code of Corporate Governance 2012).

The extent of labor participation in the board of directors, on the other hand, may greatly affect the orientation in corporate governance. In general, labor participation on the board in the Anglo-Saxon model is rare and not widely accepted in its corporate governance. Typically, there are few statutory bases for the mandatory consideration of the employees' interests. Though there are limited legislations stating the protection of employees' interests in the framework of corporate governance, they are frequently not clarified, less understood, and poorly implemented (UK Company Act, 1980; US, Principles of Corporate Governance, 2009). And, frequently, the protection of the employees' interests is reserved for some specific instances, like merger and acquisition, and is usually subject to the discretion of the board of directors. In contrast, in the Continental model countries like Germany or Japan, labor participation on the board (the supervisory board mainly) is mandatory. For instance, as an important part of the co-determination practice, the German supervisory board in large companies of over 2000 employees must have 50% members from the labor representatives, though the casting rights is slightly favorable for the shareholders (Germany Code of Corporate Governance 2012). In deciding the business strategies, meanwhile, the management has to take into account the interests of the employees as the key stakeholder.

Other significant issues with regard to the board of directors pertain to the financial and legal expertise of the board directors, the board diversity, and the check and balance mechanism. For instance, many scholars argue that directors with different backgrounds and gender will benefit the corporation, especially in times of economic difficulty. Some scholars argue that the financial crisis is largely attributed to the popular male-domination practice in financial firms while more gender-diverse boards can perform better and act as tougher monitors (Adam and Ferreira 2009). Such views are often expressed as the Lehman Brothers would not have collapsed if it had been composed of 'Lehman Sisters'; i.e., Lehman Brother's collapse was brought on by male-dominated board which favored excessive risk taking for the sake of higher investment returns (Lagarde 2010).

Board independence, as another key element in corporate governance, is drawing more attention from the legislators, regulators, and academics, especially in the context of the 2007–2009 global financial crises. It mainly focuses upon the proportion of outside directors in the board and the board committees, the standards of their independence, and duality of the CEO and the board chairman. In the Anglo-Saxon model countries, board independence is regarded as the fundamental of a good governance practice. For instance, UK Combined Code (2008) specifically stresses on the independence issues of the board of directors (the outside directors mainly) and prohibits any relationships or circumstances which will affect or likely affect the directors' judgment. This pertains to the relationships between the outside directors and the corporation in terms of employment contracts, business connections, remunerations, or family ties. Regarding the proportion of the outside directors, at least half of the board of directors should be independent outside/non-executive directors. Moreover, keyboard committees, like the nomination, remuneration, and audit committees, are expected to be composed of largely or totally of the non-executive directors. Meanwhile, there is an increasing trend of a separation of the position of board chairman from corporate CEO (UK Combined Code 2008; US Sarbanes–Oxley Act 2002).

In contrast, the standard for board independence is comparatively less strict in the Continental model countries. For instance, Germany presents laxer requirements for the board independence regarding the independence criteria, the proportion of the non-executive directors in the board and its committees (German Code of Corporate Governance 2012). Sometimes, the distinction between the membership of the supervisory board and the management board in this model is not easy to define, which may affect the independence of the supervisory board. For instance, the retired former managers may be invited back to the seats of supervisory board for the sake of their specific knowledge and expertise, the chairman of management board may turn into the chairman of supervisory board, and the supervisory memberships are offered to business partners or representatives of cross-holding corporations. This may undermine the independence and objectivity of the supervisory board and cause serious conflicts of interest (Prigge 1998).

7.3 Understanding the Board of Directors in the Context of Bank Governance

Similar to the in generic firms, the board of directors in banking organizations lies at the center of the governance structure and takes 'overall responsibility for the bank, including approving and overseeing the implementation of the bank's strategic objectives, risk strategy, corporate governance, and corporate values,' and is 'responsible for providing oversight of senior management' (BIS 2010, p. 7; 2015). However, industrial specialty is present. Adams and Mehran (2003) and Hayes et al. (2005)

find that differences in board structure across manufacturing and banking firms are statistically significant. Distinguished from non-financial corporations, the board of directors of the bank is found to play a more central role in corporate governance in banking organizations (Adam and Mehran 2003, 2008), which may attribute to the opaqueness of the bank's business activities, the fast-changing nature of the bank's balance sheet, and limited information disclosure (Morgan 2002). Meanwhile, the board of the bank is subject to more regulations and monitoring by financial regulators, such as the mandate on the composition of the board of the bank, the separation of roles between CEO and the board chairman, and the arrangement of the board committees (US, Dodd-Frank Act 2010). The specific requirements on the composition of the board of directors of the bank, for instance its proportion of the outside directors, may even determine the availability of the government financial assistance in times of financial crisis (US, TARP 2008). Moreover, the bank board, distinguished from its counterpart in generic firms, lays special emphasis on 'the bank's long-term financial interests, its exposure to risk, and its ability to manage risk effectively; approve and oversee the implementation of the bank's overall risk strategy, including its risk tolerance/appetite; policies for risk, risk management and compliance' (BIS 2010, p. 7; 2015)

7.3.1 The Orientation of the Bank Board

As the bank board plays a more central role in corporate governance in banking organizations, its orientation may take on extra significance in various governance issues, such as the bank's risk preference and management, executive pay, and legal duties. In practice, by setting the 'tone at the top,' the board of the bank develops the enterprise culture and corporate value as the foundation of its governance structure. These embrace a great variety of norms, incentives, professional standards and values that are purposed to promote integrity throughout the bank, while discouraging improper, illegal activity, and excessive risk-taking activities (BIS 2010; 2015).

Though there are some similarities regarding the protection of the interests of the shareholders and stakeholders, the orientation of the bank board varies in different model countries, which are largely founded on the different discourses of legitimacy and paradigm as discussed Chaps. 3 and 5. In the Anglo-Saxon model, echoing its paradigm of the shareholder primacy, the board of directors has been traditionally oriented toward the maximization of the shareholders' interests and best performance of the bank. For example, the board of Bank of America explicitly stresses that its mission is to 'produce strong growth and consistent, quality returns for its owners' and 'producing quality returns was, as always, our (the bank's) top priority.'(Bank of America 2002, p. 1). Though a series of financial reforms after the 2007–2009 financial crises, as it appears, greatly reshape the value of the bank in the Anglo-Saxon model and the bank starts to illustrate concerns for the interests of their clients, the discourse of the shareholder primacy and maximized profitability continue to persist. For instance, the board of the Citi Group in announcing its serious concerns over the clients that '(the bank) we will serve the true interests of our customers above anyone else,' manifests clearly that 'if we do that successfully, we will be generating real, sustainable value for shareholders.' (Citi 2009, p. II).

In contrast, the orientation of the bank board in the Continental model, apart from focusing on best investment returns for the shareholders, pertains to serious concerns for various stakeholders such as consumers, employees, and national economic development. This well represents the paradigm of the stakeholder theory which lies at the heart of the Continental model as discussed in Chap. 5. For instance, in setting its vision, the board of Commerzbank intends the bank to be the 'first choice for our customers, employees and investors' and 'customer satisfaction is at the heart of everything we do at Commerzbank' (Commerzbank 2012, p. 1). DZ Bank Group, on the other hand, lays specific emphasis on its employees' benefits and argues 'it is only with highly skilled, satisfied employees that our business can be successful, fit for the future, and deliver the improvements in performance for the clients and customers' (DZ Bank Group 2012, p. 9). In practice, banks in the Continental model are specifically oriented toward the active performance of corporate social responsibilities (CSR), which are purported to protect the interests of different stakeholders like private customers, employees, environment, and society at large (Deutsche Bank 2012; DZ Bank Group 2012).

As a hybrid of the Anglo-Saxon and Continental model, the orientation of the bank board in the State-affected model lies in sound investment returns for the shareholders and protection for relevant stakeholders (Crédit Agricole Group 2012; BNP Paribas 2012). Meanwhile, concerns for national economic development are frequently prioritized echoing the paradigm of the state-affected model as afore-discussed. For instance, the board of French Crédit Agricole Group clearly states that in 'serving the real economy, Crédit Agricole Group supports the projects of its customers in all retail banking business lines and associated specialized businesses.' (Crédit Agricole Group 2012, p. 1). And as 'the leading financial partner of the economy,' the bank knows that the 'lending of today produces the jobs and growth of tomorrow.' (Crédit Agricole Group 2012, p. 3). Specifically, Crédit Agricole Group gives priority to 'organic growth, retail banking and its associated businesses serving the real economy,' such as serving the needs of large corporations and the local economy where the bank operates (Crédit Agricole Group 2012, p. 2). The board of BNP Paribas, in identifying four pillars of its CSR policy, stresses that 'the first (pillar) is the economic pillar, which consists in financing the economy in an ethical manner' (BNP Paribas 2012, p. 10). Specifically, the bank believes that 'a bank's responsibility–indeed, its primary role–is to be able to provide financial backing for a project. This is how the real economy is financed.' and 'staying attuned to the needs of enterprises and entrepreneurs is in our DNA' (BNP Paribas 2012, p. 11).

7.3.2 The Size of the Bank Board

Another important issue for the bank board, in the context of the corporate governance of banking organizations, is the size of the board of directors. Adams and Mehran (2003, 2008) find that a positive correlation can be observed between the board size and the bank size, and a larger board of directors can be beneficial to the bank due to its increased pool of expertise, richer resources, more balanced and less extreme business decisions, and lower level of risks (Dalton et al. 1999; Cheng 2008). On the flip side, however, a large bank board may bring about inefficiencies and have negative effects on the performance of the bank (Hermalin and Weisbach 2003). For instance, it may be less effective in monitoring the management, present more difficulty in the board coordination, and bring about low efficiency in making business decisions (Jensen 1993; Cheng 2008).

The size of the bank board varies in different model countries. In general, the board of directors in the Continental and State-affected models bank has been larger than its counterpart in the Anglo-Saxon model. For instance, Ferreira and Metzger (2011) find that in 2006, the average of board size in banking organizations across countries is 15.6, with 10.7 in US, 12.4 in UK, while 21.3 in Germany. Similar results can be found in research by other scholars, though the averaged board size varies a bit due to different samples (Minton et al. 2010). As illustrated in Table 7.1, the averaged board size in sampled US and UK banks is 13.4 and 12.75, respectively, which is much smaller than the Continental model country, with Germany of 28.5. Japanese banks seem to have a smaller board size, with average of 12.5, but this figure does not include the auditor committee (which usually has 5–7 members in parallel with the board of directors). And, France, as the state-affected model country, takes middle in the spectrum, with the board size of 16. Meanwhile, in the Anglo-Saxon model, there is tendency of continuously reducing the board size without influencing its adequate functions, while such limitations are rare in either the Continental model or State-affected model.

For example, in examining the changes of the board size in US banking organizations from 2003 to 2008, Minton et al. (2010) find that the average board size decreases continuously over the years, from 12.32 in 2003 to 11.63 in 2008, as illustrated in Table 7.2. Though it is only reduced by 0.69, it is a comparatively significant change considering the already limited board size of the bank in the context of the continuous bank expansion.

The varying size of the bank board in different model countries reveals the constitutive role of varied discourses in paradigm and legitimacy. For instance, in the Anglo-Saxon model, the smart-sized bank board can be more efficient in making business decisions in the fast-changing business world and achieve better performance and profitability, which reflects the paradigm discourse of the shareholder primacy.

Meanwhile, arrangements for such efficient, small-sized bank board are a response to the more competitive business environment promoted by the financial regulators in the Anglo-Saxon model. In contrast, the larger-sized bank board in the Conti-

Table 7.1 Boards of directors cf selected banks from FTSE Top 200 and top 5 largest national banks (total assets)

Country	Bank	Total member of the board of directors	Independent/non-executive directors
US	Bank of America	18	15
	Goldman Sachs	13	10
	Wells Fargo	14	13
	JP Morgan	11	10
	Citi Group	11	9
	Total	67	57
	Ratio	100%	85.08%
UK	Barclays	12	9
	RBS	12	9
	HSBC	17	14
	Lloyds TSB	10	8
	Total	51	40
	Ratio	100%	78.43%
France	BNP Paribas	16	12
	Credit Agricole CIB	18	6
	Natixis	14	4
	Societe General	16	10
	Total	64	32
	Ratio	100%	50%
Japan	Mitsubishi UFJ Financial	16	2
	Mizuho Financial	9	3
	Resona Holdings	10	6
	Sumitomo Mitsui Financial Group	15	3
	Total	50	14
	Ratio	100%	28%
Germany	Commerzbank	30	11
	Deutsche bank	27	11
	Total	57	22
	Ratio	100%	38.6%

Note ND—no data
Source Websites of the selected banks, March 2013

7.3 Understanding the Board of Directors ...   151

Table 7.2 2003–2008 yearly summary statistics (mean) on board characteristics in US—board size

Year	Number of obs	Board size
2003	252	12.32
2004	277	12.24
2005	295	11.84
2006	314	11.75
2007	322	11.56
2008	193	11.63

Source Minton et al. (2010)

nental model, though not without concerns for efficiency, illustrates the paradigm discourse of the stakeholder theory and the idea of coordination found in the legitimacy discourse. Considering the presence of representatives of various stakeholders at the supervisory board, especially the mandatory high proportion of employee representatives, the bank board in the Continental model is likely to be considerably larger. And, reflecting the hybridization of the Anglo-Saxon and the Continental model countries, the State-affected model countries like France have an averaged bank board size which stands somewhere in between the other two models.

7.3.3 The Board Independence in Banking Organizations

Deemed as one of the most of significant elements in corporate governance in banking organizations, the independence of the bank board is said to greatly impact on the bank's performance, its market value, risk management, and survival in the financial crisis (De Andres and Vallelado 2008; Kumar and Sivaramakrishnan 2008; Minton et al. 2010). Specifically, it may enable the bank board to 'to exercise sound judgment after consideration of all relevant information and views without influence from management.' (BIS 2010, p. 26; 2015).

However, varieties can be observed in different model countries. Generally, the bank board in the Anglo-Saxon model countries appears more independent than its counterpart in the Continental and State-affected models countries, observable in much higher proportion of the outside directors (Ferreira and Metzger 2011), stricter requirement for more independent board committees, and more extensive and demanding standards upon the independence of the outside directors (UK, Corporate Governance Code 2012; US, New York Stock Exchange, 2003; US, Dodd-Frank Act, 2010).

For instance, in Table 7.3, over the period from 2003 to 2008, the percent of independent directors in US financial institutions increased from 72% in 2003 to almost 80% in 2008 (Minton et al. 2010). And, as illustrated in Table 7.1, the averaged proportion of independent board directors in selected giant banks amounts to 85.1% in US and 78.4% in UK. In contrast, in the Continental model countries, the bank board is found with fewer outside directors or supervisory directors, which accounts

Table 7.3 2003–2008 yearly summary statistics (mean) on board characteristics in US—board independence

Year	Number of obs	Independent (%)
2003	252	72
2004	277	75
2005	295	76
2006	314	76
2007	322	76
2008	193	78

Source Minton et al. (2010)

for around 28% in Japan and 38.6% in Germany. In France, the state-affected model country, there is comparatively higher board independence in the selected banks and the averaged proportion of the outside board directors reaches approximately 50%.

As a key issue of corporate governance in banking organizations, the independence of the bank board is a manifestation of the discourses of paradigm and legitimacy as discussed in Chap. 5. Resonating with the paradigm discourse of the shareholder primacy, higher board independence in the Anglo-Saxon model is believed to be one of the effective solutions to mitigate agency problems through better monitoring by independent 'outsiders.' Meanwhile, a bank board comprising a high proportion of outside directors with diversified backgrounds, professional expertise, and rich business experience may contribute to better and more efficient business decisions, henceforth enhancing the bank's performance and bringing better financial returns to investors. The higher level of the board independence in the Anglo-Saxon model banks is also shaped by key elements of the legitimacy discourses, such as financial deregulation and legal intervention. For instance, in 2007–2009 financial crisis, troubled banks with more outside directors were more easily shielded against their liabilities and procured the government financial assistance (US, TARP 2008; Adams and Ferreira 2009; Minton et al. 2010). In the context of the dominating market institutions, higher board independence is regarded as a better arrangement for the bank governance, which is assumed to bring into the boardroom the arm's length relationship and henceforth better external monitoring. Moreover, the stricter requirement over the board independence is a reflection of active legal interventions in the Anglo-Saxon model. Frequently, a bank board with higher independence can mitigate or even be immune from legal liabilities in cases alleging breach of fiduciary duties (where the independence of the board may be a key criterion for imposing liabilities).

In contrast, though the board independence is increasingly strengthened in the Continental and State-affected models, the discourses of paradigm and legitimacy imply less emphasis. In the Continental model, as a response to the paradigm of the stakeholder theory and the legitimacy of the market coordination, the board independence is said to frequently give away to coordination among representatives of different stakeholders included in the board. Specifically, echoing the regulatory mandates of the presence of the employee representatives, the bank board in this model, for instance in Germany, has a large proportion of 'inside' employee representatives which may greatly confine the board's independence (Germany, Corporate Code of Governance, 2012). Moreover, the two-tier board structure in Continental model banks, where the management board directors are all inside executives, further reduces the overall board independence. In the State-affected model countries like France, the board independence of the bank takes on a hybrid nature. For instance, due to the changes toward liberalization and 'convergence' to the Anglo-Saxon model, there is a stricter requirement in France for a significant proportion of outside directors on the bank board. Meanwhile, there is also the presence of employee representatives on the board of the directors, which may limit the board independence (French Corporate governance code of listed corporations 2010).

7.4 The Board of Directors in Corporate Governance of Chinese Banking Organizations

Manifesting both the discourses of legitimacy and paradigm on corporate governance in Chinese banking organizations, as discussed in Chaps. 5 and 6, the organization and behavior of the board of directors in Chinese banks illustrate the constitutive role of specific ideas in the frame of bank governance, which embrace the orientation of the bank board, its composition, the board's independence and relevant impediments. As discussed, the orientation of the bank board frequently plays a vital role in the bank's corporate governance arrangement. Implicated by the legitimacy and paradigm discourses in Chinese bank governance, such as the bank's intertwining with the real economy, close financial regulation, and paralleled interest concerns for the bank's shareholders and stakeholders, the board of directors in Chinese banks is observed to, not infrequently, set its 'tone' at persistently serving and supporting the sustainable development of the real economy, pursuing the bank's long-term profitability, achieving sound corporate governance, and developing enhanced risk management. Meanwhile, the bank board lays specific emphasis on providing responsible financial services for its clients, promoting training programs and career advancement for the employees and innovating new banking business and financial products in advancing green economy (Bank B 2012; Bank C 2012; Bank A 2012; Bank D 2012).

7.4.1 Organization of the Board of Directors

Echoing the influences of the international discourses illustrated in Chap. 4, the board of directors in Chinese banks presents a hybrid feature of the Anglo-Saxon and Continental model. On one side, there is a two-tier board system composed of the board of directors and the supervisory board, which is approximate to that of the Continental model. On the flip side, however, the board of directors in Chinese banks frequently includes the executive directors, non-executive directors, and outside directors, which is less different from the one-tier structured bank board in the Anglo-Saxon model. Nevertheless, national specialty is apparent and the arrangement of the board of directors in Chinese banks can be distinguished from the other two models in certain aspects. For instance, though there is a two-tier board structure in Chinese banking organizations, the supervisory board is comparatively less powerful, limited in functions, and not authorized to elect the board directors. Moreover, the supervisory board is smaller in size and embraces much fewer employee representatives (CBRC 2011). These differentiate Chinese bank boards from those in the Continental model. Meanwhile, the bank board in China presents certain differences from that of the Anglo-Saxon model, exemplified by a limited proportion of the outside directors but a higher proportion of the non-executive directors who often act on behalf of the state, typically in large-sized commercial banks (CBRC 2011).

As the rule of thumb, the composition of the board of directors in Chinese banks embraces the executive directors, non-executive directors, and outside directors. As the key component of the managing body, executive directors are inside senior executive officers responsible for managing the bank, including the board chairman, CEO, and other senior managers. Non-executive directors, for instance in the large-sized state-owned commercial banks, are largely representatives delegated from the majority shareholders such as CHI (i.e., the government directly or indirectly) and do not take any managing posts in the bank. Outside directors come from 'external,' with no any affiliations or interests to the bank or its controlling shareholders, and are expected to provide objective and independent opinions to the board of the bank (CBRC 2011).

As illustrated in Table 7.4, the averaged executive director in the sampled banks is 3.75, or 25% in proportion. Most of these executive directors are experienced banking practitioners, who have been working for a long period of time in the same bank, other comparable banks (similar nature and size), or financial regulators like PBoC, CBRC (Bank B 2012; Bank A 2012a; Bank C 2012; Bank D 2012). For instance, in Bank A, most of the executive directors have rich experience in working as the bank's CEO, the head of the bank's branch, or take posts in key bank departments like credit approval, risk management, and auditing, which enable them to be both competent bank managers and experienced financial experts (Bank A 2012). Moreover, all of the Bank A's executive directors have been working in the banking industry for over 15 years, and few of them have ever diverged from the 'dominant institutions' (i.e., the varied state-owned agencies like the government sectors, state-owned enterprises, or public universities) and the banking industry. Such industrial and institutional continuity reinforces their capability in leading the bank in the present financial system in China, though potentially at the expenses of their creativity and entrepreneurship. Strong academic background in banking or finance is another key feature of the executive directors, as all of the executive directors are awarded master's degrees in finance, economics, or management, which enable them to have a better understanding of the fast-changing banking world (Bank A 2012).

The non-executive directors in Chinese banks, on the other hand, are expected to provide advising and monitoring functions to the bank board. In the sampled banks,

7.4 The Board of Directors in Corporate Governance ...

Table 7.4 2011 statistics on board of directors of sampled banks in China in 2011

Category of bank	Bank	Board size (total)	Executive directors	Non-executive directors	Outside directors	Directors with banking experience	Directors with government official background	Duality of CEO and the board chairman
Commercial banks	Bank A	15	4	6	5	6	6	N
	Proportion in the board (%)	100	26.67	40	33.33	40	40	
	Bank B	16	4	6	6	7	7	N
	Proportion in the board (%)	100	25	37.5	37.5	43.75	43.75	
	Bank C	16	4	6	6	9	10	N
	Proportion in the board (%)	100	25	37.5	37.5	56.25	62.50	
	Bank D	13	3	6	4	5	9	N
	Proportion in the board (%)	100	23.08	46.15	30.77	38.46	69.23	
Total		60	15	24	21	27	32	
Average		15	3.75	6	5.25	6.75	8	
Average proportion in the board %		100	25	40	35	45	53	

Source Bank A (2012), Bank B (2012), Bank C (2012), Bank D (2012)

they are mainly delegated by CHI and represent the interests of the state as the largest shareholders. As observed in Table 7.4, the non-executive directors take the largest proportion in the sampled banks, which is averaged at 6 and or 40% in percentage. But as a coincidence, the sampled banks have the same number of the non-executive directors, though the proportion is a bit higher in Bank D which is 46.5% considering its smaller board size. In contrast with the executive directors, the non-executive directors are more diversified in their backgrounds and working experience. For instance, in Bank A, certain non-executive directors have profound backgrounds as senior officials from the financial regulators; others are senior practitioners from the large-sized banking organizations, insurance corporations, law firms, etc. Such diversified backgrounds may facilitate a more efficient business decision-making process in the bank board and a panorama view to avoid industrial bias (Bank A 2012).

And, observed in Table 7.4, the average of the outside directors (in the narrow senses which excludes the non-executive directors delegated from the controlling shareholders) in the sampled banks is 5.5 or 35% in averaged proportion. Due to the same institutional settings and regulatory requirements, the number and proportion of the outside directors are less variant within the sampled banks, with Bank B and Bank C higher of six outside directors and Bank D lower with only four. Contrasting with the aforesaid executive and non-executive directors, these outside directors are even more diversified in their backgrounds and special expertise, which comprise known experts, professionals, and academia engaged in finance, accounting, and taxation. More than often, the outside directors present strong international backgrounds. In Bank A, for instance, two out of five outside directors are from foreign countries. It is expected that their diversity and varied international backgrounds may bring more 'fresh air' to the boardroom of Chinese banks. In particular, the opinions of the outside directors, in contrast with those from the non-executive directors, may be more valued by the bank board and senior management (Bank A 2012).

Apparently, the bank board in China is featured with, collectively, good financial expertise and strong official background. As illustrated in Table 7.4, the bank directors with years of banking experience and practices are averaged at 6.75 or 45% in proportion in the sampled banks. This is a very sound and encouraging figure considering the limited years of development in corporate governance of Chinese banking organizations. Another interesting feature of the Chinese bank board pertains to the high proportion of directors with strong official backgrounds, either domestic or international. In the sampled banks, for instance, the 'official' directors (i.e., directors who worked in the government) are averaged at 8 or 53% in proportion. This is largely due to the selection of the samples which are large-sized state-owned commercial banks, the senior managers of which are appointed by the financial regulators and the non-executive directors are mainly from CHI on behalf of the state. Meanwhile, some of the outside directors, who are assumed to be less influenced by Chinese regulators, used to be senior government officials from Hong Kong or other countries.

In general, a large board size is prevalent in Chinese banking organizations, especially in large-sized commercial banks. As illustrated in Table 7.4, the average board size in the sampled bank is 15, with Bank B and Bank C larger of 16 while Bank D smaller of 13. Such averaged board size is a little bigger than the finding by Yv and He (2012) in 52 listed commercial banks in China from 2004 to 2009, which was around 14 on average. In general, the averaged board size in Chinese banking industry, as the research reveals, appears much larger than that of the non-financial corporation in China which is only around 9.59. And, it is also bigger than its US counterpart which is averaged at 12.9 (YV and He 2012; Pathan and Skully 2010; He and Zhou 2010).

The composition of the board of directors in Chinese banks reverberates the paradigm and legitimacy discourses as discussed in Chaps. 4 and 6. For instance, with increasing stress on better bank performance as demanded by the enhanced shareholder primacy discourse, most of the board directors, either executive, non-executive, or outside, are equipped with rich banking or financial expertise, years of experience in Chinese or international banking industry, and good knowledge and academic background in banking and finance. Implicated by the dominance of the state as the controlling shareholder (in the sampled large-sized state-owned commercial banks), there is a prominent high proportion of non-executive directors (representing the state) sitting on the bank board, which can ensure the protection of the state's interests and the orientation toward sustainable economic development. The rising outside directors in Chinese banking organizations, on the other hand, echoes strong international influences and better self-discipline in the context of financial deregulation. It also illustrates the emphasis on the financial expertise of the board directors, as many of the outside directors in the sampled banks are selected internationally and expected to bring to the boardroom valuable experience and updated banking practice from developed economies. Meanwhile, the arrangement of the bank board reflects the legitimacy discourse of ongoing financial deregulation in China. For instance, experienced banking professionals, rather than government officials, play key roles in toning the corporate governance structure of Chinese banks, and the increasing proportion of outside directors integrates more market mechanisms into the bank's governance practices.

7.4.2 The Board Independence

Another major factor for the composition of Chinese bank board is the board independence, which pertains to the proportion of the outside directors, the criteria on the director independence, and the duality of CEO and the board chairman. As illustrated in Table 7.4, the averaged outside director in the sampled banks is 5.5, or 35% in percentage, which is much higher than that of many of Chinese banking organizations averaged at around 22% or the non-financial corporations which is about 23.7% (Yv and He 2012; Pathan and Skully 2010; He and Zhou 2010). Moreover, when comparing the board independence between the large-sized commercial banks and the smaller ones, it is found that the former presents a more independent bank board (Yv and He 2012). With regard to the duality of the chairman of the board of directors and CEO, which may greatly limit the board independence and adversely affect the bank's performance, Chinese banks take a more conservative stance. As illustrated in Table 7.4, these two roles are strictly separated in the sampled banks, which intends to enhance the board's independence and strengthen its efficacy in monitoring. Furthermore, the potential duality of these two posts, which means CEO may become the board chairman after his term expires or vise visa, is rarely found in Chinese banking organizations. For instance, in a wider range survey by Bai (2010) of 14 shareholding commercial banks, it is found that the duality of CEO and the board chairman is fairly aberrant (Bai 2010).

The board independence in Chinese banks is reinforced by varied most independent board committees. For instance, different functional board committees are established to offset the adverse effects caused by the large board size and insufficient outside directors. In the sampled banks, such board committees embrace the strategic development committee, audit committee, risk management committee, nomination committee, compensation committee, and related transaction control committee, etc. (Bank B 2012; Bank C 2012; Bank A 2012; Bank D 2012). Except for the strategic development committee which is frequently led by the chairman of the board, all other committees are chaired by the outside directors. Meanwhile, the majority members of these committees are selected from the outside directors, which intends for a better overall board independence (Bank B 2012; Bank C 2012; Bank A 2012; Bank D 2012). Moreover, a paralleled supervisory board is set in place in Chinese banks to further strengthen and supplement the independence of the bank board. For instance, the supervisory board of directors, in the sampled banks, is in charge of monitoring varied major issues related to bank governance, such as the significant business strategy, risk management, and internal control. Specifically, such supervisory board, resembling its counterpart in the Continental model, is authorized to exercise effective supervision over the board of directors and senior management, which includes the appointment procedures, the evaluation of their performance, and the formation of the compensation policy. Meanwhile, the presence of the outside supervisory board directors can further improve the independence of the supervisory board, build up its monitoring functions, and in turn contribute to the board independence in Chinese banking organizations (CBRC 2011; Bank B 2012).

Last but not least, there are strict criteria imposed on the independence of the board directors in Chinese banks, especially for the outside directors. For instance, a board director is not allowed to take posts in other financial institutions which may have a potential conflict of interests with the bank (in which he acts as a board director). Should he work for other financial institutions, the board director should duly inform the bank and promises that no conflict of interests of any kinds will be incurred in the future. In case a board director is personally related to the present or planned contracts, transactions or deals with the bank, he should timely inform the board of directors of the nature and extent of his involvement and be excluded when such issues are reviewed. For the outside director, he is specifically not allowed to take posts simultaneously in over two bank organizations and the maximum of his term in a bank should be limited within 6 years (CBRC 2011). And, the independence of the board directors in Chinese banking organizations will be further explored in Chap. 9.

7.4 The Board of Directors in Corporate Governance ... 159

The arrangement of the board independence in Chinese banks is understood as a hybrid of the Anglo-Saxon model and Continental model. For instance, the increasing proportion of the outside directors, the separation between CEO and the board chairman, the independence of the board committees, and the stricter standards in selecting the board directors well reflect the influence of the Anglo-Saxon model. On the other hand, however, the presence of the supervisory board, its specified monitoring function, and the use of the outside supervisory directors articulate the impacts from the Continental model. Meanwhile, the increasingly prioritized board independence in Chinese banks is a good representation of the paradigm discourse of the enhanced shareholder primacy, which prefers efficient oversight upon the management via a more independent board structure.

However, impediments of different kinds are observable with regard to the board independence in Chinese banks. Typically, the institutional settings in Chinese context may wield strong influences, which pertain to the constraints on the monitoring function by the bank board, the overwhelming power by the majority shareholder, and the substitutive 'administrative governance' by the financial regulators. In contrast with the Anglo-Saxon model, the monitoring function by the Chinese bank board tends to be limited, and there are certain limitations on the proportion of the outside directors considering the costs it may bring about. For instance, the mechanism of the outside directors is said to produce extra hardships for the large-sized banks with long tradition and higher capital leverage, which includes more severe internal information asymmetry problems, retarded information flow from the internal directors to the outside directors, and higher costs for efficient coordination among the directors (Yv and He 2012).

Moreover, as the majority shareholder, the state may affect the board independence in the large-sized state-owned commercial banks, specifically in case of achieving policy objectives when the state is more inclined to limit the independence of the bank board to avoid unpleasant challenges to its dominance over significant business decisions. This is reinforced by the higher proportion of the non-executive directors on behalf of the state, who are expected to oversee and ensure the state's influence upon the production of the critical decisions and key business strategies by the bank board. Moreover, the independence of the bank board may sometimes yield to the 'administrative governance' by the financial regulators. For instance, the regulator, with more intervening administrative measures, may reshape the composition of the board of directors in the bank, its internal control, and the executive compensation package (Hong and Zhou 2008).

Other factors may also impede the board independence in Chinese bank governance. For instance, the institutional and cultural homogeneity of the non-executive directors, outside directors (from domestic), and their executive counterparts, most of who come from and bear the strong marks of the dominant political and economic institutions (such as public universities, large state-owned banks, and government agencies), may further constrain the board independence as they may potentially lose their independent standing due to the shared institutional paradigms. Meanwhile, the presence of the CCP membership by many of the board directors may necessarily affect the board independence, as such directors are more oriented toward the prevailing policy objectives. The few dissenting opinions regarding significant board decisions in the sampled banks, for example, may manifest limited board independence due to insufficient or reluctant challenges from the non-executive or outside directors (Bank B 2012; Bank A 2012; Bank C 2012; Bank D 2012).

7.4.3 The Arrangement of the Supervisory Board

In contrast with the Continental model, Chinese banks develop a comparatively smaller sized supervisory board of directors. As illustrated in Table 7.5, the supervisory board in the sampled banks includes seven directors in average, with the largest of nine in Bank A, and the smallest of six in Bank B and Bank D. Such supervisory board is also smaller than the bank's board of directors. In practice, the supervisory board in Chinese bank comprises the shareholder representatives, the employee representatives, and the outside directors. The shareholder representative directors are mainly delegated by the majority shareholder, namely by CHI in the sampled banks. The employee representative directors are elected through the general meeting of the bank employees. And, the outside directors are selected from practitioners with rich financial and economic experience and expertise. In Table 7.5, the averaged proportion of the shareholder representative directors in the sampled banks is 39.29%, with the Bank A the highest of 44.4%, and Bank D and Bank B lowest of 33.3%. By coincidence, and subject to the same legal mandate, the averaged employee representative directors is 39.29%, with Bank D the highest of 66.7% and Bank C the lowest of 28.6%. The averaged outside supervisory directors, on the other hand, takes 21.43%, with the Bank B the highest of 33.3%, and Bank D the lowest of 0% due to its retarded reform in governance structure (Bank B 2012; Bank A 2012; Bank C 2012; Bank D 2012).

Manifesting the paradigm and legitimacy discourses as discussed in Chap. 5, the arrangement of the supervisory board in Chinese banks presents the influence of the Continental model as well as certain Chinese specialty. For instance, the mandatory

Table 7.5 Supervisory board of sampled banks 2011

	Bank B	Bank A	Bank C	Bank D	Averaged
Shareholder representative	2	4	3	2	3.6
	33.3%	44.4%	42.9%	33.3%	39.29%
Employee representative	2	3	2	4	3.6
	33.3%	33.3%	28.6%	66.7%	39.29%
Outside supervisory directors	2	2	2	0	1.5
	33.3%	22.2%	28.6%	0%	21.43%
Total	6	9	7	6	7

Source Bank A (2012) Bank B (2012) Bank C (2012), Bank D (2012)

presence of the employee representative illustrates the labor participation and coordination in Chinese supervisory board, which intends for the proper protection of the interests of the employees as one of the key stakeholders. The inclusion of the outside supervisory directors, on the other hand, demonstrates supplementary independent monitoring over the bank's board directors and senior management. And, the high proportion of the shareholder representatives at the supervisory board manifests the close control by the state as the majority shareholder. On the flip side, however, such arrangement may as well illustrate a strong Chinese specialty. Distinguished from the Continental model, the supervisory board of directors in Chinese banks is less powerful considering its small size, limited participation by the employee representatives and outsider directors, and insufficient influences over the bank management. In some instances, the supervisory board may take an embarrassing stand and act simply as an internal monitoring department.

7.5 Conclusion

As the first cut of empirical analysis on frame of the specific corporate governance arrangement in Chinese banks, the present chapter explores the issues of the board of directors in Chinese banking industry. Referring to the board of directors in generic corporate governance arrangement and the specialty of the bank board in the context of corporate governance in banking organizations, the chapter reviews the structure of the board of directors in Chinese banks, its composition, the board size, and independence. Moreover, the chapter studies how this specific governance structure of bank board represents the discourses of the paradigm and legitimacy of Chinese institutional settings as elaborated in the previous chapters. Continuing the discursive institutional analysis, the next few chapters will explore other issues of corporate governance in Chinese banks, namely the regulation on executive pay, risk management, and legal duties.

References

Adams, R., & Mehran, H. (2003). Is corporate governance different for bank holding companies? *Economic Policy Review, 9*, 123–142.

Adams, R., & Mehran, H. (2008). Corporate performance, board structure, and their determinants in the banking industry. Staff Report no. 330, Federal Reserve Bank of New York.

Adams, R. B., & Ferreira, D. (2009). Women on board and their impact on governance and performance. *Journal of Financial Economic, 94*, 291–309.

Agrawal, A., & Knoeber, C. R. (1996). Firm performance and mechanisms to control agency problems between managers and shareholders. *Journal of Financial and Quantitative Analysis, 31*, 377–397.

Agrawal, A., & Knoeber, C. R. (2001). Do some outside directors play a political role? *Journal of Law and Economics, 44*, 179–198.

Bai, J. (2010). Comments on the independence of the governance structure of the board of directors in commercial banks against the backdrop of foreign investment. *Journal of Beijing Open University, 1*, 33–38.

Bank A. (2012). 2011 Annual Report of Bank A, Bank A. Retrieved May 25, 2012, from http://www.BankA.com.

Bank B. (2012). 2011 Annual Report of Bank B, Bank B. Retrieved May 25, 2012, from http://www.BankB.com.

Bank C. (2012). 2011 Annual Report of Bank C, Bank C. Retrieved May 25, 2012, from http://www.BankC.com.

Bank D. (2012). 2011 Annual Report of Bank D, Bank D. Retrieved May 25, 2012, from http://www.BankD.com.

Benkel, M., Mather, P., & Ramsay, A. (2006). The association between corporate governance and earnings management: The role of independent directors. *Corporate Ownership and Control, 3*, 65–75.

Bhagat, S., & Black, B. S. (2002). The non-correlation between board independence and long-term firm performance. *Journal of Corporation Law, 27*, 1231–1273.

BIS. (2010). *Principles for enhancing corporate governance*. Switzerland: Basel Committee on Banking Supervision.

BIS, Basel Committee on Banking Supervision Switzerland. (2015). *Corporate governance principles for banks*. Switzerland: Basel Committee on Banking Supervision.

BNP Paribas. (2012). 2011 Annual Report of BNP Paribas, BNP Paribas. Retrieved October 11, 2012, from http://www.bnpparibas.com.

Cheng, S. (2008). Board size and the variability of corporate performance. *Journal of Financial Economics, 87*(1), 157–176.

China Banking Association. (2011). 2010 CSR Report of Chinese Banking Industry, China Banking Association. Retrieved July 28, 2012, from http://www.china-cba.net.

China Banking Regulatory Commission. (2011). *Guidance for Corporate Governance in Commercial Banks (Consultative Document)*. Beijing: China Banking Regulatory Commission.

Commerzbank. (2012). 2011 Annual Report of Commerzbank, Commerzbank. Retrieved October 15, 2012, from http://www.commerzbank.com.

Crédit Agricole S.A. (2012). 2011 Annual Report of Crédit Agricole S.A, Crédit Agricole S.A. Retrieved December 11, 2012, from http://www.credit-agricole.com.

Dahya, J. (2002). The Cadbury committee, corporate performance, and top management turnover. *The Journal of Finance, 57*(1), 461–483.

Dahyaa, J., & McConnell, J. J. (2005). Outside directors and corporate board decisions. *Journal of Corporate Finance, 11*(1–2), 37–60.

Dalton, D. R., Daily, C. M., Ellstrand, A. E., Johnson, J. L., & Ellstrand, A. E. (1999). Number of directors and financial performance: A meta-analysis. *Academy of Management Journal, 42*, 674–686.

De Andres, P., & Vallelado, E. (2008). Corporate governance in banking: The role of the board of directors. *Journal of Banking & Finance, 32*, 2570–2580.

Deutsche Bank. (2012). 2011 Annual Review of Deutsche Bank, Deutsche Bank. Retrieved October 17, 2012, from http://www.db.com.

Duchina, R., Matsusakab, J. G., & Ozbas, O. (2010). When are outside directors effective? *Journal of Financial Economics, 96*(2), 195–214.

DZ BANK Group. (2012). 2011 Annual Report of DZ BANK Group, DZ BANK Group 2012. Retrieved October 15, 2012, from http://www.dzbank.com.

German Government Commission. (2012). *German corporate governance code*. Berlin: German Government Commission.

He, Y., & Zhou, Y. (2010). A review of the relationship between the ownership structure and corporate performance - An endogenous and dynamic perspective. *Economic Management, 4*.

Hermalin, B., & Weisbach, M. (2003). Board of directors as an endogenously- determined Institution: A survey of the economic literature. *Economic Policy Review, 9*, 7–26.

References

Hong, Z., & Zhou, Z. (2008). Internal monitoring, substitutive supervision and the value of the bank. *Journal of Financial Research, 7,* 119–132.

Hopt, K. J. (1998). *Comparative corporate governance.* Oxford: Clarendon.

Hopt, K. & Leyens, P. C. (2004). Board models in Europe-recent developments of internal corporate governance structures in Germany, the United Kingdom, France, and Italy. Retrieved June 8, 2010, from http://ssrn.com/abstract=487944.

Jensen, M. (1993). The modern industrial revolution, exit, and the failure of internal control systems. *Journal of Finance, 48,* 831–880.

Kumar, P., & Sivaramakrishnan, K. (2008). Who monitors the monitor? The effect of board independence on executive compensation and firm value. *Review of Financial Study, 21,* 1371–1401.

Lagard, C. (2010). What If It had been Lehman Sisters, May 11 th 2010. New York: New York Times. Retrieved August 26, 2012, from http://dealbook.nytimes.com/2010/05/11/lagarde-what-if-it-had-been-lehman-sisters.

Lehn, K., Patro, S., & Zhao, M. (2004*). Determinants of the size and structure of corporate boards: 1935–2000.* Working Paper, University of Pittsburgh.

Mehran, H. R., & Schaefer, H. S. (2005). board committee structures, ownership, and firm performance, Federal Reserve Bank of New York. Unpublished Working Paper.

Minton, B. A., Taillard, J. P. A., & Williamson, R. (2010). Do independence and financial expertise of the board matter for risk taking and performance? Working paper.

Morgan, D. (2002). Rating banks: Risk and uncertainty in an opaque industry. *American Economic Review, 92,* 874–888.

OECD. (2004). *Principles of corporate governance.* Paris: Organization for Economic Co-operation and Development.

OECD, Organization for Economic Co-operation and Development. (2015) *Principles of corporate governance.* OECD Report to G20 Finance Ministers and Central Bank Governors. Paris: Organization for Economic Co-operation and Development.

Pathan, S., & Skully, M. (2010). Endogenously structured boards of directors in banks. *Journal of Banking & Finance, 34*(7), 1590–1606.

Prigge, S. (1998). A survey of german corporate governance - comparative corporate governance, SSRN. Retrieved July 10, 2011, from http://ssrn.com/abstract=159562.

Rosenstein, S., & Wyatt, J. G. (1990). Outside directors, board independence and shareholder wealth. *Journal of Financial Economics, 26*(2), 175–191.

Rosenstein, S., & Wyatt, J. G. (1997). Inside directors, board effectiveness, and shareholder wealth. *Journal of Financial Economics, 44,* 229–250.

UK. (2003). *The combined code on corporate governance.*

UK. (2008). *The combined code on corporate governance.*

UK Financial Reporting Council. (2012). *The UK corporate governance code,* September 2012. London: Financial Reporting Council.

US. (2002). *Sarbanes-Oxley Act (SOX).*

US. (2008). *American emergency economic stabilization act or the troubled asset relief program (TARP) bill.*

US. (2010). *Wall street reform and consumer protection act of 2010 (Dodd Frank Act).*

Weir, C., & Laing, D. (2000). The performance-governance relationship: The effects of Cadbury compliance on UK quoted companies. *Journal of Management and Governance, 4,* 265–281.

Yv, Y. & He, W. (2012). Boards of banks in China: Endogenous innovation or passive compliance. *Journal of Shanxi Finance and Economics University 34*(2).

Chapter 8
Financial Regulation on Executive Pay in Chinese Banks

8.1 Introduction

The regulation on executive pay, as another leg of frame discourses in corporate governance in banking organizations, has drawn special attention ever since the 2007–2009 financial crisis and becomes actually the key of financial reforms across different model countries. It is in this context that this chapter reviews and explores, reflecting upon the implication of varied paradigms and legitimacies as discussed in previous chapters, the pay regulation in varied model countries, which embraces the theoretical grounds for regulation on executive pay, the different elements in the executive compensation package, and diversified regulatory measures employed by varying model countries. This enables the chapter to continue to study regulation on executive pay in Chinese banking organization, which pertains to the specific composition of the executive remuneration, specialized regulatory mechanisms and arrangements, and increasing coordination between Chinese banks and financial regulators.

8.2 Regulation of Executive Pay

In banking organizations, executive pay, or executive remuneration, has been a hot subject ever since the beginning of the 2007–2009 financial crisis, especially considering its extravagance and said correlation to excessive risk taking by the bank executives. It has become a key focus for regulators, academia, the public and media, and a core target of the 'Occupying Wall Street' movement (The Washington Times, October 12, 2011). In this context, flourishing legislations and regulations were promulgated across countries to rein this 'wild horse,' which were purposed to mitigate the executive's incentives to take unnecessary and excessive risks for the sake of their short-term interests (UK, Walker Review 2009; USA, TARP 2010; Germany, SoF-

---

© Springer Nature Singapore Pte Ltd. 2019

W. Zou, *Corporate Governance in the Banking Sector in China*, CSR, Sustainability, Ethics & Governance, https://doi.org/10.1007/978-981-13-3510-5_8

Fin Program 2009; EU, CRD IV 2013). Meanwhile, at the international level, Basel III requires financial regulators to monitor compensation structures with a compatible sound risk management (Basel Committee 2010). G20, in the mid of the global financial crisis, also revealed the leaders' determination to implement international compensation standards and eradicate highly risky, excessive risk-taking practices in banks (G20 2009).

Theoretically, many scholars argue that the executive pay should not become an issue as the manager can harvest for what he labors. However, because of the separation of control and ownership in modern corporations, the manager, as economically rational man, has unavoidably incurred the termed 'agency cost' and frequently maximized their own interests at the expenses of the owners of the firm. In this context, the executive pay becomes a serious issue to shareholders or even regulators, and several key subjects grab attention from the academic, the government, and the public. These pertain to the correlation between the executive pay and firm performance, the independence of the decision-making process on executive pay, the forms of the executive pay, and, above all, the regulation on executive pay.

However, there are competing views in the extant literature with regard to pay regulation. Opponents argue that there is no place and no need for pay regulation, as the interests of management and owners can be aligned subjectively and objectively, although entrepreneurship may not always coincide with ownership due to different orientations and preferences (Jensen and Zimmerman 1985; Bart and Bontis 2003; Georgiou 2009). This is typically observed in the positive correlation between the firm performance and executive compensations (Jensen and Murphy 1990; Kose and Yiming 2003). Meanwhile, executive pay is largely a natural product of the market force and pay for performance is self-evident as executives always have substantial holdings of stock and options of the firm, especially in USA where executives have much larger equity portions than those in any other countries. This is assumed to perfectly align the interests of the management with those of the shareholders as the management also becomes owners due to their large shareholdings (Core et al. 2005; Kaplan 2009). Similarly, there is observed good evidence, in the banking industry, for positive correlation between the executive pay and bank's profitability (Kose and Yiming 2003).

Meanwhile, other scholars argue that the harsh regulations upon executive compensation in banks, right in the aftermath of 2007–2009 global financial crisis, are actually rooted in the prevalent political idea of the 'evils' in the excessive remuneration for the bank executives, rather than careful analysis of the technical defects in the present compensation arrangement. The bankers, who are assumed to be mainly responsible for the hovering financial crisis and the plagued global economic recessions, are believed to be paid too much, and it is this flawed compensation practice that contributes to the occurrence of the financial crisis. In challenging the merits of regulation over executive pay, these scholars further argue that serious attention should be given to the board of directors and its compensation committee who are directly charged with and responsible for the pay setting process (Bhagat and Romano 2009; Core and Guay 2010).

8.2 Regulation of Executive Pay

However, proponents for pay regulation cast skepticisms on the merits of high-level executive remuneration in both financial and non-financial firms (Murphy 1999). They contend that such excessive pay does not necessarily provide proper incentives for the management, but may cause increasing income inequality (Frydman and Saks 2007), especially in the financial industry where executive pay appears excessively high (Kaplan and Rauh 2009). Specifically, the drive for the higher pay is assumed to have contributed to many of the banks' failures which are exposed by the financial crisis, as the bank managers hold a very short-term stand and take unacceptable risks. There is also said to be a prevalent 'pay for no performance' element in the current executive compensation practices, which is well evidenced by very weak sensitivity in the executive pay relating to the firm performance. Typically, the bank executives can still acquire a substantial amount of annual pay even in years when earnings and stock returns are poor and the bank operates at huge losses. And in practice, the executives have too much freedom to unwind their equity incentives and exert overwhelming powers upon the board of directors (Bebchuk and Fried 2004, 2010).

8.2.1 The Composition of Executive Pay

Basically, the executive compensation in banking organizations is mainly composed of salary, bonus, (restricted) stocks, stock options, and various forms of benefits, which can be generally categorized into cash compensation, long-term incentives (referred to as LTI), and benefits (BIS 2010, 2015). The cash compensation comprises the base salary, short-term incentives (like performance-related annual bonus), long-term bonus, and some non-monetary benefits like pension commitments, luxurious working conveniences. The long-term incentives mainly take the forms of restricted stocks and stock options. Another form of executive pay, though less visible and with limited effects, is various benefits enjoyed by the executives, such as generous leave or retirement plan, health insurance, and lower interest or interest-free credit by the bank (Burghof and Hofmann 2000).

Considering different institutional settings and paradigms as discussed, executive pay varies greatly across differing model countries, which can be observed in the composition of remuneration packages for CEOs in giant companies and banks across different model countries in Fig. 8.1. For the Anglo-Saxon model, specifically USA, LTI frequently plays an overwhelming role and largely dominates in the composition of executive pay, which frequently takes over 50% of the total compensation package (though in UK, bonus takes a larger proportion compared with the LTI). In the Continental and State-affected models countries, however, the executive pay is generally composed of less LTI but a higher proportion of basic salary and bonus. And within each model, variances are present. In Japan, for instance, executive pay is distinguished by its high proportion of basic salary but fairly limited bonus and LTI.

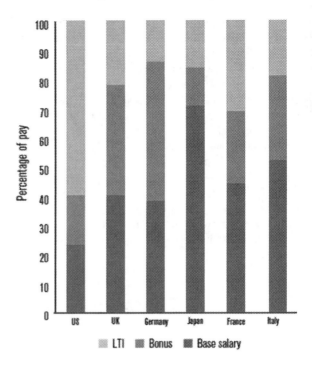

Fig. 8.1 CEO remuneration packages in companies with revenue (including banks) between 1 and 3 billion US dollars (including banking organizations), 2009. *Source* Watson Wyatt (2009)

France, though as a typical State-affected model country, is marked by a higher ratio of LTI in the composition of the executive pay, even higher than that in UK, revealing its hybridization nature of the Anglo-Saxon and Continental model (Watson Wyatt 2009).

The differences in the composition of executive pay in banks across varied models reflect the implication of various paradigm and legitimacy discourses. For instance, a higher proportion of shareholdings in executive pay (often as LTI) is readily observed in the Anglo-Saxon model, which echoes the paradigm of the shareholder primacy and the idea that shareholdings by bank managers can turn them into the 'owners' of the bank, henceforth mitigating the agency problem and motivating the management to pursue the best performance of the bank (Jensen and Murphy 1990; Core et al. 2003, 2005). In contrast, LTI is comparatively less used in the Continental and State-affected models banks due to stricter controls by the large shareholders and less agency problems in the context of the paradigm of the stakeholder theory. Instead, bonus is more frequently employed, as efficient motivations, for bank executives based on their performance. And, as a response to the long-termism for and by the bank management emphasized in the paradigm of the stakeholder theory, the base salary is comparatively high in the Continental model countries, especially in Japan. As a hybrid of the shareholder model and stakeholder model, however, France as the State-affected model country presents emphasis on using both a high proportion of shareholding and a good base salary for the bank executives.

8.2.2 Regulation on Executive Pay

In achieving effective regulation on executive pay in banking organizations, various regulatory measures are developed by the financial authorities. These pertain to limitations on base salary (especially since the financial crisis and the bailout of the banks during the 2007–2009 financial crises), caps on bonuses, more stringent disclosure requirements, increasing 'say on pay' by the shareholders, and the enhanced powers by the compensation committee within the banking organizations. Though there is now some commonality on pay regulation across different model countries, differences are still prominent(USA, TARP 2008; Germany, Soffin 2009; EU, CRD IV 2013; US Dodd-Frank Act 2010; UK Enterprise and Regulatory Reform Bill 2013).

In the Continental and State-affected models, for instance, regulation on executive pay is typically observed in the regulator's direct capping on the banker's bonuses in the aftermath of the global financial crisis. With the issuance of the latest CRD IV by European Parliament (2013), Germany and France determinedly set a cap on the bankers' bonuses, a directive intervention on executive pay in banking organizations. In this context, the banker's bonus will be capped at a ratio of 1:1 fixed to variable remuneration (variable pay), which implies the bonus will not exceed the total of the fixed salary. Though this ratio can be raised to a maximum of 2:1, it requires 'a quorum of shareholders representing 50% of shares participates in the vote and a 66% majority of them supports the measure,' or in case such quorum cannot be reached, the ratio can be approved if supported by 75% of shareholders present (EU, CRD IV 2013). Meanwhile, further regulations on the banker's bonus pertain to its composition and terms of payment. For instance, at least 50% of the variable pay should consist of shareholding or equivalent ownership interests of the bank. And, at least 40% of the variable pay should be subject to deferral payment which lasts from 3 to 5 years. Regarding the 'particularly high variable pay' by the bank executives, at least 60% of such variable pay will be deferred (EU, CRD IV 2013). In addition, the length of deferral period should take various factors like the bonus cycle, the nature of the bank's business, and its risks and activities of the staff in question. Meanwhile, all the variable pay will be subject to the strict 'claw-back' arrangement (EU, CRD IV 2013).

In contrast, instead of using most direct and intrusive regulation like bonus cap, market-based regulative measures are more frequently employed in the Anglo-Saxon model and the regulation on executive pay is largely left to the bank and its investors, which pertain to the shareholder's 'say on pay,' stricter information disclosure, and the enhanced function by the compensation committee. Meanwhile, there are specified regulations on vesting of the shareholding to the bank executives.

First and foremost, financial regulators in Anglo-Saxon model countries prefer to give extra weights to the shareholder's vote on the executive pay, which covers a great variety of pay issues and provides more detailed arrangement and frame for its functioning (US Dodd-Frank Act 2010). Typically, a new package of 'binding' say on pay has been developed in UK, which is purported to reinforce the shareholders' powers in deciding the compensation for the bank's executives (UK

Enterprise and Regulatory Reform Bill 2013). For instance, for at least every 3 years, a binding shareholder vote shall be held on the bank's compensation policy report, which sets the future plan on the remuneration package for the bank's directors and executives. These include the disclosure of key elements of the pay, maximum potential value and performance metrics, and information on contracts or terms of the board directors affecting the compensation package (UK Enterprise and Regulatory Reform Bill 2013). Meanwhile, there are further specifications on the advisory (though not binding) shareholder vote held annually regarding the implementation of the bank's compensation policy, which embraces how the bank's compensation policy is implemented, the actual payments to bank's executives, and the detailed analysis on the correlation between the bank's performance and executive pay. Other important issues include the total amount of the remuneration for the bank's directors as well as specifics of each categories of payment (including but not limited to the salary, benefits, pensions, bonuses, and long-term incentives), performance against metrics for long-term incentives, variable pay awarded in the previous fiscal year (UK Enterprise and Regulatory Reform Bill 2013).

Secondly, information disclosure, as another key element of pay regulation, attracts great significance in ensuring a fair compensation system in banking organizations. In the Anglo-Saxon model, for instance, disclosure on executive pay in banks is found to be more extensive, specific, and stricter than its counterparts in the Continental and State-affected models. As illustrated in Table 8.1, almost all the specified indicators on executive pay disclosure are covered in giant companies and banks in USA. Particularly, there is an inclusion of disclosure on the appointments of advisors for executive compensation, which are absent in either the Continental or State-affected model. In contrast, the Continental model and State-affected countries illustrate comparatively less stringent disclosure requirements. Japan, for example, stands out as the least transparent country with details of many pay aspects unavailable, and only a total amount of payment is provided (Watson Watt 2009).

Thirdly, the compensation committee (under the board of directors) frequently plays a fairly important role in setting the executive pay in the Anglo-Saxon model banks (Walker Review 2009; UK Remuneration Code 2010; US Corporate and Financial Institution Compensation Fairness Act 2009). For instance, the members of the compensation committee are carefully selected and expected to possess relevant business and financial knowledge, skills, and expertise from their long years of service as senior management, which may facilitate in setting adequate compensation objectives, negotiate and evaluate pay conditions, and hold the executive accountable for their performance (Walker Review 2009; UK Remuneration Code 2010; US Corporate and Financial Institution Compensation Fairness Act 2009). And, to guarantee a more objective, independent, and efficient function, higher independence is required for the composition of such compensation committee (US Dodd-Frank Act 2010; UK Remuneration Code 2010). Meanwhile, regulation on executive pay also extends to the LTD in the Anglo-Saxon model. In UK, for instance, there is traditionally an overall limit in banking organizations for all types of share plan amounting to 10% in any rolling 10 years period, which intends to constrain the level of dilution of the shareholder's equity (Watson Wyatt 2009). In USA, on the other hand, banking orga-

8.2 Regulation of Executive Pay

Table 8.1 Disclosure requirements for companies with revenue between 1 and 3 billion US dollars across different model countries, 2009

Country	US	UK	Germany	Japan	France	Italy
Disclosure	DRR	DRR	GR/notes of accounts		DRR for CAC40	
Policy for executives	✓	✓	✓	If it exists	✓	✓
Detail in policy disclosure	Detailed	Detailed	Brief	Brief	Brief	Brief
Aggregate		Share awards		EDs		Share awards
Detail for CEO						
Detail for board	✓	✓	✓			✓
Detail for top five highest paid	✓				✓	
Base salary	✓	✓	✓	Total amount paid	✓	✓
Incentive type and quantum	✓	✓	✓		✓	✓
Pension	✓	✓	✓		✓	
Value of benefits	✓	✓	✓		✓	✓
Termination provision	✓	✓	✓		✓	✓
Appointment of advisors	✓	✓				

Notes DRR director's remuneration report, *GR* general report, *CAC40* French top 40 listed companies, *EDs* executive directors
Source Watson Wyatt et al. (2009)

nizations under TARP are prohibited to vest restricted stocks unless all the borrowed funds are paid back, and such vesting is subject to the claw-back clauses (US, TARP 2008).

The different frames of regulation on executive pay in banking organizations reveal the influences of varied paradigm and legitimacy discourses in different model countries. In the Continental and State-affected models, for example, the direct regulatory intervention through measures like capped bonuses reflects the legitimacy discourse of relatively strict financial regulation, which is purported to rein excessive risk taking by bank executives and promote the overall financial stability. This also reflects the paradigm of stakeholder theory, which seeks to advance long-term sustainability, continuous profitability, and concerns for different stakeholders in the bank. In contrast, pay regulation for banks in the Anglo-Saxon model represents the paradigm discourse of the shareholder primacy and legitimacy of dominant market institutions. For instance, though there are concerns by financial regulators to curb excessive risk taking by the bank executives for the sake of higher pay, more attention is given to the correlation between the executive pay and their performance. Specifically, measures like 'say on pay' by the shareholders, more extensive and stricter requirements over pay disclosure, and reinforced remuneration committees reflect the discourse of protecting the shareholders' interests and mitigating the agency problem. Moreover, pay regulation on bank executives in this model reflects the legitimacy discourse of financial deregulation where the pay issues are largely left to the bank and its investors, while the financial regulator is constrained from taking intrusive regulatory measures that are legitimated by the Continental and State-affected models.

8.3 Regulation on Executive Compensation

8.3.1 Composition of the Compensation

Considering varied institutional legitimacy and paradigmatic discourses, regulation on executive pay manifests certain discursive features in Chinese banking organization, which pertains to the structure of the compensation package, specific mechanisms and arrangements in pay regulation, and the coordination between banks and financial regulators. As discussed, the composition of the executive pay can be categorized as the cash salary, the mid- and long-term incentives, and welfares of various kinds. Similar arrangement can be observed in the context of Chinese banks, but with varied priorities. Conceptually, compensation in Chinese banks is defined as payment and other forms of expenditures by the bank for varied services and contributions by the bank employees, including the basic wage, the performance-related compensation (PRC), mid- and long-term incentives, welfares, social insurances, and other non-monetary benefits (CBRC 2010). The fixed salary, or the basic salary, is the payment to bank employees based on their workload, service tenure, responsibility of the post, and the risks taken. Largely, it is decided by the bank in accordance with the mandatory principles and limited below 35% of the overall compensation package. The PRC, on the other hand, is mainly determined according to the annual assessment on the employee's performance, which takes into account different categories of risks, varied costs and trade-offs, and is expected to be consistent with the bank's sustainable development strategy. Specifically, PRC is not allowed to exceed three times of the basic salary. The welfare package, as another fairly important but less visible pay component, covers various social insurances, pensions, and extra funding for accommodation that is paid monthly by both the employees and the bank based on specified ratios (CBRC 2010). As illustrated in Table 8.2, for instance, the welfare package in Bank B takes a very high proportion in the overall remuneration for the bank executives which reaches around 21.42% (Bank B 2012).

For the variable compensation, mainly the mid- and long-term incentive plans, Chinese banks frequently take a very cautious stand. Specifically, compensation of this kind is expected not to adversely influence the bank's sustainable increase in its

Table 8.2 2011 Bank B compensation for senior management. Unit 10 thousand RMB

Post	Compensation paid (before tax)	Social insurances, funding for accommodation, pension and supplementary medical insurance paid by bank	Compensation from part-time posts	Shareholding of the bank at the end of the fiscal year	Total of compensation before tax	Compensation paid by shareholder or other affiliated institutions
Board chairman and executive director	87.6	24.1	0	0	111.7	0
Deputy board chairman and executive director	80.8	22.0	0	0	102.8	0
Chairman of supervisory board	78.6	21.8	0	0	100.4	0
Deputy CEO and executive director	75.0	21.2	0	0	96.2	0
Deputy CEO and executive director	75.0	21.2	0	0	96.2	0
Deputy CEO	75.0	21.2	0	0	96.2	0
Chairman of disciplinary Committee	75.0	21.2	0	0	96.2	0
Deputy CEO	75.0	21.2	0	0	96.2	0
Deputy CEO	75.0	16.4	0	0	91.4	0
Senior manager	73.1	19.3	0	0	92.4	0
CRO	72.5	20.6	0	0	93.1	0
CIO	72.5	19.2	0	0	91.7	0
Secretary of board of directors	72.5	17.7	0	0	90.2	0

Source Bank B (2012)

capital. Indeed, contrasting the Anglo-Saxon model banks where shareholdings and options are widely used as efficient incentives, especially before the global financial crisis, Chinese banks rarely use the mid- and long-term investment plans to motivate the executives for better performance. And, with very few exceptional instances in the sampled banks (such as the employee shareholding plan which was already halted), the directors and executives do not hold any stock or debenture investment in their own banks (Bank B 2012; Bank A 2012; Bank C 2012; Bank D 2012). For example, as illustrated in Table 8.2, no shareholding or options are vested to the executives in Bank B in their overall compensation package (Bank B 2012).

Meanwhile, there are further restrictions on the composition of executive pay. For example, the board chairman and senior management are not allowed to procure any payment from the bank's affiliated institutions or other business entities, considering the potential conflict of interests, excessive risk exposures, and insider trading. Presented in Table 8.2, none of the bank executives in Bank B receives such compensation. Moreover, the overall compensation for bank executives, specifically in large-sized state-owned Chinese banks, is comparatively low considering the stringent mandates imposed by the financial regulators. In Table 8.2, the highest pay for executives in Bank B before tax, excluding the international employees, is 1.117 million RMB and the lowest is 0.917 million RMB, averaged at around 0.97 million RMB (Bank B 2012) (similar pay restrictions are found in other sampled banks). Such income is greatly dwarfed by their counterparts in either the Continental or Anglo-Saxon model banks.

Apart from these tangible compensations as discussed, the intangible forms of remuneration that are grounded in the pay culture of Chinese banking industry are present, which includes the 'invisible' political prestige and advancement, job security, sound career reputation, excellent social perception. For instance, political advancement may frequently function as a significant incentive for the senior management in the large-sized state-owned Chinese banks. Traditionally, the senior executives of these banks, typically the board chairman and CEO, enjoy prominent political prestige and administrative rank as senior government officials. In the sampled banks (due to their specific position in Chinese banking industry), for example, the heads of the banks are entitled to comparable political and administrative status as deputy ministers in the Ministry of Finance. Other senior management (at the head office level) and the heads of the bank's one-tier branches, in turn, are said to have their administrative ranks as well which match relevant administrative posts in the central and local governments. In this context, the benefits of potential political advancement and sound political reputation, which are pecuniary in nature, can become fairly important incentives for the senior management in Chinese banking organizations. Meanwhile, there is an 'exchange of post' or 'revolving door' practice, though not frequently, between financial regulators and the large-sized state-owned commercial banks. For instance, G, who used to be the deputy head of PBoC and Head of Administrative Bureau of Foreign Currency, was assigned to act as the board chairman of Bank A and then reassigned as the chairman of China Securities Regulatory Commission (CSRC) in 2012 and the chairman of CBRC. X, who used to

8.3 Regulation on Executive Compensation

be the board chairman of Bank C, was assigned as the chairman of CSRC in 2013 (Xinhua Net, June 13, 2012).

The implicit career attachment plays another important role in the composition of executive pay in Chinese banks. In contrast with the Anglo-Saxon model where the bank managers are fairly mobile and change their job frequently, Chinese bank executives are much more stable and may choose to stay in the same bank for a very long period of time. And, many of them may work in the same financial institution for their whole life. Such career attachment in Chinese banking industry is based on the discourse that a job in the (same) bank, especially the large-sized one, is the best choice for their career development. Meanwhile, a better job security is provided in Chinese banks, and unless in extremely exceptional situations, the banks will not fire or downsize the executives, even in times of financial difficulties. Though there is now a trend of increasing mobility of young bank employees moving from the large state-owned banks to private or foreign-owned financial institutions in pursuit of higher pay, there is comparatively 'still water' in the 'big pond' of the Chinese bank executives.

The composition of the executive pay in Chinese banks is shown to manifest a hybrid paradigm of the enhanced shareholder primacy and diversified stakeholder theory, along with legitimacy discourse of close financial regulation. For instance, reflecting the state as the controlling shareholder and its close control over the management (mainly in large-sized state-owned commercial banks), shareholding, which is a major component of the executive compensation in the Anglo-Saxon model countries, is less used in Chinese banks and henceforth demonstrates resemblance to the Continental and State-affected models countries. Such pay arrangement also represents the legitimacy discourse of strict financial regulation in China, which suspects the merit of the shareholding incentives for bank executives. For instance, in July 2008, State-owned Assets Supervision and Administration Commission and the Ministry of Finance jointly issued *The Notice on Regulating Relevant Issues Regarding the Implementation of Options as Incentives in State Controlled Listed Corporations*, which explicitly constrained the abuse of options as incentives in state-owned listed corporations. Specifically, stock option plans were not allowed in state-controlled listed financial enterprises unless approved by relevant financial regulators.

Moreover, a high proportion of performance-related bonus is preferred and employed as efficient incentives for senior executives in Chinese banking organizations. And, there are also an adequate proportion of the fixed salary, a generous welfare package and implicit job security, which illustrates the orientation for long-termism by and for the bank executives in China, resembling that of the Continental model countries. Meanwhile, the political advantages and advancement by the senior bank executives in China, as an implicit but effective compensation incentive, reflect a strong attribute of the hybrid model as in the State-affected model.

The overall low remuneration package for Chinese bank executives also illustrates the legitimacy discourse of strict control by the financial regulators, resembling that of the State-affected model. Traditionally, executive pay in Chinese banks is subject to influences and limitations by different authorities, such as the government statistic agency, the State-owned Assets Supervision and Administration Commission.

176   8 Financial Regulation on Executive Pay in Chinese Banks

For instance, in January 2009, the Ministry of Finance issued *Regulations upon the Compensation Plan for the Senior Management in State-owned and State-controlled Financial Enterprises (consultative pap*er), which was targeted toward the remuneration for senior management in financial-related SOEs and set a cap of 2.8 million RMB before tax (however, the final official version of this regulative document was not officially promulgated and publicized). And frequently, the total compensation package for Chinese bank executives is compared with that of senior government officials with comparable administrative ranks. For instance, CEO of Bank C presented readily acceptance and understanding regarding the limitation on executive pay in large-sized state-owned commercial banks, 'As far as I am concerned, I am satisfied (with the present compensation plan). Specifically, compared with senior officials in the Ministry of Finance who are no less capable than me and whose workload is no less intensive, their pay is much lower' (Xinhua Net, June 13, 2012).

8.3.2 Regulation on Executive Pay

Regulation on executive pay in Chinese banking organizations, contrasting with the Anglo-Saxon model, the Continental model, or the State-affected model, manifests a few specific features resonating with China's institutional embedment and paradigmatic discourses, which are well observed in the explicit limitations upon the basic salary, mandatory deferred payment of the PRC, the 'claw-back' term and retention of the paid compensation (in cases of realization of relevant risks), and specified assessment approaches using complex indicators and metrics with regard to different risks (CBRC 2010).

Firstly, there is an explicit limitation on the basic salary by Chinese bank executives, which should not exceed 35% of the total annual remuneration. This intends for avoiding and mitigating shirking problems by the bank management when the pay is less related to their output, which are readily observable in the poor performance by the managers, the low profitability of the bank, and the corporate waste issues to the bank's shareholders (CBRC 2010). And, for many bank executives in sampled banks that are subject to heavy financial regulation and government administration, their basic salary is said to be limited within, at the annual basis, two times of the averaged remuneration of all the employees throughout of the bank group.

Secondly, there has been increasingly tight control upon the overall remuneration package by Chinese bank executives. For instance, from late 2014 to 2015, a new round, more stringent pay regulation was initiated, which aimed to further constrain the pay for senior management in SOEs administered by Chinese central government. And, based on *The Plan in Reforming the Compensation System for Heads of the SOEs administered by the Central Government*, which is approved by Political Bureau of the Central Committee of the Chinese Communist Party in 2015, the overall annual compensation for senior management in the covered state-owned financial institutions, including the sampled banks, would be reduced by around 50 percent and limited below around 600,000 Yuan RMB as in Table 8.3 and should be well

8.3 Regulation on Executive Compensation

Table 8.3 The overall compensation (before tax) for the chairman of the board of directors and CEO in sampled banks in 2014–2015. Unit 10 thousand RMB

Bank	Chairman of the board of directors			CEO		
	2014	2015	Percentage of reduction (%)	2014	2015	Percentage of reduction (%)
Bank C	118.08	61.79	48	108.32	61.33	43
Bank A	115	59.88	48	113.2	36.46	68
Bank B	113.9	54.68	52	108.9	54.68	50
Bank D	86.27	56.69	34	107.15	56.69	47

Source 2015, 2016 annual reports from Bank A, B, C, D

within seven to eight times of the averaged annual remuneration of all the employees in the enterprise.

Thirdly, the deferred payment, as another efficient regulatory measure, is widely used in PRC considering the delayed effects of varied risks. In practice, such risk-related payment is expected to match the duration of the financial risks taken, the changes in the risks, and the accomplishment of the targeted business objectives. In this regard, only a fraction of PRC, normally 1/3, would be paid periodically to the bank executives, with the rest to be granted at the end of each fiscal year after annual assessments. Furthermore, for senior managers and critical employees on key posts who are involved in substantial risk exposures, 40% of PRC would be paid in deferred terms with the time span of 3 years at minimum. And, for senior managers of the key posts, the proportion of such deferred PRC can be increased to over 50% or even 60% (CBRC 2010). Generally, PRC for Chinese bank executives should be limited within two times of his basic salary. And, with regard to the mid- and long-term incentive plans, the payment will not be made until the end of the lock-up period, which may normally last over 3 years considering the varied durations of different risks, and is frequently subject to the board's approval. Moreover, a claw-back clause is also used to withdraw the paid compensation under preset scenarios. For instance, in cases of excessive risk exposures and abnormal huge losses incurred in the risk duration, the bank is entitled to retract all PRC paid to the senior managers and relevant employees while retaining the rest of the unpaid sum. Such clause is even applicable to the former employees who already left the bank, if it still falls within the risk duration (CBRC 2010).

Fourthly, there are further restrictions on the welfare packages for senior managers in Chinese banking organizations, which aim to provide better transparency, more information disclosure, and constraints over abusive spending practices. These pertain to stricter reins over a series of invisible vocational welfares and luxuries enjoyed by the bank executives, such as: (a) limits on the expenses for the senior management with regard to business travels, training programs, business receptions and entertainments, telecommunications; (b) repeal of expenses for the senior managers' memberships in golf clubs, gyms, etc., and prohibitions on any expenses for the senior management for extra, non-business-related reception, and entertaining activities, gifts, and presents, etc.

And, a set of assessment indicators and rubrics are carefully designed and developed to enhance the efficacy of pay regulation in Chinese banks, which takes into consideration the economic efficiency, risk cost control, and performance of the bank's social responsibility. The economic efficiency indicator is determined according to mandatory requirements by relevant financial regulators. The indicator of risk cost control, on the other hand, is more inclusive and embraces a wide range of issues, such as the bank's capital adequacy, the rate of non-performing loans, and the leverage ratio. For instance, the assessment on the cost of credit risks and market risks mainly focuses on the allocation of the economic capital of the bank, the changes in the bank's capital structure, and the actual losses incurred by the bank. And, the assessment of the cost for liquidity risk pertains to the liquidity coverage under varied stress test scenarios and the cost of procuring alternative liquidity resources. The social responsibility indicator, as another important component, extends to legal compliance by the bank, business ethics issues, the enterprise value, and the customers' satisfaction (CBRC 2010).

These three mandatory indicators may greatly impact upon the overall PRC to the bank's employees. For example, if any one of these indicators is not satisfied, the averaged annual pay of all the employees in the bank group shall not be higher than the previous year. If any two of the indicators are not achieved, there will be reduction in the average PRC of the whole bank group based on the benchmark of the year before, and reduction in PRC for senior managers should be higher than that of the average employees. Failing all the three indicators, apart from the aforesaid restrictions of not satisfying any two of the indicators, the total amount of the basic salary for all the bank employees shall not be increased for the coming year. Meanwhile, complementary monitoring mechanisms are set in place, such as constraints on purchasing insurance policy for the deferred part of the compensation or the liability which may affect the correlation between the compensation and the risk (CBRC 2010).

Last but not least, there have been increasingly stricter requirements on information disclosure on executive compensation in Chinese banking organizations. For example, the board of the bank is mandated and responsible for timely, objectively, and fully disclosing all the relevant information with regard to the compensation plan for the senior management, which is deemed as a significant element of information disclosure in the bank's annual report. In practice, these embrace the structure and authority of the board compensation committee, the total volume of the annual compensation, and the mapping of the executive pay. The said disclosure also pertains to the key criteria between the compensation and the performance assessment, risk adjustment, and the non-monetary remuneration. Other information disclosures include the preparation procedure for the annual compensation plan, proper measurement on the executives' performance of the indicators related to economic effects, risk control and social responsibilities, and certain exceptional situations (CBRC 2010).

Moreover, the financial regulator in China, not infrequently, plays a fairly active role in supervising the implementation and efficacy of the compensation arrangement

8.3 Regulation on Executive Compensation

in Chinese banking organizations, such as monitoring on the achievement of the key indicators, periodical on-site inspections, and timely rectification over illegitimate business practices. For instance, the regulators will impose disciplinary measures or penalties in the instances of underperformance of the aforesaid indicators, deficiencies in the bank's risk controls, and inadequate compensation management. Meanwhile, regarding certain exceptional situations such as approaching insolvency, the compensation plan and pay level would be decided by the bailing-out institutions or government. These extend to the banking organizations which are

- Already being bailed out;
- Facing significant reputation risks which may cause substantial adverse influences upon their sustainable operations;
- Near bankruptcy or winding-up;
- Received by another institution;
- Closed (CBRC 2010).

At the firm level, the compensation committee under the board of directors plays another significant role in facilitating pay regulation, such as advising on and setting the compensation plan for the bank employees, specifically for the senior management, the board directors, and the directors of the supervisory board of the bank, which are mainly determined based on the evaluation of their performance. The compensation committee may take different forms in Chinese banks, either as an independent group in Bank B or merged with other committees like the nomination and compensation committee in Bank A (Bank B 2012; Bank A 2012). More than often, an outside director with sufficient seniority and expertise will be assigned to chair the committee, while one-third of the compensation committee members are professionals with rich accounting experience and expected to be familiar with a great variety of risks from different business lines of the bank (CBRC 2010). Meanwhile, departments like the human resources, risk control, and legal compliance are also responsible for facilitating effective monitoring over the bank's compensation practices and should be independent from any influences from the monitored business lines (CBRC 2010).

Regulation on the executive pay, as another key component of bank governance in China, is observed to have revealed the discourses of paradigm and legitimacy discussed in the previous chapters. For instance, the fairly restrictive arrangement for the proportion, standards, and terms of the executive compensation illustrates the strict financial control over Chinese banks. The deferred payment and claw-back clause on PRC, on the other hand, demonstrate the regulator's serious concerns on excessive risk taking by the bank executives and the potential threat to the national financial stability. Moreover, reflecting the paradigm of the diversified stakeholder theory, regulation on executive pay in Chinese banks presents concerns for varied stakeholders, as exemplified in including the social indicator in assessing the performance of the bank executives. And, the encouraged use of PRC as a major component of the executive compensation, the emphasis on information disclosure, and the enhanced function of the compensation committee illustrate the increasing deregulation and pro-market attitudes by Chinese financial authorities.

On the flip side, however, regulation on executive pay presents certain coordinated nature due to the increasing deregulation by Chinese government. In designing the framework of regulation on executive pay in Chinese banks, the financial regulators frequently take fairly cautious steps rather than being intrusive and dictating. For instance, CBRC had been conducting a series of research programs with regard to executive compensation in Chinese banking industry with the Ministry of Human Resources and Social Securities, the Ministry of Finance, and other related government agencies since 2008, which were oriented toward the sustainable development of the bank and sound correlation between the executive pay and the bank's risk taking. Meanwhile, CBRC actively communicated with the senior management in Chinese banking institutions and consulted their opinions regarding pay regulation, such as the annual compensation plan which could be adjusted according to each bank's respective situation and performance. On the part of senior managers from Chinese banks, especially the large-sized state-owned commercial banks, such regulative arrangement is not unacceptable, though some of them challenge the merits of the pay regulation and contend such regulatory limitation is more an impediment for the free market economy. Specifically, the pay regulation gains its ground considering the status quo of the large-sized state-owned commercial banks due to the duality of bank's senior management, the less developed market for professional banking managers, and the regulator's influence on their appointment.

8.4 Conclusion

Investigating the competing views on the merits of pay regulation, the chapter explores the composition of the executive remuneration and the varied regulative measures and policy orientations in different model countries, which are found to resonate the paradigm and legitimacy discourses as discussed in Chapters 3 and 5. In the context of bank governance in China, similarly, regulation on executive pay demonstrates the power of legitimized and paradigmatic discourses elaborated in Chapters 4 and 6. For instance, reflecting the legitimacy discourse of close financial regulation, there are outstanding and intervening mandates on the composition, ratio, and terms of the compensation package for Chinese bank executives. Pay regulation in Chinese banks also illustrates the paradigm discourse of the diversified stakeholder theory by adequate fixed salary and generous welfare package, which is designed for the long-termism orientation by the bank executives. Also, it presents the concern for the stakeholders' interests by setting the social indicator as a compulsory standard for appraising the executives' performance. Continuing the discursive institutional analysis, the next chapter, Chap. 9, will explore another major challenging issue of corporate governance in Chinese banks, risk management.

References

Bank A. (2012). *2011 annual report of Bank A, Bank A*. Available at http://www.BankA.com. Accessed May 25, 2012.

Bank B. (2012). *2011 annual report of Bank B, Bank B*. Available at http://www.BankB.com. Accessed May 25, 2012.

Bank C. (2012). *2011 annual report of Bank C, Bank C*. Available at http://www.BankC.com. Accessed May 25, 2012.

Bank D. (2012). *2011 annual report of Bank D, Bank D*. Available at http://www.BankD.com. Accessed May 25, 2012.

Bart, C., & Bontis, N. (2003). Distinguishing between the board and management in company mission: Implications for corporate governance. *Journal of Intellectual Capital, 4*(3), 361–381.

Basel Committee. (2010). Basel III: A global regulatory framework for more resilient banks and banking systems. Basel Committee on Banking Supervision, Basel.

Bebchuk, L. A., & Fried, J. M. (2004). *Pay without performance—The unfulfilled promise of executive compensation*. Harvard: Harvard University Press.

Bebchuk, L. A., & Fried, J. M. (2010). Paying for long-term performance. *University of Pennsylvania Law Review*, 158.

Bhagat, S., & Romano, R. (2009). *Reforming executive compensation: focusing and committing to the long-term*. Working paper. Yale Law School, Available at http://digitalcommons.law.yale.edu/fss_papers. Accessed March 15, 2012.

BIS. (2010). *Principles for enhancing corporate governance*. Switzerland: Basel Committee on Banking Supervision.

BIS, Basel Committee on Banking Supervision Switzerland. (2015). *Corporate governance principles for banks*. Switzerland: Basel Committee on Banking Supervision.

Burghof, H.-P., & Hofmann, C. (2000). *Executives' compensation of European banks—Disclosure, sensitivity, and their impact on bank performance*. Research paper no. 2000-01, Munich Business.

China Banking Regulatory Commission. (2010). *Guidance on regulation of stabilized compensation in commercial banks*. No. 14, Beijing: China Banking Regulatory Commission.

Core, J., & Guay, W. (2010). *Is there a case for regulating executive pay in the financial services industry?* Working paper.

Core, J., Guay, W., & Thomas, R. (2005). Is CEO compensation inefficient pay without performance. *University of Michigan Law Review, 103*, 1141–1185.

Core, J., Guay, W., & Verrecchia, R. (2003). Price versus non-price performance measures in optimal CEO compensation contracts. *The Accounting Review, 78*(4), 957–981.

European Union. (2013). European Parliament, *Capital requirements directive (CRD IV)*. Belgium: Brussels.

Frydman, C., & Saks, R. E. (2007). *Executive compensation: A new view from a long term perspective, 1936–2005*. Working Paper.

Georgiou, M. N. (2009). Government Debt Impacts on Interest Rates as Well as Entrepreneurship; A Panel Data Analysis for Western Europe, Japan and the United States (1990–2006).

German Financial Market Stabilisation Fund. (2009). *SoFFin program*. Berlin: Financial Market Stabilisation Fund. Available at http://www.fmsa.de/en. Accessed July 25, 2012.

Jensen, M., & Murphy, K. J. (1990). Performance pay and top management incentives. *Journal of Political Economy, 98*, 225–264.

Jensen, M. C., & Zimmerman, J. L. (1985). Management compensation and the managerial labor market. *Journal of Accounting and Economics, 7*(1–3), 3–9.

Kaplan, S. N. (2009). Should banker pay be regulated? *The Economists' Voice*, Vol. 6, Issue 11.

Kaplan, S. N., & Rauh, J. (2009). Wall street and main street: What contributes to the rise in the highest incomes? *Review of Financial Studies, 23*(3), 1004–1050.

Kose, J., & Yiming, Q. (2003). Incentive features in CEO compensation in the banking industry. *Economic Policy Review*, 109–121.

Murphy, K. J. (1999). Executive compensation. *Handbook of Labor Economics, 3*(Part B), 2485–2563.

UK. (2009). *Walker Review*.

UK. (2010). *Remuneration code*.

UK. (2013). *Enterprise and regulatory reform bill 2012–2013*.

US. (2008). *American emergency economic stabilization act or the troubled asset relief program (TARP) bill*.

US. (2010). *Wall street reform and consumer protection act of 2010 (Dodd Frank Act)*.

US Board of Governors of the Federal Reserve System. (2009). *Corporate and financial institution compensation fairness act*, 2009.

Watson Wyatt. (2009). *Executive pay practices around the world 2009 report*. Watson Wyatt, Available at http://www.watsonwyatt.com/research/pdfs/EU-2009-12528.pdf. Accessed December 12, 2012.

Xinhua Net (2012). Tolerance for default loans by small and micro enterprises is raised to 5% in Shenzhen, April 12th, 2012, Beijing: Xinhua Net, Available at http://news.xinhuanet.com/fortune/2012-04/12/c_122969583.htm. Accessed July 25, 2012.

Chapter 9
Risk Management System in Corporate Governance in Banking Organizations in China

9.1 Introduction

As a pivotal component in corporate governance in banking organizations, risk management has become particularly visible in the context of the 2007–2009 financial crises, the failures of which are said to be the main cause of the overwhelming financial avalanche. Indeed, risk management has become the heart of financial reforms and sound bank governance in the aftermath of the financial crisis all over the world. Based on in-depth analysis of prevalent risk management arrangements developed by BIS, the present chapter explores certain key elements in risk management system, such as generic categories of risks in banking organizations, the comprehensive risk management framework and governance structure, and specific risk management mechanisms. In this context, the chapter investigates varying risk management systems in banking institutions from different model countries and endeavors to reveal their dynamics with related legitimacy and paradigm discourses studied in previous chapters. The chapter continues to elaborate risk management issues in Chinese banking organizations, which pertains to the overall risk management framework, a moderate risk appetite, the specific risk management mechanism, and more stringent financial regulatory framework. Such risk management arrangements, in the context of Chinese bank governance, are contended to be fairly strong representations of constitutive discourses of paradigm and legitimacy in the unique Chinese institutional embedment.

9.2 Risk Management in General Banking Organizations

The word 'risk' can be traced far back to the Latin word *risicum*, understood as risk or that which cuts. It refers to uncertainty or probability from the future events which may bring certain outcomes. In a wider sense, however, the risk does not necessarily

---

© Springer Nature Singapore Pte Ltd. 2019 183
W. Zou, *Corporate Governance in the Banking Sector in China*, CSR, Sustainability,
Ethics & Governance, https://doi.org/10.1007/978-981-13-3510-5_9

lead to something bad. And it may bring about something beneficial. In the context of the banking industry, risk includes financial and non-financial uncertainties of various kinds and is generally categorized into business risks and control risks. The former originates from the bank's operation and business activities, such as risks relevant to credit, market, and liquidity. The latter arises, on the other hand, out of the defects in the control mechanisms employed by bank, including but not limited to risks in internal control, business operation, and legal compliance. Generally, four key groups of risks stand out in corporate governance in banking organization, namely credit risk, market risk, liquidity risk, and operational risk (BIS 2011).

Credit risk, by nature, is most simply defined as 'the potential that a bank borrower or counterparty will fail to meet its obligations in accordance with agreed terms' (BIS 2000, p. 1), which, for most of the banking organization, results from a great variety of business activities that are included in the banking and trading book, both on and off the bank's balance sheet. These include, but not limited to, massive bank loans, increasingly complicated and diversified financial instruments (such as acceptances, interbank transactions, trade financing, foreign exchange transactions, financial futures, swaps, bonds, equities, options), guarantees, and settlement of transactions (BIS 2000, p. 1).

In contrast, back to the end of 1997, banking organizations around the world started to be required to measure and apply adequate capital charges with regard to the market risk that is conceptualized as 'the risk of losses in on-balance and off-balance sheet positions arising from movements in market prices,' which includes two general categories, 'the risks pertaining to interest rate-related instruments and equities in the trading book' and 'foreign exchange risk and commodities risk throughout the bank'(BIS 1996, p. 1). The capital charges for the former set of risks are closely connected with the current market value of items in banks' trading books. Specifically, the trading book implies 'the bank's proprietary positions in financial instruments which are intentionally held for short-term resale and/or which are taken on by the bank with the intention of benefiting in the short-term from actual and/or expected differences between their buying and selling prices, or from other price or interest-rate variations, and positions in financial instruments arising from matched principal brokering and market making, or positions taken in order to hedge other elements of the trading book' (BIS 1996, p. 1). The capital charges for foreign exchange risk and for commodities risk, on the other hand, 'mainly apply to banks' total currency and commodity positions, subject to some discretion to exclude structural foreign exchange positions' (BIS 1996, p. 3).

Liquidity risk, on the other hand, arises out of the challenges posed to the bank's ability to 'fund increases in assets and meet obligations as they come due, without incurring unacceptable losses.' Indeed, it is the bank's essential role in the maturity transformation of short-term deposits into long-term loans that 'make banks inherently vulnerable to liquidity risk, both of an institution-specific nature and that which affects markets as a whole' (BIS 2008, p. 1). In this sense, liquidity risk can be categorized into the funding liquidity risk and the market liquidity risk. The former refers to the risk 'that the firm will not be able to meet efficiently both expected and unexpected current and future cash flow and collateral needs without affecting either daily operations or the financial condition of the firm' (BIS 2008, p. 1). The market liquidity risk, on the other hand, is a risk 'that a firm cannot easily offset or eliminate a position at the market price because of inadequate market depth or market disruption' (BIS 2008, p. 1).

A fairly challenging risk, which reoccurs times and again in varied financial crisis and banking debacles, is the operational risk, which is defined as 'the risk of loss resulting from inadequate or failed internal processes, people and systems or from external events.' Such risk, either through a great variety of historical banking scandals or flourishing banking malpractices during or *ex post* the 2007–2009 global financial crisis, is proved to be inherent and deeply embedded in all banking products, activities, transactions and systems and frequently intertwined with other risk exposures such legal risk (BIS 2011, p. 3). Considering its strong 'human nature,' i.e., significant influences from the bank employees' behaviors, operation risk differs greatly from other risks and may well test whether the bank board and senior management can effectively administer the bank's portfolio of relevant products, activities, processes, and systems (BIS 2011, p. 3).

Risks of other kinds, which also impact on the bank and are closely intertwined with the aforesaid risks, include reputational risk, legal or compliance risk, and settlement risk. For instance, settlement risk, defined as a risk that the completion or settlement of a financial transaction will fail to take place as expected, is a more complex and compound risk which may comprise varied risk exposures, such as liquidity risk, market risk, operational and reputational risk, and credit risk (BIS 2000, p. 1). Meanwhile, perceived from the financial regulator and central banking perspective, there is observed another more significant and overarching risk, the so-called systemic risk (BIS 2010), which refers to a risk scenario that 'the failure of a participant to meet its contractual obligations may in turn cause other participants to default with a chain reaction leading to broader financial difficulties' (BIS 1994, p. 177). Emphasizing on both the causation and correlation of the risk, the systemic risk implies 'strong and direct interconnections or linkages among the institutions, markets, sectors, or countries involved' and domino effects on everyone on the chain (Kaufman 2009, p. 14). For instance, should a bank default on a loan, deposit or other payment to another bank, the default may continue down the chain and may lead to the default of the whole banking system (Crockett 1997). And this is readily demonstrated in 2007–2009 financial crisis where there is 'a high correlation and clustering of bank failures in a country, a number of countries, or globally; and in currencies, by a clustering of deprecations in exchange rates in a number of countries.' (Kaufman 2009, p. 14).

9.2.1 General Risk Management Structure

For administering the aforesaid different risks, a systematic risk management framework is established in the banking organizations around the world, which 'generally encompasses the process of identifying key risks to the bank; assessing these risks and measuring the bank's exposures to them; monitoring the risk exposures and determining the corresponding capital needs (i.e., capital planning) on an ongoing basis; monitoring and assessing decisions to accept particular risks, risk mitigation measures and whether risk decisions are in line with the board-approved risk tolerance/appetite and risk policy; and reporting to senior management, and the board as appropriate' (BIS 2011, p. 3). And, for this end, a centralized overall or comprehensive risk management framework is widely employed, which determines the overall risk appetite, portfolio, and strategy for the bank group.

Such overall risk management embraces a wide range of processes, models and patterns, which motivate or constrain the bank in formulating and implementing its risk-based policies, banking activities, and financial practices. And, a great variety of techniques and management tools are used to identify, measure, monitor, and control the various risks. Meanwhile, the complicated network of risk management involves various participants in the bank, such as the board of directors, the management at all levels, the chief risk officer (CRO), the risk management department, and relevant business lines, all of whom play different but connected functions in the risk management system. Moreover, the efficient function of risk management depends upon other related departments, typically the internal control and auditing. For instance, as one of the key components of risk management system, the internal controls are 'embedded in a bank's day-to-day business and are designed to ensure, to the extent possible, that bank activities are efficient and effective, information is reliable, timely and complete and the bank is compliant with applicable laws and regulation' (BIS 2011, p. 3).

In this context, especially upon careful reflection on the cause of bank failures in 2007–2009 global financial crisis, an innovative, most consistent, and multilayered risk governance arrangement is designed, developed, and promoted for banks across different countries, which calls for a more clarified identification and allocation of responsibilities of different parts and departments within the bank in sufficiently addressing and managing relevant risks. Referred to as the 'three lines of defense' for risk management, it specifies three main 'lines' and their separate roles in controlling the risk exposures. The first line lies with the business departments of the bank, or the business line in general, 'which has "ownership" of risk, whereby it acknowledges and manages the risk that it incurs in conducting its activities' (BIS, Corporate governance principles for banks 2015, p. 5). In turn, the bank's risk management function and compliance department act as the second line, with the former responsible for identifying, measuring, monitoring, and reporting varied risks on an enterprise-wide basis and the latter engaged in ensuring that the bank operates with integrity and is in compliance with applicable, laws, regulations, and internal policies. And, the internal audit function is charged with the third line of defense, which includes 'conducting risk-based and general audits and reviews to provide assurance to the board that the overall governance framework, including the risk governance framework, is effective and that policies and processes are in place and consistently applied' (BIS, Corporate governance principles for banks 2015, p. 5).

Specifically, the role of the bank board and its risk committee is underscored in sound risk governance, which embraces 'greater involvement in evaluating and pro-

9.2 Risk Management in General Banking Organizations

moting a strong risk culture in the organization; establishing the organization's risk appetite and conveying it through the risk appetite statement (RAS); and overseeing management's implementation of the risk appetite and overall governance framework.' Moreover, there is further emphasis on the role of external risk management actors, typically the financial regulators at both domestic and international level, in monitoring and guiding the overall risk management framework and effective implementations (BIS 2015, p. 4).

In practice, tailored risk management mechanisms, which are targeted at different key risks in banking organizations, are developed industrial-wide. For instance, credit risk management is employed to 'maximize a bank's risk-adjusted rate of return by maintaining credit risk exposure within acceptable parameters' (BIS 2000, p. 1). In this process, the bank needs to address, manage, and control any credit risk exposures in the entire portfolio, individual credits, and business transactions, take into account the dynamics between the credit risk and other risks, and set such risk as a critical component of the bank's overall risk governance arrangement. Meanwhile, the bank is obligated to maintain 'a keen awareness of the need to identify, measure, monitor, and control credit risk as well as to determine that they hold adequate capital against these risks and that they are adequately compensated for risks incurred' (BIS 2000, p. 1). Procedurally, the bank would be committed to, based on its own size and nature, 'establishing an appropriate credit risk environment; operating under a sound credit-granting process; maintaining an appropriate credit administration, measurement and monitoring process; and ensuring adequate controls over credit risk'(BIS 2000, p. 1)

Liquidity risk management, in principle, embraces a 'sound process for identifying, measuring, monitoring, and controlling liquidity risk' in banking organizations and requires a 'robust framework for comprehensively projecting cash flows arising from assets, liabilities, and off-balance sheet items over an appropriate set of time horizons' (BIS 2008, p. 3). Specifically, there is increasing emphasis, based on lessons from the 2007–2009 financial crisis, upon 'the importance of establishing a liquidity risk tolerance; the maintenance of an adequate level of liquidity, including through a cushion of liquid assets; the necessity of allocating liquidity costs, benefits and risks to all significant business activities; the identification and measurement of the full range of liquidity risks, including contingent liquidity risks; the design and use of severe stress test scenarios; the need for a robust and operational contingency funding plan; the management of intraday liquidity risk and collateral; and public disclosure in promoting market discipline (BIS 2008, p. 2).' Moreover, financial supervisors are expected play the most important role in reining liquidity risk exposures by assessing the adequacy of the bank's liquidity management framework, its liquidity position, and take timely or even 'intrusive' actions in cases of any deficiency in the aforesaid areas. And, various scenarios of stress tests, either short-term, protracted institutional-specific or market-wide, are developed and used to decide the liquidity of the bank.

The market risk management is more concerned with future uncertainties of the values of both on-and-off balance sheet financial items, which are caused mainly by the sudden changes in equity and commodity prices, foreign exchange rate, interest rate and their volatility and correlations. In general, these risks can be categorized into directional and non-directional ones and measured and hence managed through the use of the maturing gap analysis, duration analysis, value at risk (VAR), stress testing (BIS 2011).

In contrast with other risk management techniques, operational risk management, at the industrial level, is more extensive and extends to the bank's portfolio of all the products, activities, processes, and systems. A three-line defense mechanism, which is similar to the generic risk governance arrangement in the bank but with a special focus, is established for such risk, including the business line management, an independent corporate operational risk management function, and an independent review, which may vary greatly among the banking organizations considering its nature, complexity, size, as well as the risk profile of the bank's specific business activities. At the frontier, the business line management at various levels and localities (such as domestic or international, head office or subsidiaries and branches) is responsible for identifying and managing operational risks within its authority. In the intermediary, a functionally independent corporate operational risk function (CORF) constitutes the second line of defense, which effectively complements the first line defense. And it is mainly composed of operational risk measurement, reporting processes, risk committees, and responsibility for board reporting. Specifically, it should emphasize upon the business lines' inputs to, and outputs from, the bank's risk management, risk measurement, and reporting systems. And its independence varies among small and large banks. The third line of defense lies with the independent review, which is composed of verification of the risk management framework and validation of the quantification systems mainly, and is designed to challenge the bank's operational risk management controls, processes, and systems. Usually, such reviews are conducted by competent internal audit, staff independent of the operational risk management framework or suitably qualified external parties. And a strong risk culture and good communication among the three lines of defense are important characteristics of good operational risk governance (BIS 2008)

9.2.2 Variance in Risk Management in Different Model Countries

In the context of the intensive financial globalization and close intertwining among banking organizations across countries, especially the sweeping influences of

2007–2009 financial crisis and the unprecedented worldwide financial contagion it brought about, an international framework by BIS on risk management is widely adopted and implemented by different financial regulators and bank practitioners around the world. And as listed in Table 9.1, these pertain to a wide range of principles, rules, and guidance on different risk managements, relevant supplementary mechanisms, and the capital requirements on the bank. The wide compliance with BIS risk management framework by regulators and banking organizations lead to a converging risk management system in different model countries and at varied firm level.

On the flip side, however, BIS risk management framework works largely as guidance rather than mandatory requirements, and variances are unavoidable at the national and firm level. For instance, many adjustments have been made by varying regulators to accommodate their own national institutional settings. And in implementation, further changes are initiated by different banking organizations to adapt to their specific nature and complexity. These well manifest the different discourses of legitimacy and paradigm as discussed in previous chapters. In practice, these differences pertain to, in particular, the risk appetite, mechanisms for managing risks, and variations in risk management focuses.

As a key element of risk management, risk appetite refers to 'a high-level determination of how much risk a firm is willing to accept taking into account the risk/return attributes; it is often taken as a forward-looking view of risk acceptance' (BIS 2010, p. 7). It is sometimes used synonymously with risk tolerance, which is defined as 'a more specific determination of the level of variation a bank is willing to accept around business objectives that are often considered to be the amount of risk a bank is prepared to accept.' (BIS 2010, p. 7). Frequently, risk appetite is closely connected with the bank's risk culture and strategy, and implemented in various financial activities in different business lines.

Risk appetite is found to vary in different models of corporate governance in banking organizations. Generally, banks in the Anglo-Saxon model have a greater appetite for risks than their counterparts in the Continental and State-affected models. As it is frequently the investment banker who sits at the top of the bank as CEO or Chairman, it is not rare to find that the board of the banks in the Anglo-Saxon model sets a tone for higher risks and preferences for risky financial trading and innovations (Goldman Sachs 2012; Citi Group 2012; Bank of America 2012). In USA, for instance, highly risky bank loan products like NINA loans (No Income and No Asset loans), NINJA loans (No Income, No Jobs, No Assets) or Light Doc loans (Documents for loan application are very light, i.e., very limited credit record) were fanatically developed and extensively marketed to the public before the 2007–2009 financial crisis. Especially the NINJA loan, the very low-quality subprime loan, had extended the bank's risk appetite so far as it did not need any record of income, job, or evidence of assets, but just a simple borrower's credit rating which is no more than showing his willingness and ability to pay. These subprime bank loans frequently lead to extravagant risks and pose great threats to the whole financial system, as evidenced in the past 2007–2009 financial crisis (Langley 2008). Although such loans vanished, reluctantly, like a vapor in the desert, other transformed substitutes

190   9   Risk Management System in Corporate Governance …

Table 9.1 Selected key guideline, principles, and rules for risk management in banking organizations by BIS under Pillar I, II, and III

Categories of risk	Key guideline, principles, and rule for risk management in banking organizations
General structure	Principles for enhancing corporate governance, October 2010 Compensation principles and standards assessment methodology, January 2010 Enhancements to the Basel II framework, July 2009; and Principles for sound stress testing practices and supervision, May 2009
Capital adequacy	Revisions to the Basel II market risk framework (updated as of December 31, 2010), February 2011 Minimum requirements to ensure loss absorbency at the point of non-viability, January 2011 Consultative document on capitalization of bank exposures to central counterparties, December 2010 Sound practices for back-testing counterparty credit risk models, December 2010 Guidance for national authorities operating the countercyclical capital buffer, December 2010 Basel III: A global regulatory framework for more resilient banks and banking systems, December 2010 Guidelines for computing capital for incremental risk in the trading book, July 2009 Enhancements to the Basel II framework, July 2009 Range of practices and issues in economic capital frameworks, March 2009 International convergence of capital measurement and capital standards: a revised framework, comprehensive version, June 2006 International convergence of capital measurement and capital standards, July 1988
Credit risk	Sound practices for back-testing counterparty credit risk models, December 2010 FSB Report on principles for reducing reliance on CRA ratings, October 2010; Enhancements to the Basel II framework, July 2009 Sound credit risk assessment and valuation for loans, June 2006 Principles for the management of credit risk, September 2000; Sound credit risk assessment and valuation for loans, June 2006 Principles for the management of credit risk, September 2000 Joint Forum cross-sectoral review of group-wide identification and management of risk concentrations, April 2008 Sound credit risk assessment and valuation for loans, June 2006; Principles for managing credit risk, September 2000 Principles for the management of credit risk, September 2000
Market risk	Revisions to the Basel II market risk framework (updated as of December 31, 2010), February 2011 Interpretive issues with respect to the revisions to the market risk framework, February 2011 Guidelines for computing capital for incremental risk in the trading book, July 2009 Supervisory guidance for assessing banks' financial instrument fair value practices, April 2009 Amendment to the Capital Accord to incorporate market risks, January 2005 Principles for the management and supervision of interest rate risk, July 2004

(continued)

9.2 Risk Management in General Banking Organizations

Table 9.1 (continued)

Categories of risk	Key guideline, principles, and rule for risk management in banking organizations
Liquidity risk	Basel III: International framework for liquidity risk measurement, standards and monitoring, December 2010 Principles for sound liquidity risk management and supervision, September 2008
Operational risk	Principles for the sound management of operational risk, June 2011; Recognizing the risk-mitigating impact of insurance in operational risk modeling, October 2010 High-level principles for business continuity, August 2006 Joint Forum outsourcing in financial services, February 2005
Internal control, compliance, audit, and reporting	Consultative document on the internal audit function in banks, November 2011 Enhancements to the Basel II framework, July 2009 Compliance and the compliance function in banks, April 2005 Framework for internal control systems in banking organizations, September 1998 Supervisory guidance for assessing bank' financial instruments fair value practices, April 2009 External audit quality and banking supervision, December 2008 The relationship between banking supervisors and banks' external auditors, January 2002
Disclosure and transparency	Pillar 3 disclosure requirements for remuneration, July 2011 Enhancements to the Basel II framework, July 2009; Basel II International measurement of capital measurement and capital standards, June 2006 Enhancing bank transparency, September 1998
Abuse of financial services	FATF AML/CFT Methodology, 2004, as updated FATF 40 + IX, 2003 Consolidated KYC risk management, October 2004 Shell banks and booking offices, January 2003 Customer due diligence for banks, October 2001

Source BIS Principles and Guidance on risk management in banking organizations

are innovated and marketed aggressively in the USA in the aftermath of the crisis, which are best exemplified by the car loans with minimum requirement for collaterals or guarantees.

Secondly, banks in this model are frequently involved in financial transactions or innovations, in which the risks are hard to be measured due to the complex financial trading structure and complication of risks inherited in nobody-understand *mysterious* financial products. For instance, as a part of the 'gambling culture,' the banks are aggressively engaged in trading speculative and highly risky financial derivatives like credit default swap (CDS), which are highly leveraged, too complicated to be measured accurately, and involve great uncertainties. This is well evidenced, for example, by the 'sinking' of the London Whale, where JPMorgan Chase took a highly risky derivative bet on CDS and lost around $ 5.8 billion but its risk officer apparently could not totally understand the risks of the transactions and the potential for ensuing losses (US 2013). Meanwhile, banks in the Anglo-Saxon model have been fanatically engaged in 'originate to distribute' pattern of riskier securitized loan business, which creates a long chain of risks, involves too many participants, and brings about many difficulties in precisely measuring the risks.

Thirdly, banking organizations in the Anglo-Saxon model are more proactive in global expansions, typically through transnational mergers and acquisitions, which frequently bring in more risks of various kinds and even go beyond the banks' financial limit. An illustrative example is the takeover of ABN AMRO by RBS, the said largest takeover in the banking history, which proved to be a 'bad mistake' and contributed to the falling of the RBS. In the process of this merger, various excessive risks are involved, such as risky transaction structure, increasing exposure to risky trading assets, and funding the acquisition by debts instead of equity (FSA, RBS Report 2011). Another example was the charge against HSBC for financing terrorisms, which was said to involve a bank merged by HSBC in its international expansion. Meanwhile, banks in this model may choose to over-extend the risk appetite to the extent that they 'take in more than they can chew,' which is typically observed in their reckless engagement in illegal transactions like the manipulation of LIBOR, mis-selling of ill-designed financial products, and money laundering as discussed in previous chapters.

In contrast, banks in the Continental and State-affected models, to some extent, are said to have a comparatively lower risk appetite, which reflects an orientation for the sustainable profitability and close integration into the real economy. For instance, banks in these models are actively engaged in traditional retail banking business which involves comparatively more direct and measurable risks, clearer lending and borrowing relationships, and specified counterparties. Moreover, the banks are more closely connected to the regional economic development and frequently finance the enterprises that they know well. Nevertheless, banks in these models may also have a high risk appetite and take risks beyond their reach, although in different perspectives. For instance, though the banks in both models are generally less active in initiating securitized loans, they may purchase such risky financial products as part of their investment portfolios, as best exemplified in buying voluminous subprime mortgage loans issued by US banks in 2008 financial crisis. Excessive risk taking in these models may also be connected with the banks' over-financing the industrial sector and enterprises in the real economy. For instance, in the banking crisis in 1990s in Japan, Japanese banks took excessive risks and over-extended bank loans, which had inflated the 'bubble' in the real estate industry. This kind of extravagant risk taking resulted in a high level of non-performing loans and might feed into deep economic recession. Another risky activity of the bank in Japan is the holding of shares or common stocks in the balance sheet, and the bursting of the stock price eroded a tremendous value of the bank's capital (Hoshi and Kashyap 2004; Fiji and Kawai 2010).

The divergence of the risk appetite by banking organizations across different model countries can be understood as a manifestation of varied legitimacy and paradigm discourses discussed in previous chapters. In the Anglo-Saxon model countries, the overwhelming paradigm of the shareholder primacy, which stresses on maximized profitability and best investment returns to the shareholders, apparently motivates the bank management to pursue excessive risks for higher returns. Specifically, constraints on excessive risk taking in banks are enfeebled due to the

9.2 Risk Management in General Banking Organizations

congruence of the interests of the management and shareholders, and inefficient monitoring by the depositors and the deposit insurance agency. Moreover, the significant correlation between executive compensation and risk taking encourages the bank executives to take in more risks without second thought. Such fanatic risk taking is further aggravated by various is further aggravated by various factors in the legitimacy discourses. For instance, the increasing financial disintermediation and separation from the real economy by the bank make the risks it faces more complicated, less direct, and less measurable. The pro-competition and deregulative posture by the financial regulators further encourage higher risk taking by the banking institutions. Indeed, such hands-off regulatory attitude empowers the banks to take more freedom in practicing whatever financial activities they prefer. On the flip side, however, strong orientation for free-market competition by regulators may also force the bank's managers to follow the 'jungle rule' in order to survive the challenges from within and beyond the banking industry, by means of taking more risks for better profitability. And, major legal impediments for charging liabilities on the bank's directors and managers, typically the prevalent irrational rationale of the bank's TBTF (Too big to fail) and defensive principles like business judgment doctrine, may render bank's management less subject to personal liabilities even in case of the bank failure caused by excessive risk taking and in turn motivates them to make bolder business decisions and take in risks beyond control.

In contrasting Continental and State-affected models countries, the paradigm discourse of the stakeholder theory and serious concerns for economic development, however, largely constrain the bank from pursuing excessive risks. Frequently, bank managers voluntarily focus on the long-term, sustainable, and steady profitability of the bank rather than the best performance in the short run by taking in higher risks. Meanwhile, illustrating the implication of the legitimacy discourse, typically the bank's integration into the real economy, close connections with the industry, and intertwining with enterprises, banking organizations in these models may have a more direct and better understanding of the risks they face. The strict financial regulation, manifested in explicit limitations on financial competitions and concerns for financial stability, also helps rein the excessive risk taking by the bank managers. And, considering the less significant correlation between executive pay and excessive risk taking, and the general long-termism held by most bank managers, the bank management in the Continental and State-affected models is less motivated to seek for riskier investment.

Alongside risk appetite, differences are also prominent in varied risk management mechanisms and diversified focuses across different model countries. Regarding credit risk management, for instance, many banks in the Anglo-Saxon model are more concerned with the potential default or degrading in the credit quality of the over-the-counter (OTC) derivative counterparties and issuers of the securities, considering the bank's proactive involvement in financial derivative products and trading. For example, US banks may identify that credit risk largely arises from the client transactions in OTC derivatives, securities financing transactions like resale or repurchase agreements and securities borrowing and lending activities, and receivables from brokers and dealers (Goldman Sachs 2012; Citi Group 2012). In contrast, credit risk management in the Continental and State-affected models lays specific emphasis on credit situations of industrial sectors, public finance, and key financial institutions. For example, in the Continental model countries like Germany, banks may closely monitor their massive lending to major sectors such as the mechanical engineering, automotive industry, and specific industry like shipping, which takes an outstanding proportion in the bank's balance sheet (Commerz Bank 2012). By supporting public finance, banks may hold a large part of the government's lending exposures and the borrowers are 'sovereigns, federal states, regions, cities and local authorities as well as supranational institutions' (Commerz Bank 2012, p. 172). Meanwhile, due to in-depth involvement in the passing Euro Crisis, banks in Germany are also subject to sovereign exposures to other falling EU countries like Greece, Ireland, Italy, Spain, and Portugal. There are further credit exposures to selected financial institutions, such as the national Federal Reserve Bank, the European Central Bank and certain European issuing banks classified as 'exceptional debtors.' Moreover, further credit risk exposures come from investments in Central and Eastern European economies where there is continued uncertainty as a result of the sovereign debt crisis (Commerz Bank 2012).

And, contrasting with their counterparts in the Continental and State-affected models, banking organizations in the Anglo-Saxon model countries, especially after 2007–2009 financial crisis, have experienced more stringent financial re-regulations and are henceforth subject to more prescriptive specific regulatory rules, principles, and various additional regulatory requirements, which result in further emphasis on the regulatory or compliance risk management. Meanwhile, considering their proactive global expansion and extensive international merger and acquisition activities, banks in this model are more prone to diversified financial regulations in various host countries. These lead to uncertainties of various kinds regarding the regulatory risk exposures which make legal compliance even more complicated. For instance, in USA, the Volcker Rule and regulation on the derivative markets have actually brought about a few new uncertainness regarding the standard and content of legal compliance. The new agencies created by Dodd-Frank Act, like the Bureau of Consumer Financial Protection, also result in some dubiety considering their authority to regulate. Moreover, regulatory uncertainties may also come from ongoing international changes, such as the financial transaction tax, capping on the bonuses of the bankers by EU, and varied impacts by Brexit (Citi Group 2012).

The variance in specific risk management in banking organizations across different model countries well echoes legitimacy discourses as discussed in Chap. 3. Steps away from the real economy, banks in the Anglo-Saxon model have most complicated risk management mechanisms to deal with more diversified and complex risks of different kinds. In credit risk management, for instance, the banks are more concerned with credit exposures to financial derivatives and securitization loan business from the 'fictitious economy.' Meanwhile, due to the proactive international expansion and financial re-regulation movements, banks in the Anglo-Saxon model are increasingly subject to more compliance and regulatory risks. In contrast, banks in the Continental and State-affected models, due to their close connection to the real economy, are more concerned with repayment of loans borrowed by varied enterprises and sovereigns.

And, though there are increasing requirements on regulatory and compliance risk management by the banking organizations, they are comparatively less extensive and stringent compared with their counterparts in the Anglo-Saxon model.

9.3 Risk Management in Chinese Banking Organizations

Similar to discussions on the aforesaid risk management, key risks in Chinese banks are categorized as credit risk, market risk, liquidity risk, and operational risk, though risks of other kinds are equally highlighted. Manifesting the legitimacy discourses elaborated in Chapter 6, risk management in Chinese banks reflects strong international influences and regulatory orientation. For instance, Chinese banking industry has been actively implementing the New Basel Capital Accord and well proceeded with Basel Pillar I, II and III, which are observable in the enhancement of the banks' risk management mechanism, relevant rules and procedures, IT systems, data and personnel. Specifically, a mature framework for the overall risk management under the New Basel Capital Accord is set in place. According to on-site inspections by CBRC, for example, most of the large-sized commercial banks met the requirements and submitted the application for implementing the New Basel Capital Accord (Bank B 2012; Bank A 2012; Bank C 2012; Bank D 2012). Meanwhile, the regulatory discourse plays a dominant role in the 'landing' of the international norms with respect to bank risk management. For instance, CBRC has been actively facilitating the establishment of the overall framework of risk management for Chinese banks in accordance with BIS principles and rules, and issues timely related guidance, rules and directives. However, the coherence of the aforesaid discourses can only be achieved through joint efforts from Chinese banking organizations, typically the large commercial banks, which reflects increasing financial deregulations and the trend of coordination between the government and the financial institutions. For instance, in preparing for relevant guideline on risk management, CBRC frequently invites representatives from major commercial banks, financial institutions, other relevant financial regulators, and academia for extensive consultation and discussion. In this process, Chinese commercial banks, not infrequently, take great initiatives to argue and bargain for their advantages. Moreover, the guidance by CBRC sometimes acts as an advisory official document, leaving to Chinese banks sufficient discretion in producing, ad hoc, their own risk management systems.

9.3.1 Overall Risk Management Framework

Given the great impact by the international influence and regulatory discourses, risk management system in Chinese banking organizations, in a wider sense, embraces a great variety of elements such as the internal control, auditing, and specific risk management mechanisms. First and foremost is the establishment of an overall risk management system, which is said to be a product of the BIS influence and regulator 'translation.' Such comprehensive risk management framework is purported to extend to the overall process of the bank's business operation, control all the perceivable risks in the bank's business activities at various levels, and cover personnel from the board of directors, senior managers to the general employees (Bank B 2012; Bank A 2012, Bank C 2012; Bank D 2012). This overall risk management system, in Chinese context, is founded upon the principles of compatibility between profits and risks, balance between efficiency and internal check and balance, mixed use of qualitative and quantitative methods, the dynamic adaptability and sustainable operational process (Bank B 2012).

In practice, the overall risk management system is well embedded in Chinese banking organizations, though not without variances. In Bank A, for example, the risk management committee under the board of directors takes full responsibility for formulating the bank group's risk strategy and policies, monitoring and evaluating the overall risks on a regular basis. Employing a more centralized structure, the bank develops a vertical risk management pattern, from 'head to hand' and through the channel of 'chief risk officer—risk supervisors—heads of risk management department—risk managers.' At the head office level, the chief risk officer (CRO) is responsible for the overall risk management and reports to the board of the directors. The risk management department, headed by CRO, is mainly engaged in formulating risk management policies, conducting risk measurement and analysis. Meanwhile, there is a specialized market risk management division and a risk management team for overseas entities set within the risk management department. The credit management department is engaged in credit approval and monitoring over related credit risk exposures. Other departments, at the head office level, take responsibility for managing related risk exposures within their own operations. At the branch level in varied localities, the one-tier branches for instance, the risk officers are obligated to head risk management and relevant credit approval issues and report directly to the CRO. At lower levels of the branches, such as the two-tier branches and subbranches, the risk officers take due responsibility in managing the specific risks in their local financial business (Bank A 2012). In this context, a matrix system of risk management is established where two reporting lines are set for controlling overall risk exposures throughout the bank group. The first reporting line goes vertically to the risk management officers at higher levels, while the second line extends horizontally to the management within their respective entities or business units. Moreover, an internal 'firewall' and a risk reporting system are further designed to prevent 'risk contagions' within the bank group (Bank A 2012).

As another key component in risk management framework, internal control plays an increasingly significant role in Chinese banks, which are largely shaped by various policy discourses, such as *The Basic Norms for Enterprise Internal Control*, *The Guidance for Internal Control for Commercial Banks* (CBRC 2007), and *The Guidance for Internal Control for Listed Corporations* (Shanghai Stock Exchange 2006). In practice, these policy orientations are well echoed by Chinese banking organizations. For instance, based upon related policies and guidance by CBRC, a wide range of internal policies for specific risk management are carefully drafted and implemented in Bank B, as exemplified by the bank's *Plan for the Establishment of Internal Control System for 2012–2014*, *The Strategic Planning for Bank B's Development for 2012–2014*, and *Handbook of the Compliance Management for Commercial Banks* (Bank B 2012). Such internal control system, meanwhile, is joined by various departments of the bank, such as the board of the directors, various board committees, and IT department. The internal auditing system, on the other hand, is also active in facilitating efficient risk management and stresses on certain significant aspects in the bank's business operations, such as financial profitability, economic efficiency, financial innovations, and controlled risk exposures throughout the bank group. Meanwhile, for better and sound internal control practices, renowned international auditing firms are hired to review and issue independent auditing opinions regarding the bank's risk management practice (Bank B 2012).

9.3.2 Risk Appetite and Specific Risk Management Mechanism

Distinguished as the starting point of good risk management in banking organizations, risk appetite is pivotal in deciding the overall risk strategy, mechanisms for risk management and control, and resilient business operations. In the context of Chinese banking industry, risk appetite is shaped by many factors, such as expectations from key stakeholders like creditors and depositors, the state as the majority shareholder, and the orientation by the financial regulator. As observed in the sampled banks, moderate risk appetite is widely adopted in large-sized Chinese commercial banks. For instance, Bank D implements a 'steady' risk appetite that reinforces strict compliance with laws, regulations and the new BIS capital agreement, which aims to achieve the balance of varied objectives, such as the financial stability, profitability, and sound liquidity. These are well demonstrated in the bank's overall business strategy of moderate risk taking for moderate profit returns, maintaining capital adequacy, and facilitating enhanced risk management to cope with its business expansion and financial innovations (Bank D 2012). Targeted at 'steady and stable business operations', Bank C stresses upon optimizing allocation of the bank's capital and maximizing the shareholders' interests within tolerable range of risks. And, by establishing a well-measured risk appetite for the whole bank group, the bank pursues the risk principles of 'Rationality, Steadiness, and Prudence' and strikes a balance between the bank's risk taking and profitability (Bank C 2012, p54). Bank B, on the other hand, issues the internal *Regulations on Risk Preference (Trial)* and clarifies its general risk appetite throughout the bank group. For example, targeted at the risk-adjusted profit maximization, the bank reinforces the implementation of risk preference which is monitored by means of periodical reviews and the well-designed efficient reporting system (Bank B 2012). Similarly, in setting the risk appetite of the bank, Bank A pursues a steady and sustainable profitability strategy within tolerable range of various risks (Bank A 2012).

The specific risk appetite in risk management framework by Chinese banks is found to manifest the discourses of legitimacy and paradigm discussed in previous chapters. For instance, echoing the paradigm of the diversified stakeholder theory, Chinese banks are inclined to take moderate risk appetite and concentrate on the long-term profitability, sustainable development, and steady growth. This is reinforced by the fact that the state acts as the large shareholder (in the large-sized state-owned commercial banks specifically), who can be more patient with the bank's performance and focuses on the bank's viable profitability and its significant financial contribution to the national economy. In particular, as risk taking and maximized profitability is less related to the executive compensation in many large-sized Chinese banks, the senior management is responsively less motivated to take excessive risks which will not necessarily advance their personal interests. Low risk tolerance in Chinese banks is also a reflection of the legitimacy discourses. With great emphasis on national financial stability, Chinese financial regulators have been maintaining close supervision over the bank's risk taking and restrict the banks from excessively risky activities. Meanwhile, as the banking industry is heavily regulated in China, such as strict market entrance control, more restrictions on financial innovations, and implicit containment over interests rate (though such control is being removed gradually), competitions among banks are comparatively limited and many bank boards and senior managers (especially in large-sized banking organizations) are under less stress to compete and thereof have even less incentives to take in higher risks for the sake of best performance and maximized investment returns to safeguard their posts (in contrast with what happens in the Anglo-Saxon model countries). This is reinforced by the general culture on risks in China which is risk-averse rather risk loving.

To address, control, and manage various risk exposures, tailored risk management mechanisms are developed in Chinese banking organizations, such as credit risk management, market risk management, liquidity risk management, and operational risk management. Among them, credit risk management is frequently prioritized, which is purported to adjust and optimize the structure of the bank's credit in accordance with policy orientations, fast changes in macroeconomic situations, and requirements by the financial regulators. In practice, this mainly involves varied credit policies on different industries and key financial products. Moreover, credit risk management in Chinese banks has to take into account, in particular, the preferential regional credit policy targeted at satisfying the needs of the local development, timely repayment for the bank loans, and optimization of the bank's monitoring and information system (Bank B 2012; Bank A 2012). For instance, there is increasingly stricter control over financial lending to the financing platform by the local government, the real estate industry, and enterprises categorized as 'Highly Polluting, Highly Energy Consuming, and Over-Capacity' (Bank B 2012; Bank A 2012; Bank D 2012; Bank C 2012).

With regard to risk management in bank loans to the financing platform by local governments, for example, various mechanisms are employed to mitigate credit risk exposures, which embrace more restrictive credit policy, centralization of credit approval (from the branches to the head office), and constraints over annual increase rate. Specifically, for the outstanding government platform loans,

9.3 Risk Management in Chinese Banking Organizations

the banks conduct further reassessments, reconfirm the sources for repayment, and initiate specialized inspections (Bank B 2012; Bank C 2012; Bank D 2012). And, with regard to credit risk management on bank lending to the real estate industry, Chinese banks develop industrial-specific loan policies, which is purported to cope with latest changes in Chinese real estate market and enhance the bank's capacity in managing fast-changing risk exposures. In practice, different measures are innovated, such as the quota management, controlled credit scale, and list management on targeted real estate developers. Meanwhile, Chinese banks have started to impose higher standards for market entrance, set stricter conditions for funded estate projects, optimize relevant loan products, and differentiate investment preferences for various regions. Regarding loans to ongoing real estate projects, for instance, stricter scrutiny and preventive measures are taken, such as requirements for complementary collaterals or guarantees, periodical assessment on the value of the mortgage and the mortgage ratio, and timely re-evaluation of the mortgaged assets (Bank B 2012; Bank C 2012; Bank D 2012).

For credit risk management in financial lending to environmental protection sectors, which actually poses new challenges to Chinese banking organizations, there is observed increasing repression on bank loans to 'Highly Polluting, Highly Energy Consuming, and Over-Capacity' industries while strong support for the green industry, i.e., the environmental friendly businesses (Bank B 2012; Bank C 2012; Bank D 2012). Meanwhile, new industrial-specific credit policy is initiated to strengthen risk management for differentiated sectors, which aims to efficiently adjust bank investment in highly credit-concentrated industrial sectors, facilitate development of emerging industries with national strategic importance, and update the manufacturing and modern service industries (Bank B 2012). Another 'minefield' for credit risk management in Chinese context is increasingly massive loans to SMEs, which requires more intensive and complicated risk control due to less mature market environment and vulnerable credibility of such under-developed enterprises. These pertain to enhanced administration over approval procedures for SME-related credits, effective ongoing supervision and specialized analysis, routine and structured monitoring, and periodical on-site inspections. Other measures embrace designing prudential credit policies for SMEs loans, promoting digital management, and standardizing relevant business processes (Bank B 2012; Bank C 2012; Bank D 2012). Meanwhile, internal credit rating system is established within Chinese banks to achieve better control over the loan assets, which, based on the possibility of repayment for principals and interests, is categorized into five categories: normal, concerned, subprime, suspicious, and losses. In Bank A and Bank B, in particular, a more specific and tailored twelve-grading system is developed which takes into account of the number of the default months, the expected loss rate, the credit conditions, the adequacy of the guarantee, and other qualitative and quantitative factors (Bank A 2012; Bank B 2012).

The specific risk management mechanisms are shown to manifest the discourses of paradigm and legitimacy embedded in corporate governance in Chinese banks. For instance, implicated by the paradigm of the diversified stakeholder theory and legitimacy of bank's integration into the real economy, credit risk management in Chinese banks focuses more on risk exposures in financing national economic development and regional economic growth. Echoing the close connection between the bank and industrial sectors, credit risk management pays close attention to bank loans to the real estate industry and the polluting, over-capacity, and excessive energy-consuming sectors. And, resonating with the bank's support for enterprises, especially the SMEs, credit risk management in Chinese banks lays special emphasis on SME-related financial lending. Meanwhile, the bank's credit risk management is also representation of China's strict financial re-regulation, such as restrictions and containment over credits to the local government financial platform, the real estate industry, and the 'High Polluting, High-Energy Consuming, and Over-Capacity' industries.

9.4 Conclusion

Continuing the discursive institutional analysis, the present chapter explores another significant element of corporate governance in banking organizations, risk management, and focuses specifically on varied categories of risks, the risk appetite, and specific key risk management mechanisms in different model countries. Specifically, the chapter reveals the impacts of the varied paradigm and legitimacy discourses in shaping key practices in risk management in divergent institutional settings, such as risk appetite and risk management arrangements. In Chinese institutional scenario, however, risk management in the banking industry is found to be greatly influenced by international and domestic regulatory discourses, which centers on the formation of the overall risk management framework, the complementary functions of internal control and auditing, and moderate risk appetites for the sake of sustainable profitability. And, subject to implications of legitimacy discourses discussed in Chapter 6, certain key risk management mechanisms are designed, in particular, to address risk exposures from financing the real economy, industrial sectors, and SMEs, which are readily observable in the bank's credit risk management. The next chapter, as the final piece of the whole jigsaw, will explore legal duties in Chinese bank governance, which have gained great weight in the aftermath of the global financial crisis.

References

Bank A. (2012). 2011 Annual Report of Bank A, Bank A. Retrieved May 25, 2012 from http://www.BankA.com.

Bank B. (2012). 2011 Annual Report of Bank B, Bank B. Retrieved May, 2012 from http://www.BankB.com.

Bank C. (2012). 2011 Annual Report of Bank C, Bank C. Retrieved May 25, 2012 from http://www.BankC.com.

Bank D. (2012). 2011 Annual Report of Bank D, Bank D. Retrieved May 25, 2012 from http://www.BankD.com.

References

Bank of America. (2012). 2011 Annual Report of Bank of America, Bank of America. Retrieved October 15, 2012 from http://www.bankofamerica.com.

BIS, Bank for International Settlements & Group of Ten. (1994). Macroeconomic and monetary policy issues raised by the growth of derivatives markets. Bank for International Settlements.

BIS. (1996). *Amendment to the Capital Accord to Incorporate Market Risks*. Basel Committee on Banking Supervision.

BIS. (2000). *Principles for the Management of Credit Risk*. Switzerland: Basel Committee on Banking Supervision.

BIS. (2008). *Principles for Sound Liquidity Risk Management and Supervision*. Switzerland: Basel Committee on Banking Supervision.

BIS. (2010). *Principles for Enhancing Corporate Governance*. Switzerland: Basel Committee on Banking Supervision.

BIS. (2011). *Principles for the Sound Management of Operational Risk*. Switzerland: Basel Committee on Banking Supervision.

BIS, Basel Committee on Banking Supervision Switzerland. (2015). *Corporate Governance Principles for Banks*. Switzerland: Basel Committee on Banking Supervision.

China Shanghai Stock Exchange. (2006). *The Guidance for Internal Control for Listed Corporations*. Shanghai: Shanghai Stock Exchange.

China Banking Regulatory Commission. (2007). *Opinions on guiding the credit extension regarding energy saving and pollution reduction* (Vol. 83). Beijing: China Banking Regulatory Commission.

Citi Group. (2012). 2011 Annual Report of Citi Group, Citi Group. Available at http://www.Citigroup.com. Accessed 15 October 2012.

Commerzbank (2012). 2011 Annual Report of Commerzbank, Commerzbank, Available at http://www.commerzbank.com. Accessed 15 October 2012.

Crockett, A. (1997). Why is financial stability a goal of public policy?. *Economic Review-Federal Reserve Bank of Kansas City, 82*, 5–22.

FSA. UK Financial Services Authority (2011), The failure of the Royal Bank of Scotland. Report, Financial Services Authority, UK.

Fujii, M., & Kawai, M. (2010). *Lessons from Japan's banking crises 1991–2005*, (Working Paper, No. 222). Retrieved June 9, 2010.

Goldman Sachs. (2012). 2011 Annual Report of Goldman Sachs, Goldman Sachs. Available at http://www.goldmansachs.com. Accessed October 15, 2012.

Hoshi, Takeo, & Kashyap, Anil K. (2004). Japan's financial crisis and economic stagnation. *Journal of Economic Perspectives, 18*(1), 3–26.

Kaufman, H. (2009). *The road to financial reformation: Warnings, consequences, reforms*. John Wiley & Sons.

Langley, P. (2008). Sub-prime mortgage lending: A cultural economy. *Economy and Society, 37*(4), 469–494.

US Securities and Exchange Commission (SEC) (2013). Summary of Charges by SEC against the Financial Industry and the Collection of Fines and Compensation, Revised on January 9th, 2013. Retrieved January 25, 2013 from http://www.sec.gov/spotlight/enf-actions-fc.shtml.

Chapter 10
Legal Duties in Chinese Bank Governance

10.1 Introduction

As the final piece of the puzzle, Chap. 10 explores legal duties of the bank in the context of corporate governance in banking organizations, which has been prioritized both by the banking industry and financial regulators across countries since and in the aftermath of the 2008 global financial crisis. Starting with discussion on legal duties in generic corporate governance, the chapter investigates specialized legal duties in the scenario of bank governance, which mainly embrace the compliance duty and fiduciary duty, with the former focusing on the duty to comply with the regulatory requirements and the latter comprising the duty of care, duty of loyalty, and duty of disclosure. On such basis, the present chapter continues to elaborate legal duties in Chinese bank governance, namely, the specific compliance duty and fiduciary duties in Chinese institutional settings. Representing, predominantly, the paradigm discourses of the diversified stakeholder theory and the legitimacy discourse of financial regulation, the compliance duty analyzes how Chinese banks comply with the laws and regulations in their business operation, anti-money laundering campaigns, and anti-corruption efforts. The fiduciary duties in Chinese banks, on the other hand, explore how the duty of care, the duty of loyalty, and the duty of disclosure are constituted by the regulatory discourses, which well resonate the paradigm discourses of the enhanced shareholder primacy.

10.2 Legal Duties in Generic Corporate Governance

As a significant element in corporate governance, legal duties start to attract great attention in the aftermath of the 2007–2009 global financial crises, especially the fiduciary duties owned by varied major corporate participants like the board directors, managers, and controlling shareholders. Originating from the trust law

© Springer Nature Singapore Pte Ltd. 2019

W. Zou, *Corporate Governance in the Banking Sector in China*, CSR, Sustainability,
Ethics & Governance, https://doi.org/10.1007/978-981-13-3510-5_10

in the Anglo-Saxon legal system for describing the nature of the duties imposed upon a trustee, fiduciary duty is now frequently used in corporate law and corporate governance. It requires that officers, directors and controlling shareholders own enforceable duties to the corporation and through the corporation to the shareholders (Bauman et al. 2007, p. 639). Generally, the fiduciary duty is composed of the duty of care and duty of loyalty, though sometimes the duty of disclosure is included as well. The fiduciary duty is now widely accepted and enforced in different model countries, but differences can be readily observed, such as the standard of the duty, the possibility of incurring a civil liability, and the role of the judge.

The duty of care, in the context of corporate governance, refers to the duty by the directors and managers to act in the best interests of the corporation, exercise reasonable care in making business decisions, and perform efficient monitoring upon the operation of the corporation (OECD 2004). In the Anglo-Saxon model, typically, the duty of care largely employs an objective standard which defines the care 'as an ordinarily prudent person in a like position would use under similar circumstances.' (US, Model Business Corporate Act 2002). It specifically stresses upon efficient oversight by the board directors, their adequate competence and qualifications (such as professional knowledge, skills, experience), and due diligence (Francis v. United Jersey Bank 1981). Furthermore, the duty of care pertains to reasonable monitoring and inquiry on corporate business operations, though there is a dispute regarding the standard, whether applying the red flag event criterion (Graham v. Allis-Chalmers Manufacturing Co. 1963) or the establishment of a permanent monitoring system (Irem Caremark 1994). Similar settings on the duty of care can be observed in the Continental model, though not without variances. For example, German corporate code requires that the board of directors and management must act with diligence of a prudent businessman and the breach of which will lead to personal liabilities (Germany Code of Corporate Governance 2012). In contrast, the standards and rules regarding the duty of care are less rich and detailed than those developed by its Anglo-Saxon counterpart, considering the limited and passive role by the court in 'making law' and legal precedents only used as reference without sufficient legal enforceability.

The duty of loyalty, on the other hand, requires the directors, managers, and controlling shareholders prioritize the interests of the corporation over their own private interests, and restrain from the conflict of interests activities like self-dealings or related transactions with the corporation (OECD 2004). In the Anglo-Saxon model, the key concern on the duty of loyalty is the self-dealing by the management, defined as 'transaction between a corporation and one or more of its directors or officers…or an organization in which one or more of its directors or officers are directors or officers, or have a financial interest.' (US Del. Code Ann. tit. 8, § 144 2005). More than often, such deals must be approved by a majority of disinterested directors or shareholder after full disclosure or proved to be of fair value to the corporation, which is not different from a general arm-length transaction in the market. In practice, however, the application of such principle is complicated due to the confusing coverage, the different meaning of 'disinterested director' at ad hoc basis, and the difficulty in defining the fairness of the transaction. Other concerns of the duty of loyalty can

10.2 Legal Duties in Generic Corporate Governance

be observed in expropriation activities by the managers such as embezzlement of corporate assets (Bauman et al. 2007).

In the Continental model country, similarly, the duty of loyalty pertains to the board of directors, management, and controlling shareholders. In Germany, for example, different requirements on the duty of loyalty are prescribed for the management board and supervisory board, with the former subject to much stricter and wider restrictions. Specifically, the management board directors are prohibited from competing with the corporation in any means or taking advantages for personal interests. With regard to related transactions involving the member of the management board, they will not be valid unless approved by the supervisory board while the management board has no *say*. For the duty of loyalty by the supervisory board, in contrast, a demanding requirement of independence is set in place, which explicitly separates its members from the management board. However, though restrictions are imposed upon deals between the corporation and the member from either the management board or supervisory board, they do not necessarily pertain to the related transactions between the corporation and relatives of the directors or firms in which directors have a substantial shareholding (Baums and Scott 2005).

In particular, the Continental model, differentiated from the Anglo-Saxon model, lays extra emphasis upon the problem of competing interests between the majority and minority shareholders. For instance, German corporate law specifically addresses related transactions between its majority shareholders and the corporation and requires the duty of loyalty be owned by the majority shareholder toward the minority ones. It demands full disclosure of such (relevant) transactions in the firm's annual report prepared by the external independent auditors, though such information is only available to the supervisory board instead of the shareholders (Baums and Scott 2005).

As the third pillar of the fiduciary duty, the duty of disclosure requires the board directors and managers to disclose all the relevant information regarding the corporation business and operation, which may affect the decision making by the investors. And, the key component of this duty is the materiality of information. Applying the objective standard, the materiality of information frequently involves the significance or certainty of the omitted or misrepresented fact in influencing the decision making by a reasonable investor (OECD 2004). In general, standards for the duty of disclosure are much stricter and more extensive in the Anglo-Saxon model than those in the Continental model. In USA, for example, the Securities and Exchange Commission (SEC) requires that the corporation should provide all the material information to the shareholders for making an informed voting decision. Conceptually, the test of materiality is that 'there must be a substantial likelihood that the disclosure of the omitted fact would have been viewed by the reasonable investor as having significantly altered the "total mix" of the information made available' (Bauman et al. 2007, p. 256). And, with regard to the contingent or speculative information or event, the standard of materiality expands to consider 'a balancing of both the indicated probability that the event will occur and the anticipated magnitude of the event in light of the totality of the company activity' (Bauman et al. 2007, p. 258). The materiality of misstatement of omissions can be categorized as quantitative or qualitative.

The former, widely used by US courts and SEC, stresses upon economic benchmarks as the investor is most concerned with the financial returns on their investment. The latter, which is drawing increasing attention, takes into account 'the subjective intentions and motivations of those involved in making disclosure decisions without reference to the economic significance of the information in question' (Bauman et al. 2007, p. 259). However, the test of materiality is not limited to the investor protection and can extend to some other goal, typically the public interests (SEC, Sect. 14 a; Russell, 1976).

In contrast, the duty of disclosure is less restrictive in the Continental model. In Germany, for instance, the liability for breach of the duty of disclosure is incurred mainly in cases of release of false and misleading material information or omission of major information to the shareholders in securities prospectus, interim reports, and financial statements. The board of directors and managers will not be imposed liability unless proven to maliciously deceive in the process of information disclosure (Baums and Scott 2005). In general, breach of the fiduciary duty by the board directors, managers, and controlling shareholders may lead to personal liabilities or even criminal charges. However, there are barricades for effective enforcement of the fiduciary duty, and it is not an easy job to find the directors and management liable for violation due to varied standards, hardship in procuring persuasive evidence, and complementary protection for corporate directors and managers. In cases of the duty of care, for instance, there are obstacles like inconsistency on the standard of care, and prevalence of the business judgment rule which restrains the court from second-guessing the merit of the business decision (Aronson v. Lewis 1984; Smith v. Van Gorkom 1985; US Principles of Corporate Governance, 2009). Meanwhile, the 'Director and Officer' insurance, which is widely used in corporations nowadays, may cover a wide range of liabilities by the board directors and managers for their wrongdoings. Similar obstacles can be found in cases of the duty of loyalty and duty of disclosure, though not without variances (Bauman et al. 2007).

Another barrier lies in the difficulty in initiating legal actions by the shareholders against the liable directors and managers. Due to the 'fictitious' legal personality of the corporation, to whom the directors and managers may be held liable, the shareholders can only bring about indirect suits, i.e., the derivative suits, through the corporation to seek legal recourses against the directors and managers for breaching their fiduciary duties (Bauman et al. 2007). This is made even harder by the fact that it is the board of directors (in the Anglo-Saxon model) or the supervisory board (in the Continental model) who is entitled to decide whether to proceed the legal actions or not. In most cases, the board of directors is reluctant to initiate the charges as such legal actions may indeed challenge their duty of monitoring. Even if a case is filed, obstacles of varying kinds exist which may dilute its merit and efficacy, such as defensive maneuvers, appeals, and delay for different reasons. Comparatively, the derivative suit is more popular in the Anglo-Saxon model than its continental counterpart considering more active roles by the judges. And, due to the allowance on contingent fees in fiduciary duty cases, the lawyers in the Anglo-Saxon model are also more motivated to solicit such litigations from the grievance shareholders.

10.3 Legal Duties in Corporate Governance in Banking Organizations

In the context of corporate governance in banking organizations, legal duties can mainly be categorized into the compliance duty and fiduciary duty. The former falls under the umbrella of extensive regulatory responsibilities, where financial regulators play dominant roles and violations will incur disciplinary, administrative, or even criminal penalties. The latter, similar to the discussion of legal duties in generic firms, largely refers to the fiduciary duty by the board directors and management of the bank and embraces the duty of care, duty of loyalty, and duty of disclosure, where the court plays most important function and the breach will lead to personal or economic liabilities.

The compliance duty in bank governance mainly focuses on complying with laws, regulations, and relevant standards. In a wider sense, this duty goes beyond legally binding norms and embraces broader standards of integrity and ethical conducts. It involves a great variety of sources such as primary legislations, rules, and standards issued by regulators, market conventions, codes of practice by the industrial association, and the bank's internal codes of conduct. In practice, the compliance duty pertains to 'observing proper standards of market conduct, managing conflicts of interest, treating customers fairly, and ensuring the suitability of customer advice', as well as some specific areas like prevention of money laundering and terrorist financing and meeting tax laws related to certain banking products and services (BIS 2005, p. 12). Frequently, the compliance duty is intertwined with risk management, such as legal or compliance risk management, as briefly discussed in risk management Chap. 9.

The other set of legal duty in banks, similar to those discussed in generic firms, is the fiduciary duty which requires the board of directors and managers 'exercise their "duty of care" and "duty of loyalty" to the bank under applicable national laws and supervisory standards', and includes 'engaging actively in the major matters of the bank and keeping up with material changes in the bank's business and the external environment, as well as acting to protect the interests of the bank' (BIS 2010, p. 27). Meanwhile, the duty of disclosure, as another key component of the fiduciary duty, may play a significant role in corporate governance in banking organizations, especially considering the 2007–2009 financial crises when the banks were said to hold back material information of various kinds from the investors, creditors, and the regulators.

In general, the fiduciary duty extends mainly to the bank board directors, the management, and the controlling shareholders. Considering the industrial specialty of the bank, however, the fiduciary duty may be more extensive and subject to higher standards in contrast with generic firms. For instance, not only does the fiduciary duty cover the interests of the bank's shareholders, it may also extend to protections of varied stakeholders such as creditors, depositors and clients, or even regulators who provide deposit insurance for the bank and bail it out in times of financial crises. Furthermore, the bank is argued to bear a wider fiduciary duty to the public due to its immense impacts on national economy and the society at large (US, Dodd-Frank Act 2010).

However, similar to legal duties explored in generic corporate governance, variances can be observed in different models of corporate governance in banking organizations. In general, the fiduciary duty in banks is observed to be more specific, diversified, and stringent in the Anglo-Saxon model countries compared with its counterparts in the Continental and State-affected models. For instance, in the Anglo-Saxon model, the fiduciary duty in bank governance is distinguished case by case and a careful distinction is made for different circumstances. Meanwhile, a set of more extensive criteria is developed, along with higher standards and stricter liabilities. And, the fiduciary duty by the board of directors and management may be further integrated into specific corporate governance system of the bank. In JMPC for instance, a mechanism of fiduciary risk management is established as part of the business risk committees, which is specifically designed to deal with particular issues of fiduciary duties and ensure that the investment and risk management products or services (which may give rise to fiduciary duties to clients) will be provided at appropriate standards relative to their fiduciary relationship with a client (JP Morgan Chase & Co. (2012). In contrast, the fiduciary duty for banks in the Continental and State-affected models are comparatively less specified by the regulators and legislators and frequently referred to general norms in the corporate law and code of corporate governance (Misawa 2005).

The variances of the fiduciary duty in corporate governance of banking organizations across different model countries, though present in the duty of loyalty and the duty of disclosure, is best exemplified in the duty of care. Contrasting with the Anglo-Saxon model, there are comparatively less specified principles or rules, in generic firms, on the duty of care by the corporate board directors and managers in the Continental model or State-affected model. And, in the context of banking organizations, even fewer stipulations are found with regard to the specific standards imposed on the bank board directors and managers for their duty of care and relevant civil liabilities (Misawa 2005). In the Continental model, for instance in Germany, the bank board directors and managers are generally required to perform their duties based on the generic standard of duty of care. And 'If they violate the due care and diligence of a prudent and conscientious Managing Director or Supervisory Board member, they are liable to the company for damages' (Germany Code of Corporate Governance 2012, p. 5). Meanwhile, 'The Supervisory Board must take care that he/she has sufficient time to perform his/her mandate' (el. at. Germany Code of 237 Corporate Governance 2012, p. 12).

In contrast, more specific and detailed requirements on the duty of care by the bank board directors and managers are readily observed in the Anglo-Saxon model, especially in USA. For instance, the US court cyclically raises the standard of care by the bank's directors and managers and imposes a more stringent liability, which is largely a fairly positive legal response to the occurrence of the financial crisis. Typically, the court may shift from considering the fairness of the business decision-making process to the scrutiny of the more substantive decision, its end result, and consequence in relevant bank cases (Villa 2013).

10.3 Legal Duties in Corporate Governance in Banking Organizations

In contrast with the board directors in generic firms, bank directors are said to be subject to a higher standard for the duty of care considering the trust invested in them by the creditors and depositors. 'While legalistically the relation between the bank and its depositors is that of debtor and creditor, practically the directors are charged with the trust responsibility to see that depositors' funds are safely and providently invested' and 'the main responsibility of the director is for the safe and legal application of the bank funds in the form of loans and investments' (Broderick, as Superintendent of Banks of the State of New York v. Marcus 1934). In this scenario, the duty of care by bankers who are positioned as financial specialists, goes beyond the standard of ordinary care and 'a bank director should perform his or her duty as banking professional in such a manner that a violation of duty as a professional constitutes a violation of a bona fide manager's duty of care' (Misawa 2005, p. 19). Specifically, subject to a more stringent standard of care as a 'prudent banker' (Litwin v. Allen 1940), the bank director 'shall bear fiduciary duty of providing reasonable monitoring relative to bank operations' and 'properly monitor lending functions, — ascertaining the situations of the bank, and monitoring them exercising their monitoring right in reasonable manners' (Misawa 2005, p. 26). Meanwhile, financial regulators may further enhance the standard of care born by the bank director and managers. For instance, the Dodd-Frank Act authorizes FDIC to claw back up to 2 years of compensation paid to the bank's directors and managers, if they are found substantially responsible for the failure of the bank. These may involve the board directors and senior managers who are responsible for the strategic policy making or company-wide operational decisions for the bank, or found liable by the court for breach of his duty of loyalty, or removed from the post by FDIC due to his responsibility in the failure of the bank (Dodd-Frank Act 2010; Villa 2013).

The variances of legal duties in different models manifest different paradigm and legitimacy discourses as discussed in Chap. 3. In contrast with the Continental and State-affected models, the Anglo-Saxon model, reflecting the paradigm of shareholder primacy, apparently provides stronger and better legal protections for investors by means of more extensive fiduciary duty, stringent standards, and stricter liabilities, which aim to mitigate the agency problem and maximize investment returns to the investors. For instance, to bring about a better performance of the bank and mitigate the shirking problem, a higher standard of duty of care is set in place which requires the bank board directors and managers to perform their due diligence, adequate prudence in decision making, and sufficient monitoring over the bank's operations as banking professionals. Meanwhile, the variances in legal duties are also representation of different legitimacy discourses of legal intervention. For instance, the Anglo-Saxon model presents more legal interventions by the court, the regulator, and the law firm, and the dominance of the market institutions and the arm's length relationship between and among different market players reinforces the status of the judiciary to resolve disputes by private parties. And, such active legal intervention is, typically, observed in higher standards of fiduciary duty by the bank directors and managers.

In contrast, reflecting the paradigms of the stakeholder theory and the hybrid of model, strong legal protections for shareholders are comparatively less prevalent in the Continental and State-affected models. The fiduciary duty on the bank board directors and managers, for example, is less extensive, less strict, and frequently less possible to lead to the imposition of the legal liabilities. Though there are laws, guidance, and rules regarding the generic fiduciary duty of corporate directors and managers, specific legal standards for bank directors and management are not abundant as their counterpart in the Anglo-Saxon model (another possibility is that many of the specific rules regarding the bank directors and managers are in German or French and not available in English version). Moreover, legal duties in the Continental and State-affected models countries manifest certain legitimacy discourses. For instance, resonating with limited legal intervention and comparatively self-constrained posture of the courts, legal duties in the bank are less diversified.

10.4 Legal Duties in Corporate Governance of Chinese Banks

In Chinese institutional settings, similar legal duties are observed in corporate governance in banking organizations, which embrace the compliance duty at public law and fiduciary duty at private law. The former largely falls under the umbrella of extensive regulatory responsibilities, where financial regulators, like PBC, CBRC, and MoF play dominant roles, and the violations of which will frequently lead to disciplinary, administrative or even criminal penalties. The latter set of obligations, on the other hand, embrace the duty of care, duty of loyalty and duty of disclosure, which, given the powerful influence of the regulatory discourse in Chinese context, is largely produced and shaped by varied financial regulators rather than the court. For instance, CBRC issues a great variety of guidance and principles on the fiduciary duty by Chinese banks' board directors and managers.

10.4.1 Legal Compliance Practices

The compliance duty, in Chinese context, requires that the bank's business operation, activities, and practice comply with various formal or informal norms, such as laws, rules, regulations, and principles. In a wider sense, this may include a great variety of duties under administrative ordinances, directives by ministries and regulators, industrial standards, operational rules and business ethics by self-governing organizations like the industrial association or trade union. Frequently, the compliance duty falls into the terrain of compliance risk management targeted at controlling different legal risks faced by the bank. In practice, however, it extends far beyond and may

10.4 Legal Duties in Corporate Governance of Chinese Banks

be closely intertwined with relevant issues like internal control, business operations, and the fiduciary duty (CBRC 2006).

As a key component, the compliance duty is prioritized and integrated into corporate governance in Chinese banks, the overall enterprise culture, and good business ethics. In particular, an effective dynamic is established between the internal self-disciplinary compliance practice and the external financial supervision. For instance, CBRC, by close monitoring, inspection and evaluation, supervises the validity and effectiveness of Chinese banks' compliance practice on a continuous basis (CBRC 2006). Meanwhile, the compliance duty involves various participants, including but limited to the board of directors, the supervisory board, and managers at different levels. And, a specific department, frequently the compliance department or legal affair department, is established to be responsible for compliance issues throughout the bank group.

Moreover, Chinese bank sets the compliance duty as one of its major social responsibilities, as discussed in previous chapters. For instance, Bank B, by strictly conforming to relevant laws, rules, and regulations, develops the principle of 'Regulated Conduct, Moderate Authorization, Sound Monitoring, Efficient Inspection and Effective Control' for its internal control mechanism, which aims for better performance of its compliance duty and strengthen a sound compliance culture throughout the bank group (Bank B 2012b). Specifically, the bank enhances its internal control guidance, *Basic Regulations for Internal Control*, which is targeted at fully 'explicating the codes of conduct, authorization management, standard regulations, supervision and inspection, accountability and penalty and internal control assessment' (Bank B 2012b, p. 15). Regarding the business policy, Bank B stipulates *Basic Regulations for Compliance Management* which 'clarifies the organizational structure and managerial obligations of the Group's compliance management' (Bank B 2012b, p. 22). Bank D, in contrast, reinforces its self-discipline practices, duty of compliance with relevant laws and regulations, and active implementation of internal control measures, which aims to boost the bank's image as 'a responsible giant bank'. Typically, in accordance with *The Self-discipline Convention for the Banking Industry of China* by CBA (2009), the bank intends to contribute to maintenance of a sound financial market order, fair competitions, and sustainable development by initiating compliance programs like *Top 100 Model Outlets* (Bank D 2012). Bank A, by referring to *The Basic Norms for Enterprise Internal Control by* MoF, assesses and evaluates its internal control system to diagnose potential deficiencies which may substantially impact upon the operation and management of the bank. And, the bank lays specific emphasis on supervising compliance practices by its domestic and overseas branches in the context of fast business expansion at both international and domestic level (Bank A 2012b). Moreover, diversified training programs are designed by Chinese banks to promote the employees' awareness of the compliance practice. For instance, Bank B initiates campaigns of 'Year for Implementing Internal Control and Violation Prevention Systems' and 'Compliance Management and Prevention of Operational Risks' to reinforce the employees' awareness and understanding of legal compliance (Bank B 2012b). Bank D, on the other hand, sponsors various events ranging from *Compliance Culture and Prevention System* to *Risk Inspections*, and has complemented over 6,000 legal compliance sessions and 900 specific knowledge contests for its employees (Bank D 2012).

Secondly, the compliance duty lays specific emphasis on anti-money laundering (AML) and anti-terrorism financing practices. For instance, Bank B designs its own AML model which focuses on the customer identification, the global control list, and the overall monitoring system for domestic and overseas departments (Bank B 2012b). Specifically, the bank reinforces its reporting system on suspicious transactions and AML compliance for its international subsidiaries and branches, sponsors tailored training programs at different levels, and cooperates with financial authorities on AML investigations, all of which enhance the bank's risk control over potential money laundering activities. Bank A, on the other hand, develops a similar categorization mechanism overseeing clients suspected of money laundering, strengthens its AML monitoring and diagnosis systems, and improves reporting channels on suspicious financial activities. Moreover, a series of training sessions are put in place to alert the bank employees against any possible money laundering attempts (Bank A 2012).

Thirdly, anti-corruption and establishment of a clean business environment are also set at the top of the agenda by Chinese banks as part of their compliance duties. For instance, developing its own principles of 'striking at the root of problems and its harmful effects, taking precautious measures, and imposing punishment' regarding the corruption activities (Bank B 2012b, p. 55), Bank B sets up efficient preventive systems and sanction measures to promote a sound operational environment. And, many internal rules and guidance are produced such as *Administrative Measures for Preventing the Conflict of Interests*, *Regulations on Honest Operation by the Management*, and *Commitment of Honest Operation by the Managers* (Bank B 2012b). Specifically, an 'Honest Management System' is innovated which traces and collects information on business conducts by 29,552 managers from 1,975 subsidiaries and branches. In 2011 alone, for instance, 1,677 investigations on commercial bribery were conducted and 1,245 measures were taken to redress relevant improper transactions. Moreover, 15,406 training sessions, themed on campaigns against business corruption and promotion of ethical professional behaviors, were organized and actively attended by around 757,569 participants (Bank B 2012b). Bank A, on the other hand, develops its own daily monitoring mechanisms sponsors tailored training programs, educational exhibitions, case diagnosis, and organizes various anti-corruption lectures and seminars, all of which are intended to reinforce sound business ethics and 'clean practice' throughout the bank group (Bank A 2012).

The arrangement of the duty of compliance in Chinese banks reveals implication of the discourses of paradigm and legitimacy as discussed in Chaps. 4 and 6. For instance, echoing the paradigm of the diversified stakeholder theory and emphasis on CSR performance, Chinese banks hold themselves accountable to the regulator as one of their key stakeholders and implement the duty of compliance, which is best exemplified by legitimate practices in business operation, anti-money laundering, and anti-corruption. Meanwhile, the compliance duty also represents the paradigm discourse of the enhanced shareholder primacy, which is purported to protect the interests of the shareholders by constraining from profitable but illegal business activities.

Such compliance duty illustrates as well the legitimacy discourses of strong financial regulation and paralleled deregulation. On one side, the compliance duty by Chinese banking organizations is largely shaped and produced by regulatory discourses and closely supervised by Chinese financial authorities, violation of which may incur administrative fines, penalties, and punishments. Moreover, the compliance duty is purported, by the regulators, to reinforce the stability and sustainability of Chinese financial system. On the flip side, however, the compliance duty reveals a trend toward market-oriented self-discipline by Chinese banks, which reflects increasing financial deregulation and less intervention by the state.

10.4.2 Fiduciary Duties in Corporate Governance in Banking Organizations in China

Similar to the legal duties discussed both in generic firms and banks across different model countries, the fiduciary duty in corporate governance in Chinese banking organizations pertains to the board directors, the management, supervisory directors, and the controlling shareholders, and is generally categorized into the duty of care, duty of loyalty, and duty of disclosure. Specifically, the fiduciary duty in Chinese banks is subject to various regulations, industrial rules and guidance, and changing policies (China Banking Regulatory Commission 2011).

A. Duty of care

The duty of care, in the context of Chinese bank governance, mainly extends to issues such as qualifications of the board directors and senior managers (D&M), the duty of due diligence, and the duty of adequate monitoring (China Banking Regulatory Commission 2011). First and foremost, the qualifications of D&M in Chinese banks are prioritized and expected to meet the regulatory requirements, which include a record of good business ethics and reputation, adequate professional knowledge, and related financial experience and expertise, along with sound personal and family financial situations (China Banking Regulatory Commission 2011). Meanwhile, there are even mandatory stringent requirements upon academic backgrounds and terms of financial practices by D&M, which may become more demanding for the outside directors (Bank B 2012). Meanwhile, the qualification standards for D&M are not static, but dynamic. With fast-changing economic, financial, and political environments, increasingly complicated banking business, and financial innovations of various kinds, continuous upgrading on the qualifications of D&M is mandated in Chinese banking industry. For instance, in 2011, the board directors in Bank B were invited to participate in specific survey and research programs in selected key business departments at the bank's head office and overseas branches, which intended to enable the directors to have better understanding of latest developments in core banking business, such as the bank's competitiveness in deposits attraction, financial assistance to SMEs, new assets management, and renovation of the internal (credit) rating system. The research programs also aimed to update the board directors of the changes with regard to the bank's external economic and financial environments, its key business activities, and related management procedures, all of which may reinforce the director's role in proposing effective advice to the bank's management. Meanwhile, to enhance D&M's competency in banking and finance better performance, periodical training programs on varied subjects are organized by financial regulators at different levels, such as training sessions for directors in listed corporations sponsored by Beijing Bureau of CSRC, which concentrates on prevention against insider trading, better internal control system, and efficient performance by D&M (Bank B 2012a). And, the bank's nomination committee and financial authorities are also actively engaged in examining and assessing whether the standards of such qualifications are met. Moreover, financial regulators are actively engaged in strict reviews on practices by D&M candidates (which are recorded in the financial supervisory information system), their personal files, and opinions consulted from other financial regulators or related administrative agencies. Such regulatory monitoring may even extend to D&M's personal credit records, his professional knowledge and capability, and other issues deemed appropriate based on prudential supervision principles (CBRC 2012).

Another important element of the duty of care is due diligence, which requires D&M to perform their duties with adequate diligence and commitment and be restrained from negligence, shirking or other kinds of reckless activities. In practice, these pertain to active attendance at the board meetings, completion effectively of required working hours, and understanding fully their due obligations (China Banking Regulatory Commission 2011). Firstly, the bank directors are expected to input sufficient time to deliver their duties. For instance, he is obliged to attend over two-thirds of the board meetings personally on annual basis. In case of absence with due course, other qualified directors can be delegated, but not without written consent (from the absentee director). Annually, the outside directors are required to work at least 15 working days in the bank, physically. And for outside directors acting as the head of the auditing committee, the related-party transaction control committee, or the risk management committee, they are obliged to work at least 25 working days. And, the completed minimum working hours, attendance at the board meetings and presentation of independent opinions by the board director will be recorded in his profile and used for assessing his performance (China Banking Regulatory Commission 2011).

This can be well observed in Bank B, where the bank's executive directors, non-executive directors and outside directors well performed their duties of diligence by full attendance at all the board meetings and meetings by board special committees, with the attendance rate reaching 100% (though this satisfactory percentage embraced those of delegated attendance), as illustrated in Table 10.1. The outside directors were also actively proposing independent opinions with regard to the bank's business development and strategic planning.

Meanwhile, the outside directors initiated a wide-range on-site research programs, which focused on major changes of the bank's business operation, organizational adjustment, risk management, internal control, and the compensation arrangement.

10.4 Legal Duties in Corporate Governance of Chinese Banks

Table 10.1 2011 Bank B statistics on attendance by board directors at board meetings and meetings by board special committees

Directors	Times of attendance/times of attendance mandated						
	Board of directors	Special committees under the board					
		Strategic committee	Auditing committee	Risk management committee	Nomination committee	Compensation committee	Related transaction control committee
Executive directors							
A	10/10	6/6					
B	10/10	6/6			2/2	3/3	
C	10/10			5/5			
D	10/10						6/6
Non-executive directors							
E	10/10	6/6				3/3	
Non-executive directors							
F	10/10	6/6				3/3	
G	10/10			5/5	2/2		
H	10/10		6/6	5/5			
I	10/10			5/5	2/2		
J	10/10	6/6	6/6	5/5			
Independent and Non-executive directors							
H	10/10	6/6	6/6	5/5	2/2	3/3	6/6
I	10/10	6/6	6/6	5/5	2/2	3/3	
J	10/10	6/6	6/6		2/2	3/3	6/6
K	10/10		6/6	5/5	2/2	3/3	6/6
L	10/10	6/6		5/5	2/2		
M	10/10		6/6			3/3	6/6

Source Bank B (2012a)

And, seminars on specific subjects were also organized with the bank's management for better communication (Bank B 2012a).

Secondly, the duty of due diligence demands that the bank directors be capable of understanding and analyzing the complicated financial activities of the bank, its periodical reports, and various independent opinions (on the bank's operation) issued by the regulators, external auditors, and the public. In this scenario, the board directors are expected to lay special emphasis on major issues such as formulation and implementation of the bank's business strategy, appointment, and monitoring over the bank's senior management, the bank's risk preference, risk strategy and risk management, and the compensation plan and related assessment standards (CBRC 2010). Meanwhile, a special duty of care can be observed for the non-executive directors, who are responsible for facilitating smooth communication between the bank and the controlling shareholders, and preventing the prioritization of the majority shareholders over those of the bank and other (minority) investors. For instance, with regard to implementation of the board's decisions by the senior management, especially when there are deficiencies in the bank's relevant rubrics which do not meet the requirements of the prudential bank supervision or may possibly deviate in the foreseeable near future, the non-executive directors are obliged to require the bank to make due rectifications. Another issue falling into the non-executive's duty of care is efficient monitoring over transactions between the shareholders and the bank, which demands legality, reasonableness, and fair valuation.

For the outside directors, on the other hand, they are positioned to provide objective and independent opinions to the bank board, and focuses, in particular, on the protection for the interests of various stakeholders (typically depositors) and minority shareholders. And, the outside directors are expected to monitor specifically following issues with sufficient care, such as the legality and fairness of related-party transactions, completeness, and authenticity of information disclosure, events which may incur substantial losses to the bank, and issues which may damage the interests of the bank's depositors and the minority shareholders (CBRC 2010)

Performance of the duty of care by D&M is accordingly appraised by the bank regulators and related financial authorities. Based on relevant guidance, Chinese banks are required to establish the adequate monitoring and assessment system which intends to evaluate performance of fiduciary duties by D&M and sets up an official record for tracing their practices. And, the assessment process can be divided into different categories for varied stages, such as self-assessment, mutual assessment by peer directors, and assessment by the board of directors and the supervisory board. Meanwhile, CBRC may review such assessment and take relevant measures in case of need. For instance, if there is any non-compliance by the bank regarding its assessment system and procedures, or the assessment result is largely untruthful, CBRC will impose penalties and demand rectification. Furthermore, on-site inspection is conducted by CBRC, periodically, based on the bank's assessment reports (CBRC 2010).

B. Duty of loyalty

The duty of loyalty, in the context of bank governance in China, mainly pertains to the board directors, senior managers and majority shareholders, and involves various issues of conflict of interests, such as holding posts in other competitive financial institutions, pursuit of undue benefits at the price of the bank's interests, and direct or indirect involvement in present or planned business contracts, transactions or arrangements with the bank (China Banking Regulatory Commission 2011). In particular, to prevent the instances of conflicting interests which may adversely affect D&M's duty of loyalty, the following situations are explicitly prohibited by the financial regulators,

10.4 Legal Duties in Corporate Governance of Chinese Banks

(i) by the time of his appointment, D&M or his spouse owns a large amount of unpaid debts, including those owned to the present financial institution to which he is to be appointed as D&M;

(ii) D&M or his relatives jointly hold over 5% of the stocks of the present financial institution and the total credit granted by this institution exceeds the fair value of the aforesaid stocks;

(iii) D&M and the institution he controls jointly hold over 5% of the stocks of the present financial institution and the total credit granted by this institution exceeds the fair value of the aforesaid stocks;

(iv) D&M or his spouse takes posts in other institutions which hold over 5% of the stocks of the present financial institution and the total credit granted by this institution exceeds the fair value of the aforesaid stocks unless such credit grant is not related to him or his spouse by any means;

(v) D&M's post in other institutions will conflict with his present or future post in the present financial institutions or greatly distract him from properly performing his duties such as working hours, working efficiency,

and other situations defined by CBRC in accordance with prudential regulation principles (CBRC 2012).

And for outside directors, more stringent standards are imposed and the following scenarios are not allowed,

(i) the outside director and his spouse jointly hold over 1% of the stocks or options of the present financial institution;

(ii) the outside director or his relatives take post in other institutions which hold shares in the present financial institutions;

(iii) the outside director or his relatives take post in the present financial institutions, or other institutions controlled directly or indirectly by the present financial institution;

(iv) the outside director or his relatives take post in institutions which default in repaying loans to the present financial institution;

(v) the outside director or his relatives take post in institutions which have business relations or conflict of interests as creditors or debtors with the present financial institution due to their relationship at law, in accounting, auditing, management consulting, guaranteeing or cooperation, which may hinder the sound performance of his independence;

(vi) the outside director or his relatives may be subject to great influences or control by the majority shareholders or senior management in the present financial institution which may hinder his performance of independence,

and other situations defined by CBRC based on financial prudential regulation principles. Furthermore, for senior management of the bank, he is prohibited from taking any post in other business institutions unless such institutions are affiliated to the bank and the intended post is approved by China Banking Regulatory Commission (2011).

In practice, the duty of loyalty by D&M pertains to varied business activities by the bank. For instance, D&M is responsible for protecting the secrets of the bank and forbidden to procure any improper profits or interests in performing his duties. Meanwhile, the director is not allowed to take advantages of his directorship to pursue undue personal benefits, maximize the shareholders' interests at the expense of the bank's interests, or get involved in any transactions which may cause conflict of interests with the present banking organization (CBRC 2010). Specifically, if the director is, directly or indirectly, engaged in the present or future contracts, transactions, or business arrangements with the bank, the nature and degree of his involvement should be notified to the control committee over related-party transactions and the director should be excluded when the transaction is reviewed by the bank board (China Banking Regulatory Commission 2010, 2011). For the duty of loyalty by specific categories of directors, such as the non-executive directors who represent the controlling shareholders, it is expected that the directors should actively promote the communication between the majority shareholders and the bank. In particular, related transactions between the controlling shareholders and the bank should be carefully scrutinized, while complementary capital planning is to be arranged to avoid extra risk exposures in the bank's capital adequacy (China Banking Regulatory Commission 2011).

C. Duty of disclosure

In contrast with generic firms, information disclosure by the banking organizations is highly sensitive and ambivalent. On one side, it is necessary and mandatory for the bank to disclose adequate information to protect the interests of the shareholders and stakeholders. On the flip side, however, due to the specialty of the bank, typically its highly leveraged capital structure, fast changing financial activities, 'unstable' balance sheet and complicated financial innovations, extensive information disclosure may cause serious problems and unnecessary public panics, especially the systemic one like the bank run which may pull down even the healthiest bank. As discussed, information disclosure can generally be divided into the mandatory information disclosure and voluntary information disclosure. The former refers to the information which may significantly influence the investors in making their investment decisions and is mandated to be disclosed. The latter, based on the bank's own arrangement and without revealing its sensitive financial information or business secrets, embodies information which may exert certain influences upon the shareholders and other stakeholders, such as the bank's development strategy, management orientation, and the relationship between the bank and other stakeholders. In general, the duty of disclosure pertains to the board directors, supervisory board directors, senior managers, and controlling shareholders. Meanwhile, information disclosure is expected to comply with the principles of authenticity, accuracy, completeness and timeliness, and readily accessible to the public (China Banking Regulatory Commission 2011).

These can be well observed in Chinese banking institutions, especially in large-sized commercial banks. In Bank B, for instance, the board of directors is responsible for information disclosure, which generally embraces periodical reports, temporary reports, and other mandatory disclosure (Bank B 2012). The periodical information

10.4 Legal Duties in Corporate Governance of Chinese Banks

disclosure comprises the bank's basic information, financial and accounting reports, risk management reports, and information regarding the bank's corporate governance and annual major events. For instance, disclosure on the bank's risk management should include but not limited to, (1) the conditions of the bank's key risk exposures such as the credit risk, liquidity risk, market risk, operational risk, reputation risk, and national risk; (2) the risk control conditions, including the capability of the board of directors and senior management in monitoring and controlling the risks, tailored policies and processes for overall risk management, risk measurement, the information system for risk management and monitoring, and internal control, and (3) the risk assessment and measurement approaches. Specifically, the bank will consult external auditing firms regarding the adequacy of information disclosure on its risk management system (Bank B 2012).

Meanwhile, the duty of disclosure embraces D&M's opinions on periodical reports in forms of written confirmations. For instance, the supervisory board is obliged to provide opinions in written forms and demonstrates whether preparation and reviewing procedures (on the periodical reports) conform to relevant laws, regulations, and rules, and whether periodical reports can truthfully, accurately and fully reveal actual economic and financial conditions of the bank. Specifically, D&M and the supervisory directors are responsible to provide explanations in cases when they cannot guarantee or hold dissenting opinions with regard to the authenticity, accuracy, completeness of such reports. Meanwhile, the supervisory board is responsible for monitoring the performance of the duty of disclosure by D&M and the overall information disclosure by the bank. And, in the instance of any illegality or breach of the duty of disclosure, relevant investigation and solutions should be reported to the financial regulators by the bank timely (China Banking Regulatory Commission 2011).

In practice, the duty of disclosure varies for the board directors, senior management, supervisory directors, and the majority shareholder. In Bank B, for instance, the board directors are expected to guarantee that disclosed information well comply with the principles of authenticity, accuracy, completeness, and any misstatement, misguiding or gross lapse of information are prohibited. And, in case of breach, the board directors may take several or joint liabilities for unduly disclosed information. For the senior management, the duty of disclosure embraces reporting timely to the board of directors any material events that occur in the bank's business operation, financial conditions, etc. Meanwhile, the senior management is expected to respond timely to inquiries by the board of directors regarding the bank's periodical reports, temporary reports and other relevant issues, reinforce administration on information disclosure and its efficient implementation in daily business operations and management activities (Bank B 2012). The duty of disclosure also pertains to the bank's shareholders, especially the controlling shareholder. For example, the bank's controlling shareholder or shareholders with over 5% shareholding will be required to timely notify the bank's information disclosure department if they notice or know any material information which needs to be disclosed (Bank B 2012). And, positioned as an specialized effective monitoring mechanism, the supervisory board of the bank and its members frequently play an important role in reviewing and supervising performance of the duty of disclosure, including but not limited to periodical and random inspections over the bank's information disclosure system, requirements upon the board of directors to rectify any deficient information disclosure practices, and preparing written opinions on the bank's periodical reports with regard to their compatibility with laws, regulations and rules. Specifically, the supervisory directors may initiate investigations in cases of any verified violations or malpractices by D&M (Bank B 2012).

However, there are exceptional instances in the duty of disclosure, where the information, though substantial and material, can be delayed or even excluded from disclosure, if it is classified as uncertain, temporary business secrets, or other circumstances recognized by the stock exchange where the bank is listed, and disclosure of such information may damage the bank's interests, misguide the investors, or violate relevant laws, regulations or rules. In these circumstances, applications for delayed disclosure or exclusion can be filed to relevant regulators and D&M of the bank will be exonerated from their duty of disclosure (Bank B 2012).

As another key component of legal duties in bank governance in China, the fiduciary duty presents the constitutive discourses of legitimacy and paradigm explored in the previous chapters. Manifesting the paradigm discourse of the enhanced shareholder primacy, the fiduciary duty in Chinese banks lays increasing emphasis on legal protections for the investors. For instance, to bring about a better performance, the duty of care demands stricter qualifications of D&M, more stringent review over their due diligence, and close assessment on their performance. To control the conflict of interests in various activities by D&M and the bank's controlling shareholders, Chinese regulators initiate more demanding rules on the duty of loyalty such as the mandate on the independence of D&M and constraints over related-party transactions. Meanwhile, reinforcement in the duty of disclosure is purported to mitigate information asymmetry between the bank management and the shareholders, hence, providing sufficient material information to the investors and facilitate the implementation of the duty of care and duty of loyalty as well. Moreover, responding to strong impacts of the regulatory discourses, the fiduciary duty in Chinese banks is largely founded upon, apart from the laws and statutes, the regulatory guidance, rules, and principles, while Chinese court is found to have limited influences. For instance, with regard to the duty of care, the qualifications and the standards of due diligence by the bank D&M are mainly prescribed and closely monitored by CBRC. Moreover, the performance of the duty of care by D&M is partly subject to the supervision and assessment by Chinese financial regulators. Regarding the duty of loyalty, strong regulatory influence is prominent and it is always the financial regulator that clarifies the qualification requirements of D&M and illustrates various prohibited scenarios which may adversely affect the performance of the duty of loyalty and incur varied conflict of interests. For instance, CBRC specifies the duty of loyalty by the non-executive directors in Chinese banking organizations in related-party transactions between the bank and the controlling shareholders and produces detailed requirements on information disclosure by D&M which embrace key principles of disclosure and relevant standards.

10.5 Conclusion

Continuing the discursive institutional analysis, the present chapter reviews the legal duties in the banking organizations, mainly the compliance duty at public law and fiduciary duty at private law. Reflecting on the paradigm and legitimacy of different models, prominent differences can be observed for the intensity of compliance obligation and the standards and boundaries of the fiduciary duty by the bank board directors and managers across countries. In corporate governance of banking organizations in China, however, the legal duties are found to be subject to legitimacy discourses of international influence and regulatory impacts, and the paradigm of the hybridity of the enhanced shareholder primacy and diversified stakeholder theory. The compliance duty summarizes various compliance practices in the bank's business operations under the great influences by the financial regulators. The fiduciary duties, on the other hand, generalize sophisticated and varied standards and requirements on the board of directors, senior managers, and the controlling shareholders of the bank regarding the delivery of their duty of care, duty of loyalty, and duty of disclosure.

References

Aronson v. Lewis. (1984). 473 A. 2d 805, 812 Del.
Bank A. (2012). 2011 CSR Report of Bank A, Bank A. Retrieved May 25, 2012, from http://www. BankA.com.
Bank B (2012). 2011 Annual Report of Bank B, Bank B. Available at http://www.BankB.com. Accessed May 25, 2012.
Bank B. (2012a). 2011 Annual Report of Bank B, Bank B. Retrieved May 25, 2012, from http://www.
Bank B. (2012b). 2011 CSR Report of Bank B, Bank B. Retrieved May 25, 2012, from http://www. BankB.com.
Bank D. (2012). 2011 CSR Report of Bank D, Bank D. Retrieved May 25, 2012, from http://www. BankD.com.
Bauma, D. Jeffrey, Palmiter, R. Alan, & Partnoy, F. (2007). *Corporations Law and Policy* (6th ed.). NY: West Publisher.
Baums, T., Scott, K. E. (2005). Taking shareholder protection seriously? Corporate Governance in the United States and Germany, SSRN. Retrieved October 15, 2009, from, http://papers.ssrn. com/abstract=473185.
BIS. (2005). *Compliance and the compliance function in banks*. Switzerland: Basel Committee on Banking Supervision.
BIS. (2010). *Principles for enhancing corporate governance*. Switzerland: Basel Committee on Banking Supervision.
Broderick. (1934). Superintendent of Banks of the State of New York v. Marcus, 272 NYS 455, 152 Misc. 413, 272 NY 455, 1934.
China Banking Association. (2009). *The self-discipline convention of the banking industry of China*. Beijing: China Banking Association.
China Banking Regulatory Commission. (2006). *Guidance for compliance risk management in commercial banks*. Beijing: China Banking Regulatory Commission.
China Banking Regulatory Commission. (2010). *Assessment method on performance by directors in commercial banks* (Trial), No.7, Beijing: China Banking Regulatory Commission.

China Banking Regulatory Commission (CBRC). (2011). *Guidance for corporate governance in commercial banks (consultative document)*. Beijing: China Banking Regulatory Commission.

China Banking Regulatory Commission. (2012). *Regulation on qualifications of directors and management in banking financial institutions (consultative document)*. Beijing: China Banking Regulatory Commission.

Francis v. United Jersey Bank. (1981). 87 N.J. 15, 432 A.2d 814.

Graham v. Allis-Chalmers Manufacturing Co. (1963). 188 A.2d 125, Del, 1963.

German Government Commission. (2012). *German corporate governance code*. Berlin: German Government Commission.

JP Morgan Chase & Co. (2012). 2011 Annual Report of JP Morgan Chase & Co. Available at http://www.jpmorganchase.com. Accessed 19 Oct 2012.

Litwin v. Allen. (1940). 25 NYS 2d 667, 168 Misc. 205, 25 NY 2d 667, 1940.

Misawa, M. (2005). Bank directors; decisions on bad loans: a comparative study U.S. and Japanese standards of required care. *Banking Law Journal, 122,* 429–466.

OECD. (2004). *Principles of corporate governance*. Paris: Organization for Economic Co-operation and Development.

Smith v. Van Gorkom (1985). 488 A. 2d 858, Del.

US American Bar Association. (2002). *The Model Business Corporation Act (MBCA)*, Washington D.C.: American Bar Association.

US Delaware. (2005). *Delaware general corporation law.*

US. (2010). *Wall street reform and consumer protection act of 2010 (Dodd Frank Act).*

Villa, J. K. (2013). *Bank directors', officers', and lawyers' civil liabilities*. Aspen: Aspen Publishers Inc.

Chapter 11
Book Conclusion

11.1 Key Findings

In conclusion, this book has drawn on insights into the discursive institutionalist works and the varieties of capitalism literature in order to explore corporate governance of banking organizations in China. With its three-tier canvass of discourses, proceeding from legitimacy, paradigm, to frame, the book demonstrates that corporate governance in Chinese banks is symbiotically linked to the specific Chinese national configuration. At the legitimacy level, bank governance in China is found to be justified by the relationship between the bank and the economy, the impacts of paralleled powerful financial regulation and deregulative moves, and the increasing international influence. At the paradigm level, corporate governance in Chinese banks is illustrated to be shaped by a specific hybrid model with concerns for the shareholder primacy and broader stakeholder interest groups. At the level of the frame discourse, corporate governance in Chinese banking organizations is presented in the development of specific governance mechanism, typically represented by the organization and practice of the board of directors, regulation on executive pay, risk management, and legal duties.

The detailed empirical work undertaken suggests that the governance of Chinese banking organizations is best characterized as a part hybrid and part uniquely Chinese institutionalism. Hybrid is demonstrated through the mix of the shareholder model, the stakeholder model, and the state-affected model. In governance practice, there is represented by the mix of the models, such as the structure of the board of directors where there is a hybrid characteristic of the Anglo-Saxon model and the Continental model. On the other hand, the book finds strong evidence of an emerging 'Chinese model'. Embedded in China's institutional settings ideologically structured as the *Market Economy with Chinese Specialty*, the Chinese model is found to be characterized with the enhanced shareholder primacy theory, the paralleled diversified stakeholder theory, concerns for national economic development, and increasing exposures to international influence. In contrast with the generic

© Springer Nature Singapore Pte Ltd. 2019
W. Zou, *Corporate Governance in the Banking Sector in China*, CSR, Sustainability, Ethics & Governance, https://doi.org/10.1007/978-981-13-3510-5_11

shareholder primacy theory as popular in the Anglo-Saxon model, Chinese model of bank governance presents a distinctive nature of the enhanced shareholder primacy, in which the state acts as the controlling/large shareholder (in large-sized commercial banks) and the banks are oriented toward the balance of the best performance and sustainable development, and maintenance and increase the value of the state assets invested in the banks. In parallel, Chinese model emphasizes on protecting the interests of diversified stakeholders and present serious concerns for a great variety of the bank's constituencies, from the state, regulator, depositor, to environment and society at large. Specifically, this model sorts out efficient solutions for coordinating the enhanced shareholder primacy and concerns for diversified stakeholders in the context of the state acting as influential bank shareholder. Moreover, Chinese model lays great emphasis on facilitating national economic strategy, regional economic development, and financial assistance to industries and sectors. Another feature of Chinese model lies in its 'opening' to international influence, which is comparatively less observed in other established models. With the spirit of 'Reform and Open Up to the Outside', Chinese model is positioned to welcome international norms and practice, which is reinforced by China's increasing presence and membership in international economic organizations and involvement in financial globalization, fast growth of foreign banks in China in number, geographic coverage, and financial activities, and expansion of Chinese banks in global financial markets. All these features lead to the 'specialty' of corporate governance in Chinese banking organizations and henceforth produce the specific 'Chinese model'.

From the institutional perspective, the book finds that corporate governance in Chinese banks is a composite of three-level discourses and the dynamics within. At the level of the legitimacy, bank governance in China gains its legitimate grounds by 'Serving the Real Economy', i.e., integration into the national economy, close connections with industrial sectors, and intertwining with enterprises. Regarding the constitutive role of the financial regulation, there is a parallel discourse of continued close control by the government and increasing orientations for opting for deregulation. In terms of legal intervention, Chinese courts present a paradoxical characteristic of passivism and activism and are frequently influenced by political discourses. Meanwhile, the discourse of the international competition and influence is increasingly significant in legitimating particular corporate governance arrangements in China. As the idea at the background of the cognition, the legitimacy of corporate governance in Chinese banks is found to provide great implications in constituting the discourses of paradigm and frame. For instance, attributed to the hybrid nature of the legitimacy discourse, the paradigm discourse in Chinese bank governance exhibits a strong hybridization of the shareholder model, stakeholder model, and state-affected model. Meanwhile, such legitimacies may constitute specific bank governance structure in Chinese banks, such as the orientation of the bank board toward serving the real economy, preference for moderate risk appetites and specific risk exposures, and a social responsibility nature in the duty of legal compliance.

At the paradigm level, corporate governance in Chinese banks is found to be constituted by the paralleled discourses of the enhanced shareholder primacy theory and

11.1 Key Findings

diversified stakeholder theory. The enhanced shareholder primacy theory, in Chinese context, is formed through the specific concerns for the state as a majority shareholder of the bank, the balance of the maximization of shareholder interests with stakeholders' interests, and a specific agency problem. The diversified stakeholder theory, on the other hand, highlights the bank's serious concerns for the interests of a great variety of stakeholders, from general economy to individual employees, from the regulators to the clients, and from the environmental protection to the social welfare at large. Such hybrid paradigm is found to provide significant implications on the development of the frame in Chinese bank governance. For instance, the enhanced shareholder primacy influences the arrangement of a high percentage of non-executive directors at the bank board representing the state, specific risk exposures to the real economy and industrial sectors, and the discouragement of using shareholdings as part of the composition for executive pay. The paralleled paradigm of the diversified stakeholder theory, on the other hand, leads to the mandatory presence of employee representatives as the supervisory directors, the board's orientation for protecting various constituencies, and comparatively less risky appetites by Chinese banks.

At the frame level, echoing the legitimacy and paradigm discourses as so discussed, the book illustrates a specific set of corporate governance structure developed in Chinese banks, which mainly includes the organization and behavior of the bank board, the regulation on executive pay, risk management, and legal duties. The present study shows, in the organization and behavior of the board of directors, Chinese banks have developed a comparatively large-sized bank board with rich banking experience, good financial expertise, and increasing independence. Specifically, it is found that the bank board is oriented toward sustainable profitability to the shareholders, active support for the economic development, and the balance of interests among various stakeholders. The regulation on executive pay in Chinese banks exhibits that the remuneration composition is oriented toward the long-termism of the bank executives. Specially, the intangible element of political prestige and advancement plays a significant role as part of the compensation for the bank's senior executives. The special regulatory measures, on the other hand, reveal that the pay regulation is closely supervised and assessed by Chinese regulators. In risk management, the book demonstrates the risk management framework in Chinese banks is largely constituted by the international influence and regulatory discourses. In practice, the bank risk management is found to be characterized with moderate risk appetites and particular risk exposures to the real economy. Regarding the legal duties in Chinese banking organizations, the present study presents that there is a significant role of the regulatory discourse in shaping the compliance duty and the fiduciary duty. As the duty at the public law, the compliance duty is found in a wide range of practices like business operation, anti-money laundering moves, and anti-corruption efforts. The fiduciary duty, with its increasing significance in Chinese banks, demonstrates the standards and boundaries of the duty of care, duty of loyalty, and duty of disclosure.

As the discourse at the third level, the frames in the bank governance in China are observed to manifest the discourses of the paradigm and legitimacy. For instance, implicated by the enhanced shareholder primacy and the dominance of state as the controlling shareholder, a very high proportion of non-executive directors are set in the composition of the bank board. The increasing presence of the outside directors, on the other hand, echoes the international influence and reinforced self-discipline of the board of directors, though the institutional settings in China may limit the independence of the board to some extent. The frame of the regulation on executive pay, reflecting the state as the controlling shareholder and strict financial regulation, discourages the use of shareholdings or options as the incentives for the bank executives. Instead, an adequate proportion of the fixed salary, generous welfare packages, and implicit job security resonate with the specialty of the paradigm of the stakeholder model in Chinese bank governance. The specific regulatory measures on executive pay present the regulator's close control over Chinese banks and emphasis on the national financial stability. And, reflecting the paradigm of the stakeholder theory, pay regulation on Chinese banks also illustrates the concerns for the stakeholders, exemplified by the social indicator as a key assessment of the bank's performance. In risk management, echoing the paradigm of the stakeholder theory, Chinese banks take moderate risk appetites and concentrate on the long-term profitability and sustainable development. This also represents the concerns for the financial stability by the regulators and their close supervision over the banks' risk taking. For special risk managements, implicated by the paradigm of the stakeholder theory and legitimacy of bank's integration into the real economy, credit risk management in Chinese banks focuses on the risk exposures to the local financial platforms, the real estate industry, and to SMEs. In the frame of the legal duties, echoing the paradigm of the stakeholder theory and the CSR performance, Chinese banks hold themselves responsible to the regulator as one of their stakeholders and implement the duty of compliance. Moreover, the duty of compliance by Chinese banks illustrates the legitimacy discourses of the strong financial regulation and paralleled deregulation. Manifesting the paradigm discourse of the enhanced shareholder primacy, the fiduciary duty in Chinese banks lays increasing emphasis on the legal protection for the investors, such as stricter requirements on the qualifications of D&M in Chinese banks, stringent rules on the duty of loyalty, and attention to the duty of disclosure. Meanwhile, responding to the strong influence of regulatory discourse, the fiduciary duty in Chinese banks is largely founded upon, apart from the laws and statutes, the regulatory guidance, mandates, and principles, and is frequently subject to the supervision and assessment by Chinese financial regulators.

11.2 Policy Recommendation

The book has argued that corporate governance in Chinese banking organizations should be understood as constituted through three levels of discursive institutions that I have termed legitimacy, paradigm, and frame. While primarily of academic importance, this argument and the findings which support it ensure that the book also holds important insights for financial regulators and banking practitioners. Though the model of the bank corporate governance promoted by international organizations or other developed economies may appear alluring, it may not be totally suitable for China considering the specific national configuration. In this context, a careful consideration of the legitimacy discourse should be explored as the starting point, such as Chinese bank's legitimacy in serving the real economy, integration into the national development strategy, close connection with the industrial sectors, and intertwining with the enterprises, SOEs or SMEs. Meanwhile, the constitutive role of the regulatory discourses should be given extra emphasis, considering both the close financial supervision and deregulation in present China. The international discourse, on the other hand, may provide good references and lessons for Chinese banks, especially for those actively engaged in the global expansion. The legitimacy as discussed should be analyzed further for the formation of next two levels of discourses, the paradigm and frame. At the level of the paradigm, corporate governance in Chinese bank is constituted through orientations for priorities of the varied interest groups. In Chinese context, specifically, these may pertain to the increasingly significant enhanced shareholder primacy and the stakeholder model. Particularly, a thorough study on whose interests should prevail and how to balance the interests between the shareholders (minority) and the stakeholders may be helpful in constituting the adequate governance structure in Chinese banks. At the level of frame, an overall governance arrangement should be constituted in the context of the specialty of Chinese banking industry, which covers the key issues like the balanced and more efficient board of director, better regulation on executive pay with proper incentives and concerns for risks, the more adaptive and efficient risk management system, and the effective legal obligation development. Specifically, though the arrangement of the specific governance structures in Chinese banks seems highly technical, serious concerns should be given for its resonance with the national paradigm and legitimacy discourse.

The discursive institutional analysis of corporate governance in Chinese banks may be helpful to Chinese regulators as well. In financial reforms targeted at improving the governance structure in Chinese banks, not only should the regulator consider how to enhance the particular governance mechanisms, but they need to consider the discourses at the level of the paradigm and legitimacy. For instance, the regulator should take into account what is the dominant discourse oriented in the bank group, whose interests are prioritized, and what is the significance of such paradigm on the development of the specific governance structure. More fundamentally, the regulator needs to explore the legitimacy discourse and seeks out the prevalent institutional settings for the bank governance, such as how the bank is positioned in the economy, what is the influence on the bank by the regulator and legal intervention, and what is the implication of the international discourse. And resiliently, the regulator should figure out how the legitimacy is projected onto the discourses of the paradigm and frame of the bank governance and henceforth propose adequate institutional changes.

11.3 Limitations of the Book and Further Research

In spite of the researcher's efforts, the present book necessarily has certain limitations. For instance, the research mainly focused on four sampled Chinese banks as a case study of corporate governance in the Chinese banking industry, and the sample was small considering the total number of banks in China. Moreover, the sampled banks were all the large-sized financial institutions, and it was medium and small-sized banks that were not included. And, regarding the ownership structure, though the sampled banks are listed commercial banks, they are largely dominated by the state as the controlling shareholder. Banks with other types of ownership structures, such as those with less state ownership or highly privatized, were not included in the study. That said, and considering the total assets of the sampled banks and their prestigious places in Chinese banking industry and national economy, their corporate governance arrangements are of particular significance to corporate governance in banking organizations in China. It is also the case that the sampled banks are the 'model' banks for Chinese banking institutions, and they are certainly prioritized by Chinese financial regulators and frequently consulted in the preparation of various principles and guidance regarding corporate governance reforms in Chinese banks.

Another limitation in the research undertaken by this book relates to the focus on four key issues of corporate governance in Chinese banks, namely the board of directors, the regulation of executive pay, risk management, and legal obligation. Other issues, such as transparency and the ownership structure, were not included. Meanwhile, in discussing the aforesaid four issues, the book could have potentially explored each in greater detail. For instance, regarding the board of directors in Chinese banks, the research only briefly considered the board committees. Nevertheless, the present research explored the main and 'hottest' issues in the study of corporate governance in banking organizations in China, and the prioritization of these issues in the study was in part a reflection on the findings of the research process wherein representatives of banks and regulatory institutions identified and/or confirmed these issues as their principal concerns.

Finally, the present research has confronted certain methodological limitations. Due to confidentiality policies and sensitivity to external interviews in Chinese banking organizations, field work was reliant upon semi-structured and non-structured interviews. Other methods, such as non-participant observation, ethnography, or survey, could not be employed in the study. It would, moreover, have been beneficial if the research process had included a greater number of interviews. However, the interview methodology provided a highly effective basis for the present research, particularly as it enabled the study of the constitutive force of certain discursive institutions in corporate governance of banking organization in China. In addition, although the research interviews were comparatively limited in number, they were all undertaken with participants with roles and responsibilities closely connected to the present research.

11.3 Limitations of the Book and Further Research

To enhance the present research, improvements are planned for the future and allied research projects. For example, in order to further explore the general arguments made here about the constitution of corporate governance in Chinese banks, future research will consider a broader sample of banks. Specifically, the research will include the medium- and small-sized banks, and banks with less state influence such as the joint-equity commercial banks and highly privatized banks. Meanwhile, the future study may consider a longer time span for the sampled banks and collect more historical data, depending on the availability, and accessibility of such data. For a deeper understanding of the governance practices in Chinese banks, the future research may include more key governance issues that have particular weight in Chinese context, such as the ownership structure and its influence on the bank's performance, and issues of transparency. It would also be possible for the further research to consider issues of risk management, for instance, in greater detail as national and global standards continue to evolve and change. The future research is expected to refine the research methodology as well, such as further interviews in more sampled banks, non-participation observation by means of joint research. Specifically, the future study may lay further emphasis on the quantitative method and take in more quantitative data for comparing with the qualitative data to achieve better viability.

Printed in the United States
By Bookmasters